The Art of Rudyard Kipling

The Art of
Rudyard Kipling

J. M. S. TOMPKINS

UNIVERSITY OF NEBRASKA PRESS · LINCOLN

Copyright © 1959 by J. M. S. Tompkins
Second edition 1965
All rights reserved
Library of Congress catalog card number 65-26135

PRINTED IN ENGLAND

TO THE MEMORY OF
A. J. TOMPKINS, M.A.
SCHOOLMASTER
AND
LT.-COL. E. C. ATKINS, C.B.
MANUFACTURER AND FARMER
LOVERS OF KIPLING'S WORK
THIS BOOK IS DEDICATED

The Appeal

If I have given you delight
 By aught that I have done,
Let me lie quiet in that night
 Which shall be yours anon:

And for the little, little, span
 The dead are borne in mind,
Seek not to question other than
 The books I leave behind.

RUDYARD KIPLING

Contents

	Preface	page ix
I	Kipling and the Novel	1
II	Laughter	33
III	Tales for Children	55
IV	Simplicity and Complexity	85
V	Hatred and Revenge	119
VI	Healing	158
VII	Man and the Abyss	185
VIII	Change and Persistence	222
	List of tales and poems by Kipling mentioned in this study, with the dates of their first printing and the volume in which they were collected	260
	Index	270

Preface

Seven years ago, when I finished writing this book, the renewed and refocused criticism of Kipling had hardly begun to make itself felt. This is not to say that there were not, from time to time, serious evaluations of his work, proceeding mostly from senior scholars who had retained the habit, or at least the memory, of reading him. Mr Andrew Rutherford's recent collection of essays, *Kipling's Mind and Art*, enables us to inspect some of these signposts of a reputation. On the whole, however, these appreciations were short and, again on the whole, directed to the work of the first half of Kipling's writing life. Mr Edmund Wilson's well-known essay 'The Kipling that Nobody Read' in *The Wound and the Bow* did indeed extend to the later tales and had the great interest of offering, for the first time, a coherent theory of his subject's emotional and intellectual development. It was a theory, however, that commended itself rather to those who did not know their Kipling than to those who did, and involved a number of isolated misunderstandings of English life, the content and bearing of specific tales and the extent to which they had been read, which cumulatively deflected the course of the study. It remains as a challenge to later interpreters rather than a guide.

None of these studies, however rich in perception, tallied closely enough with my own experience to persuade me that the ground had been thoroughly worked over already. In particular, none of them seemed to give enough attention to the substance and art of the later tales. It was from these that my own interest had sprung. Setting aside the children's books and *Captains Courageous* (known from early youth) and also *Kim* (begun on Armistice Day 1918, while I sat in a train at Liverpool Street, on the way to my first job, with all the engines whistling on their tracks and the distant rumpus assaulting the emotions) it was the tales in *Debits and Credits* that first stirred my eager response. They seemed to me adult, masterful art, suited to my generation; reading them in the nineteen-twenties I felt no time-lag in their point of view. From this stage I worked backwards over the earlier tales and verses, tracing the emergence of the themes and qualities that chiefly interested me. In so doing, I readily assembled arguments against the statements, common then, that Kipling's art ceased to develop before his fortieth year, that he was at no time a conscious or deliberate artist, and that his later tales were confused and miscarried attempts to repeat the successes of his youth.

The odd appearance now of these baseless generalizations is the evidence of the rapidity with which the critical scene has changed. Whatever problems Kipling presents, whatever reactions are provoked by his aggressive brilliance and his copious, vital, imperfect art, it is no longer pretended that he is not an important writer. His works have refused to perish, and on this ground alone, if there were no others, would demand reassessment. This they are receiving from English, American and Continental critics. There is, indeed, a great deal of activity in this field, and approaches are made from different angles and sometimes along unfamiliar paths. The enquiry into 'Kipling's Place in the History of Ideas' by the Provost of King's in *Victorian Studies* demonstrates the relevance of his work to the sociologist, and Professor C. A. Bodelsen's *Aspects of Kipling's Art* analyses the symbolic structure and experimental novelty of the later tales. It is perhaps too early still for a dispassionate, informed and comprehensive view of Kipling's genius and the material it worked in, though in this, his centenary year, it must be attempted. 1911, however, was too early for such a view of Thackeray, and 1912 for Dickens. We may hope, however, to accumulate new facts and insights and to watch the action of time on criticism and the substance criticized. Perspectives alter and language shifts, however imperceptibly. What was an offence becomes an explicable matter of history; what was self-evident becomes hard to take. Types, once fully recognizable, disappear from the scene and have to be reconstructed, and words and locutions modify their emotional charge if not their lexical definition. I become more aware of my place in time in relation to changes of sensibility and assumptions of principles, and this lends added interest to any literary study I undertake. It also adds force to my conviction that no one should pass judgment on the 'tone' of a writer, more than a generation away from him, without some historical knowledge of his language and the manners of his society.

The centre of Kipling's work, nonetheless, is permanent human nature, the motives, reactions and relationships of men within a defined territory, notably though not exclusively that of the work they do. Any mode of criticism which for too long a time obscures the narratives, their scenes and the figures that move in them, which too completely strips down what is sometimes pejoratively called the 'surface' of the 'mere' tale to expose the underlying sociological or symbolic structure, is running the risk of overbalancing itself. Kipling tells us that he asked the cousin who suggested a Roman tale to him to provide the hero's name, for 'I move easiest from a given point'. It is from given points of situation and type that he moves. The illustrative value, often very strong, is nevertheless secondary to the dramatic datum; the symbolic vibrations may deepen the theme profoundly, they may even have helped to direct his choice, but the story has primacy and is self-justifying. If the 'surface' were not so brilliant, if the Kipling world were not so stuffed with human beings under various stresses of duty, command, anguish, error, hatred and love, we should not give ourselves so much trouble about his ideas or the 'private marks' on his bales of merchandise. This solid centre I took for granted in my book, since it is what holds the majority of his readers.

It is obvious that I do not offer either a comprehensive study of Kipling's work or a strictly critical assessment of it. I omit, as far as is possible, its political relations, which cannot be profitably studied out of their historic context. I do not forget them or undervalue their great importance, but they did not seem to be my business. I have assumed only the outline knowledge of the history of the last hundred years that everybody has. In what I have said of the Indian and South African stories I have been concerned with the permanent human and moral themes that run through all the tales, and with the writer's craftsmanship; and the same thing is true of my treatment of his tales of the Great War. In selecting my subjects, I had two principles of choice. One was to please myself and work within my own limits. The other was to assemble, order and examine in detail the parts and qualities of Kipling's work which were, at that time, too frequently ignored, and of which the casual generalizations about him in the press took no account at all. It seemed to me that, until the existence and persistence of these unfamiliar aspects of his art were acknowledged, it was impossible to deal with the whole justly. I also wished to accept in my study the limitations proposed by Kipling himself in the lines printed at the beginning of it, and to see what I could find inside them. I have worked consistently within the tales, with support from the verses, the travel-books and speeches, and from Kipling's autobiographical sketch, *Something of Myself*. I have only twice gone outside his published and acknowledged works, and that is to quote from an account by H. Rider Haggard of what Kipling said in conversation with him, printed in Miss Lilias Rider Haggard's life of her father, *The Cloak that I Left*. Seeing that my study was intended to be selective, there seemed no reason to repeat in full such established critical observations as C. S. Lewis's assertion of Kipling's originality in opening up the vast and important field of man in relation to his work and those that share in it, or Professor Bonamy Dobrée's enlightening passage about the theme of Breaking Strain in his later work. It may be that I took too much for granted here.

In the seven years since I finished writing this book my general view of Kipling has not changed, but naturally I have had cause to reconsider some of my detailed interpretations. I had begun to doubt, while my book was still in proof, whether Jim Wickenden's hatred in 'Friendly Brook' was quite so inactive as I had believed, but I still maintain that his loosening of the bridge was merely tentative, a committal of his cause to chance and the brook. Lady Castorley in her impatience may perhaps have added poison to her mental murder of her husband—I am still not sure, and it makes Gleeag's part difficult—but Manallace is the centre of 'Dayspring Mishandled'. Professor Bodelsen has pointed out to me that Moira Sichliffe may have been more conscious of her abnormal powers than I supposed; and I myself think I have elucidated the way Kipling intends his psychic mechanism to work in ' "The Dog Hervey" '. It seems to be (to use an anachronism) a sort of chain-reaction. Moira imposes the image of the man she loves upon the brain of the sickly little dog. It is naturally a blurred impression, and what the narrator, another sensitive, sees under the dog's eye is only a shadow by the door; but he remembers clearly Moira's odd and alarming dog, her familiar in fact, and it is this image which is passed from his consciousness to that of

Shend, in the storm. I have no recantation to read about 'Mrs Bathurst', for I have never had a complete theory about that tale. Professor Bodelsen's seductive idea of a Mrs Bathurst already dead when her figure appears on the screen runs into difficulties in the last pages of the tale, and the illumination shed by Mr Elliot L. Gilbert's 'What Happens in "Mrs Bathurst" ' (*P.M.L.A.*, 1962) wavers at the same point. I would only say that, if the second figure on the railway siding in the teak forest is a completely new and arbitrary intrusion at that late point in the tale, Kipling has used a very uncharacteristic technique.

The chapters of my book are placed in chronological order, as far as this is possible where each has to cover a large part of Kipling's work. I begin with his return to London from India at the age of twenty-four and with his attempts to master the novel. The defeat of this ambition confines him to the short story, with which the rest of the book is concerned. The same crowded London months also see the publication of his first highly-wrought farce, and this type of tale is the subject of the second chapter. I next consider the children's tales, which he began to write in Vermont at just under thirty and continued for some fifteen years. The discussion of simplicity and complexity in his work that follows takes its position from the appearance of 'Mrs Bathurst', the first of the really difficult tales, in 1904, his thirty-ninth year. The fifth chapter, dealing with the theme of revenge, which recurs in its various mutations throughout Kipling's whole work, is placed at the beginning of the second half of the book to correspond with its importance in alienating the sympathy of the younger generation during the second half of his career, and delaying the comprehension of the later phases of his art. It stands in close relation of contrast with the chapter on the theme of healing. Here we have the new theme, emerging some years before the War and strengthening to the end. The seventh chapter, 'Man and the Abyss', puts all that has preceded in a new perspective, and the last exemplifies both the truth and the untruth of the common statement that Kipling did not change. The book is meant to be cumulative in its effect. I hope to leave with the reader a stronger sense of the variety, the resource and the depth of Kipling's art.

I have sought to lighten the text of dates and references by providing a list of the tales, verses and speeches, to which I refer, with the year of their first appearance and the volume of Kipling's works in which they can be found most easily. The list is meant as a practical convenience, not a formal bibliography. I have preserved his spelling of the names of his characters, even where it was inconsistent (M'Phee and McPhee of the same character, and Quabil and Qabil in the same book). He spells his Demon of Irresponsibility both with the single vowel and the diphthong, but keeps to the diphthongal form for his Personal Daemon of inspiration in 'Something of Myself', so I have reserved the anglicised form for the Demon of the farces. The inverted commas that distinguish some twenty titles have been preserved. Besides doing their usual work, they sometimes indicate a double meaning. ' "Bread upon the Waters" ' has both a literal and a scriptural sense, and there are two kinds of transmission in ' "Wireless" '. ' "My Son's Wife" ' is a quotation from Jean Ingelow's 'High Tide on the Coast of Lincolnshire'. Allusions to this poem run through the tale. It is the subject of the winter cantata in which Connie Sperrit sings, and the little flood that brings her and Midmore together recalls the great one that took away 'my son's wife, Elizabeth'. It seemed a pity to obscure these characteristic elaborations. Lastly, I have committed myself to the clumsiness of writing of the 'I' of the tales, wherever, as is often the case, 'narrator' is ambiguous. This character is sometimes indistinguishable from Kipling the writer, but by no means always, and I am forced to employ this irritating little pedantry to keep the point clear.

The passages from Kipling's works appear by the permission of his daughter, Mrs Bambridge, to whom I wish to express my gratitude. I also acknowledge the courtesy of Messrs Macmillan and Co., the publishers of Kipling's works. Miss Lilias Rider Haggard has kindly consented to my using two extracts from her biography of her father, Rider Haggard, *The Cloak that I Left*. Part of my sixth chapter appeared in an article in *The Modern Language Review* in 1950; the material has been revised and extended.

My book received much kindly and understanding comment, professional and private. It was a pleasure to me that a study aimed primarily at fellow-academics carried so far outside these circles. It was also an assurance of the living power of my subject.

Royal Holloway College J. M. S. TOMPKINS
February 1965

CHAPTER ONE

Kipling and the Novel

It was one of Kipling's disappointments that he did not prove a novelist. In India he had worked on a novel that was never completed, and within a few months of his arrival in London he had set himself down to another, drawing a good deal on his own experiences (as *Something of Myself* clearly shows) and expressing at full and eloquent length the relation of a young artist to his art. *The Light that Failed* was not the complete success that he must have hoped for, and sooner or later he saw that it was not the novel he hoped to write. In *Something of Myself* he calls it 'that *conte*' and puts it in its place as 'not a built book', while taking some comfort in the fact that the French liked it. The ambition to proceed novelist did not, however, desert him for a long time, and he tells us that it was often discussed in the family. For some ten years he made various approaches to it, but after *Kim* he gradually accepted his restriction to the short story, and learnt in the end to make it carry the weight of a novel.

There is no need to dwell on his next long book, *The Naulahka*. It is a matter of obvious incentives and readily available resources. Much of it parallels 'Letters of Marque', the newspaper articles he had written on his tour in Rajputana, and in his collaboration with the American Wolcott Balestier he may have looked primarily for the impulse of a substantial, continuous story, in the turns of which he could stow the memories of his travel. The writing of the Indian scenes is in the main better than that in the original articles, but it is impossible to think that much effort went to this book. No doubt, however, pleasure did, a rare taste of partnership in writing, perhaps a pleasure in letting the collaborator have his head, perhaps a glee in angling for the American public with a book of which hero and heroine were American. It resulted, however, in artistic confusion and nullity. At the end the reader can have it all ways at once. Kate's missionary zeal is defeated by Kipling's India, while Kate's young man defeats India on another level, winning the Rajah's treasure by a mixture of naïve audacity and bluff. His success is short-lived, for the candid American maiden, helped by his perception of the impasse they are in, forces him to return it. Perhaps Kipling thought the ambiguity of the issue characteristic of life in India; perhaps, with the conclusion of the book left on his hands, he simply got home as he best could. Certainly East and West fail to meet to any profitable purpose, and the book is scrambled together rather than 'built'.

The Naulahka is not mentioned in *Something of Myself*, but '*Captains Courageous*' and *Kim* are. Neither is presented as a novel. In '*Captains Courageous*', Kipling says, he tried to record a 'rather beautiful localized American atmosphere that was already beginning to fade'. The narrative substance of the book is so slight that it is little more than a way of organizing the descriptive substance; we become acquainted with the conditions, physical and moral, of life on the fishing schooner 'We're Here' and in her home port of Gloucester as they are impressed on Harvey Cheyne, the spoilt, rich boy, and contrasted with his world and that of his father, the western multi-millionaire. Harvey's conversion to hard work and responsibility is presented as the Elizabethan dramatists presented changes, natural in themselves, which they did not care to develop, by means of a dramatic shock and a short verbal summary; what the change is is worked out in action. Kipling used much the same technique with Frankwell Midmore's conversion in ' "My Son's Wife" ', seventeen years later. *Kim* was one of the books the Daemon was concerned in, that is, it was a work of inspiration as distinguished from one of keen interest and craftsmanship. It was 'a thing imposed from without', but no claim is made for it as a 'built book', and it is described as 'nakedly picaresque and plotless'.

Apart from structure there is the question of expansion. Much of Kipling's narrative style is highly condensed. In the earliest published work, what is condensed is often simple in itself; the condensation gives it impact, edge and a spectacular quality. In the later works, what is condensed is complex, and the condensation makes for pressure and high vitality at the cost of some difficulty. *The Light that Failed*, however, is not particularly condensed in utterance. It is allowed, or encouraged, to flow. The writing never runs to waste, but it is explicit and fully expressive. Scenes and feelings are worked out, and people declaim and debate their opinions. Nothing is hinted or bitten back; it is a style of full statement. There are examples of a similar style to be found in the tales, from the time that Kipling was free from the two-thousand-word limit of the *Civil and Military Gazette* until about a dozen years later. It is not a matter of bravura-pieces, like the seascapes in '*Captains Courageous*' or ' "Their Lawful Occasions" ', but of the space allotted to the movement of a tale and especially to conversations. *The Story of the Gadsbys* is positively leisurely in its literal record of the ordinary experiences of the ordinary good fellow, with the 'soft drop' in him. 'William the Conqueror' extends to two parts and seems to wish to be a novel, if it could, but has not got the principle of growth in it. It moves as if the author were consciously practising a long-distance stride to keep himself supple for the course that he may one day run. In it, moreover, and in 'The Brushwood Boy', he has tried to find a version of the man-and-maid theme that will suit his range of tones. The novel, however, did not come of these exercises; or not the novel as Kipling, the traditionalist, understood the *genre*. What he meant by it is seen in the well-known description at the end of *Something of Myself* of the three-decker that he never built, 'each curve melting deliciously into the next that the sea might nowhere meet resistance or weakness . . . a vessel ballasted on ingots of pure research and knowledge, roomy, fitted with delicate cabinet-work below-decks . . . an East Indiaman worthy to lie alongside *The Cloister and the Hearth*'. Critics have been surprised at the comparison, but it connects with his account of writing *Rewards and Fairies*, into which he put 'the bones of one entire historical novel for any to clothe who cared'. These bones can hardly be other than 'Brother Square-Toes' and ' "A Priest in Spite of Himself" ', and we see that the three-decker would indeed have been laid down on ample lines and would have plied on that Atlantic crossing which was so much in his mind.

This was in 1910, a little more than half-way through Kipling's writing life, and much more than half-way along the row of his volumes on the shelf. After that the hope must have faded, if not the regret, for there seem to be no traces of the aborted novel in the later tales. There is, however, in the last three collections a development that should have assuaged his disappointment; for here, to some extent in '"My Son's Wife"' and 'Mary Postgate' and triumphantly in 'The Wish House' and 'Dayspring Mishandled', he found a way to make the reader perceive the substance of a novel in the words of a short story. This was a reversal of direction from the expansive to the concentrated method. 'William the Conqueror' had (perhaps) failed to develop, but in 'The Wish House' and 'Dayspring Mishandled' we are given, in no more than thirty pages, a tangle of individual lives, desires and frustrations through a generation. *Captains Courageous* was constructed by agglutination, but here every fact is structural, every word purposive. The expansion is transferred from the page to the reader's imagination, where the brief statements and their implications gradually ripen and shed their contents. These tales have the capacity of spreading and solidifying in the memory till they lie like tracts of experience in our minds.

'The Wish House' is a marvel of structure in its special kind, and it is a kind directly opposite to the delicate exploration of a limited subject, towards which critical taste tended when it was published in 1924. The tale includes, perhaps, some fifteen years —Kipling does not specify, but it covers the change from horse-drawn vehicles in town and country to charabancs and tractors— and there are glimpses of the years before it begins. The house of the title is the little house, long empty, in a London by-street where Mrs Grace Ashcroft, the cook from Sussex, goes to speak to the Token through the letter-box and take upon herself the pain and death that she believes to be in store for the lover who has left her. I discuss elsewhere in this book whether the reader is to regard the occasion of the sacrifice as real or illusory; to Mrs Ashcroft it is real. It is the act towards which all the lines of her life tend and from which they decline. It is not, however, final in its nature; the decision has to be painfully renewed, again and again, until it becomes habitual and, at last, irrevocable. When Mrs Ashcroft tells her tale, she is dying of cancer and knows that her time will be short.

The story emerges in the stoical talk of two ageing women in a Sussex village, meeting for the last time, since Liz Fettley is going blind and will not be able to visit her friend again. They sit in the little room, shaken by the charabancs that roar past to the football match, with the spring light falling through the geraniums on the window-sill and an abundant tea laid out, 'buttered toast, currant bread, stewed tea, bitter as leather, some home-preserved pears, and a cold boiled pig's tail to help down the muffins'. This Dutch picture is kept before our eyes, but out of the window, as it were, over the shoulder of Mrs Fettley who sits there, pretending to sort the quilt-patches that she will never sew, layer on layer of the past appears—the London of horse-drawn traffic, with the acrid horse-dung piled high in the gutters in summer, the unholy little house in Wadloes Road with the basement-kitchen and the strip of walled garden in front, and beyond that the pastoral Sussex of their youth, a landscape with figures. All the while the interplay goes on between the two friends. Mrs Fettley is 'free-tongued' and inquisitive about things past and present, the new parish visitor, the demands of Mrs Ashcroft's grandson and his striking likeness to Jim Batten from Rye; but nothing stirs Mrs Ashcroft's smooth, weighty self-containment until Liz has told her how the 'death-notice' of a long-ago lover of her own has been read out to her from the newspaper, and then, but not immediately—for the light and air have changed and the kitchen-door has been closed against the chill—she deliberately 'pays' Liz for her confidence with her own story. In this unaccustomed plain-speaking near the end of life old curiosities are satisfied, but the women do not press on each other. Each has carried her pitcher of griefs after her own fashion all her life, and there is no jostling or spilling at the narrow end of the journey. Liz Fettley's story is secondary, and we get no more than a hint of it; it is part of the technique, needed to provoke Grace Ashcroft's proud sense of justice to tell what would otherwise never have been told, and useful in doubling the reflection of the changing conditions of country life. Into her mouth are put the questions that drive to the marrow of the tale, and by her comments she helps to define the social climate in which it takes place and to give an outside view of Grace. Her character is shaped for this function. But Grace's life-story is coherent and intense. There is nothing detached about the incidents that stud the wide expanse, and the curiosity of the detail is never merely decorative. Harry Mockler is a mother's boy, and this explains his one love-affair with a middle-aged woman. We learn this fact when Grace does, when the conviction that he will never turn to another woman is needed to strengthen her to renew her obscure sacrifice. Ashcroft is seen briefly at the beginning of her narrative; he is on

his death-bed and says he is 'death-wise' and can see what is
coming to his amorous and stubborn wife. The few words that
are exchanged between them are as full of matter as the remarks
of the men and women in the sagas, and, together with Mrs
Fettley's query about the six months in Chichester gaol and her
memory of Polly Batten and the hay-fork, indicate the nature of
Grace's married life. A mere inflection of Mrs Ashcroft's voice
hints calmly that her husband's roving eye had rested on Liz,
and sets us considering the nature of the bond between the two
elderly women. All this is conveyed in some thirty lines, and all
of it comes back to the memory, extended by the rational and
humane imagination that Kipling, in this phase, knew so well
how to activate, when Mrs Ashcroft, on her return to her village,
goes with emotionless decorum to put a jam-jar of flowers on her
husband's grave. There are other pointers—Mrs Fettley's stare at
the grocer's bright calendar on the wall long before the admission
that she is 'blindin'' up' is wrung from her—but the patterns are
not overdone; the tide of life flows smoothly through the tale and
through the talk of the women, for it is against a background of
regional and national changes that the individual life suffers its
mutations. Grace's respectable service as cook in London takes
shape beside the picture of her walking with Harry, a middle-
aged woman with painful feet, following on the pavement the
accustomed miles of the countryman. Harry, the groom and
carter, is driving a tractor by the end of the story, or off with
lorries as far as Wales, so that Grace, working through the end of
her life in thirst and deprivation, has yet the drop of jealous
comfort that his job keeps him from settling down. Mrs Fettley's
daughter pays the butcher to chop the suet for her, and her
grandson asks her for as much as three shillings at a time for 'them
aireated wash-poles folk puts up in their gardens to draw the
music from Lunnon, like'; but the friends can remember when
there was 'no cheap-dog pride to folk' and man or woman would
lay hold of any job that promised a shilling, when a London cook
on holiday would take a hand at potato-lifting, in men's boots
with her petticoats shortened. As for their grandsons—'No odds
'twixt boys now an' forty year back. Take all an' give naught—
an' we to put up with it.'

If ever there was a 'built' story, it is this. Almost every paragraph, besides doing its narrative or descriptive work, adds a

stroke to the figure of Grace Ashcroft, that formidable woman. She is immersed in circumstance, but not dominated by it. The *Manchester Guardian*, Kipling reminds us, suggested that in Mrs Ashcroft he had revived Chaucer's Wife of Bath, even to the 'mormal on her shinne', and Kipling leaves us in some doubt whether he is sharing or humouring the mistake. It is Chaucer's Cook, a man, who has the mormal. Nor does Kipling admit the proposed origin. And, indeed, there is not much resemblance between Chaucer's Wife and Mrs Ashcroft, except that both had been mistresses in the 'olde daunce' of love and that both were mastered at length (though the Wife only temporarily) by a younger man. Mrs Ashcroft, too, could have said with the Wife:

> *For certes I am al Venerien*
> *In Feelynge, and myn herte is Marcien;*
> *Venus me yaf my lust, my likerousnesse,*
> *And Mars yaf me my sturdy hardynesse.*

But Grace Ashcroft is a tragic figure; she is like a woman in the sagas, with much the same range of sensibility, the same ancient acceptance of the dark forces in life, and the same stark courage and laconic speech. She goes her own way and keeps her own secrets; what she wants she takes, and pays the price. When Harry Mockler leaves her, her fierce possessiveness finds a way to force him to 'take his good' from her, without knowing it, to her life's end; and her love is purified by its very intensity. There is more shading to the picture than there is room to show, but every touch rises easily out of the conversation. 'But you've 'ad your satisfactions?' she says to Mrs Fettley when she has heard of the engine-driver's death. 'Then you've naught to cast up about.' Early in the tale she is the pensioned cook, remarking thoughtfully in front of her loaded tea-table: 'I dunno as I've ever owed me belly much.' At the end, she is the agonized woman, murmuring in face of death her tenacious hope that 'the pain *do* count to keep 'Arry—where I want 'im. Say it can't be wasted, like'. Then the District Nurse comes in, and the two elderly women pull down the shutters over their whole essence and experience, present a bland and decent front to her, and go to their several sufferings.

This, then, is the way in which Kipling came to master the material of the novel, but he did it by relinquishing the novel form. He did it, he tells us, by thoroughly and honestly imagining all that he afterwards omitted. The dead coal and ash were poked out of the bars of the grate, and the fire burnt brighter, but a great deal of fuel had first been consumed before it reached that pitch of heat. It is with 'The Wish House' in mind that we can turn back more than thirty years to *The Light that Failed*, for nothing of that kind can have taken place here. We have rather the sense of the young author, unleashed on a full-length fiction, speaking from the middle of the experiences on which he bases it, telling himself that he must put this in, and this, and this, and locking the tumultuous stuff into a somewhat arbitrary pattern. It is natural for a young writer to want to write about art; his mind is full of his *métier* as a personal fact, and he has neither solved nor shelved the problems it presents. It is also natural that he should write about love, and if he chooses to write about them together, and to make his hero both lover and artist, he must be prepared to see most of his readers concentrate on the love and ignore the art. This is inevitable, because only a minority can understand the problems of art. It may be because the general reader in France is more ready to sympathize with the problems of the artist as such that the French have been kinder to Kipling's *conte* than the English. They judge it more favourably, because they weigh both sides of it.

The basis of *The Light that Failed* is personal. A great deal that befalls Dick Heldar in the earlier part of the book can be matched in *Something of Myself*. It does not match exactly, partly because Kipling, like Browning, has chosen to write in the terms of another art, not his own, and partly because, proceeding from his own experience, he has imagined alterations of important circumstances. What really happened to him as a child, at the end of his captivity in the House of Desolation, is recorded in 'Baa Baa, Black Sheep', and again in *Something of Myself*. After the loveless misery that he and Punch suffered, both little boys, the real and the fictitious, were returned to their parents and immersed in healing trust and love. Both, however, were scarred for life. Kipling was left, not, as has been loosely said, a cruel man, but certainly with an emotional comprehension of cruelty and an intellectual interest in it. But he was also left with an experience of the natural action of family love, more conscious, one supposes, than that of most children, and this was confirmed by what he saw and met in India. The allusions all through his work to 'men's Mothers', like the hymns of Thackeray to maternal love, are off-key for the present generation, but in both cases substantial truth is conveyed. Throughout *Something of Myself* Kipling insists on his debt to his parents, and in 'The Interregnum', the chapter that describes the heavy toil of the first London months and the confusion and excitement of sudden fame, hyperbolical praise and attack, their arrival, he says, 'simplified things', and his Indian training gave him ballast. Dick Heldar, by a natural action of the creative imagination, is stripped of family and ballast. He is an answer to the question: 'What might have become of me if I had been left in that house for years, without parents or relations, and if the other child there had not been my sister?'[1] What becomes of Dick is that his strong and unexercised affections fasten on Maisie, his partner in hardship, as later on Torpenhow, his partner in work, but that otherwise he is a buccaneer, tough, resentful, arrogant—'an aggressive, cocksure, you-be-damned fellow', say his friends, the war-correspondents, whose soul has been 'fired' before they came across him. At least, these are the facets of his character presented in the first scenes of the book. Having no ballast, and no Wesleyan ministers as grandparents, Dick falls into the pitfalls of his sudden fame. He is not only above himself and greedy for the oats that have at last been poured into his starveling manger, but he succumbs to the temptation of trading deliberately inferior work, and smartens up and sentimentalizes the Rifleman of his picture, 'His Last Shot', because the art-manager of *Dickenson's Weekly* says his readers will not enjoy anything so brutal as a true sketch of a man fighting for his life. Then Torpenhow addresses him for his good; and here, and in the conversations between Dick's friends, and again when Dick, graduating from culprit to dominie, tries to instruct Maisie in the nature of good work, his creator, who like Dick had been 'called up to notoriety' at twenty-four, cleared his mind of the problems that beset him, as he tried to come to terms with his genius and the world it operated in.

[1] I leave this passage as it was first written before Professor Charles Carrington's *Rudyard Kipling* (1955) made it known that, when Kipling revisited Southsea as a schoolboy, there was indeed another girl there, with whom he fell in love. It is plain from the evidence about Florence Garrard that the presentation of Maisie, and Dick's relations to her, also derive in large measure from personal experience. Working entirely from within the text of Kipling's books, I could not risk a guess; but this evidence must confirm the suspicions of a great many readers.

Through the lips of Dick or Torpenhow or the Nilghai the supposedly hard-bitten young journalist speaks enthusiastically of the sacredness of art; he insists that to think of success is to produce bad work, but admits remorsefully to pleasure in the praise that even bad work brings him. He considers the ignorance of his audience, which yet it is suicidal to cheat or despise, and offsets his perception of the infinitesimal proportion of the world's population that cares for art as art by the pleasure of the untaught admirers—the two artillery men outside the print-shop and Yellow Tina at Port Said, recognizing in Dick's sketches the truth of the facts they dealt in. He records his spleen at artistic circles, where untravelled critics questioned the authenticity of Dick's colouring and queried if his work was art; and he declares that colour is a natural gift but that what matters to the artist who has it is line, which he can be drilled into. All this boiled up and spilled over, and was strained as well as it is possible to strain when there has been no time for the sediment to settle. Some of the ingredients of the brew had lasting virtue. The sarcastic definition of art—'find out what the public likes and give it them again'—which marks the nadir of Dick's wilful debasement of his work for money, shows that Kipling had already accepted the clause in his contract with his Daemon, never to follow up a success. Others were of less durable quality, distilled by the contemptuous astonishment of the returned Anglo-Indian for the ways of his home-keeping kin and the 'heathen' City of London, and they can be matched in the verse and prose that he sent from London to the *Pioneer*, to be found in *Abaft the Funnel*.

It is not in India but in the Sudan that Dick Heldar learns to love the soldier, but the upshot is the same as it was for his creator, a determination to set down without evasion the conditions of his life and the cost of his services. Dick has roughed it about the globe to a much greater extent than Kipling ever did; he has seen battle and brutality, and Torpenhow, who finds him at Suakin sketching 'a clump of shell-torn bodies', describes his work sardonically as 'Verestchagin-and-water'. Dick, like Kipling at that date, looks in his art for 'subjects under the influence of strong excitement', such as those he produces from his sketch-book: 'Row on a Chinese pig-boat. . . . Chief mate dirked by a comprador. . . . Somali muleteer being flogged. . . . Star-shell bursting over camp at Berbera. . . . Soldier lying dead in the moonlight outside Suakin—throat cut by Fuzzies.' Maisie is later to tell him that his 'things smell of tobacco and blood'. This zest for the masculine excitement of violence stands very much in Kipling's light at present. It is not the nature of the record—that has been outdone, again and again, by much respected writers—but the zest. The artist's satisfaction in drastic pose and startling colour seems to come uppermost in the effect, and to obscure from a generation conscripted for violence his honourable effort to force the physical conditions of warfare into the imaginations of an uninformed public. Certainly both elements may be detected. Kipling, moreover, was not at Suakin, though he saw to it that Dick Heldar was. This should not in itself be a valid objection to subject or treatment, but the recent course of history has given it an accidental weight. He tried to meet a similar objection with good humour in the light verses 'The Story of Ung', but the answer is intentionally superficial. Violence is a permanent expression of human nature, and its potentialities must always stimulate the imagination of certain types of artists; the more so if it is seen to be evaded and falsified in contemporary art. Dick in his buccaneer days has no qualms; he rejoices in what is 'given' him and later, leaning out of his London window, addresses the great city with the usual misinterpretation of Blücher's words: 'What a city to loot.' By this time the looting is not primarily financial, but it is clear that in this greedy, intense acquisition of human types and experience he has no scruples and no compassion. It is a brutal hand that, in Port Said, turns the face of Binat, the ruined artist, to the light and at the cost of an extra half-sovereign records his 'degradation so tremendous'. On Westminster Bridge, just before he sees Maisie again, he exults to think that the misery and wretchedness in the crowds that flow past him are all material for his art.

It is, however, very flighty reading that thinks that here Kipling is applauding his hero. Dick is, as Bagehot says of Browning's characters, the type in difficulties; he has fallen into the spiritual dangers of which his maker was more aware than he. In the eighth chapter of *From Sea to Sea* Kipling describes his exploration of the night-life of Hong-Kong, the nerve-ridden women he met in its haunts, and how, being taken for a doctor, he spent hours trying to soothe one of them in horror of cholera. He puts it all down for the *Pioneer*, and he also puts down, with youthful and embarrassing fervour, his sense of guilt in having 'made capital out of her extreme woe'. Yet the opportunity was 'given' and not to be rejected. Many young writers pass through a phase of this trouble, and later, having done its sensitizing work, the trouble recedes. Writers, however, do not appear in Kipling's tales (except Eustace Cleever, who is not relevant to this point) and the problem is translated into terms of the painter's art. Much later, in 'The Eye of Allah', we meet John Otho, the only other artist among his characters, except the old lama in *Kim*. This young man regards men as 'matter for drawings', and paints his beautiful Virgin from his memory of the face of his dead mistress. His artist's concentration and ruthlessness are part of the story, since he alone, having used the microscope—'The Eye of Allah'—for what it was worth to his art, does not protest at the Abbot's destruction of it; but his sensibility is not explored. Consciously or unconsciously, he has accepted his nature and function. Dick, who is forced to plumb his mind by what he conceives to be Maisie's need, gets no further than saying that men—living men or the twelve hundred dead on the Sudan battlefield, whose number roughly equates that of the people in the world who understand art—are to the artist strictly only material to work with, but that unfortunately one must be either a man or a woman, and that, 'even if one were an angel and painted humans altogether from outside, one would lose in touch what one gained in grip'. The balance is not struck; it cannot, in fact, be struck by thinking about it. The artist does, or does not, draw on the whole extent of his experience, and his art can, or cannot, cope with all he knows. In *The Light that Failed* Kipling was trying to put everything in, and Dick Heldar is blurred in consequence. At times his maker is too much in his skin, at times he is too deeply moved with pity for him or with exaltation at his deserved chastisement, for him to stand out, defined and whole, as Maisie does. Kipling trims the joints carefully. 'There are the makings of a very fine prig in you, Dick', says Torpenhow to the whilom buccaneer; but the care betrays some embarrassment. He does better with the question of compassion. Dick qualifies for the 'tremendous thrashing' that Torpenhow promises him, and recognizes that he is getting it in his infatuation for Maisie and his inability to prevent her from following the false god of success or to help her overtake it.

The red-haired girl, sketching his face as he sits looking at Maisie, treats him as he treated Binat, but, with a compunction he had not shown, burns the sketch. For that Dick shall be disciplined and acknowledge it is part of Kipling's intention.

There is nothing in *Something of Myself* that relates closely to Dick Heldar's love-story. Kipling tells us that in his boyhood he saw a picture of the death of Manon Lescaut and read the book when he was eighteen. It made a great impression on him, and he thinks that 'London' brought it out in a 'metagrobolised' form. These glances into the workings of the artist's mind are always interesting, but they are not always useful for criticism. We should not have guessed it, any more than we should have guessed that the *Alcestis* underlay Mr Eliot's *Cocktail Party*. When we are told we see points of contact, but the 'metagrobolism' has been too complete to leave them much significance. Another 'metagrobolism' suggests itself. The misplaced, enslaving love, the impoverished art and the spoilt picture are all in Browning's 'Andrea del Sarto'. There they are satisfyingly interrelated. Loosen the connection and you have the themes of the main movements of *The Light that Failed*. In all three works love is the destroyer: Manon destroys the gentle, inexperienced Des Grieux as Maisie destroys her much tougher victim. By making her an artist, laborious, devoted, craving for success and limited in power, and by making her incapable of love, Kipling has presented Dick with a problem that brings his whole nature into play. She uses him as he used Binat, and he concedes her right to do so; she is ashamed of herself, but her shame does not generate love. She is Blake's pebble; one of them has to be broken, Dick says; but Maisie is incapable of it. Therefore, we may say, the unloving woman destroys her lover, and the half-artist destroys the master in his art. It is by this conception that much of the emotion in the book is generated, and its predominance appears to be confirmed by the title and by the strong pattern of recurrences within the narrative. In the first chapter the boy Dick is nearly blinded by Maisie's pistol, and later exclaims: 'Spoilt my aim', when her hair blows across his eyes as he is sighting his target. Elements of this pattern, with its accompaniments of a red gleam and the noise of the sea, are repeated when he gets the wound in the desert which ultimately destroys his optic nerve, and just before he meets Maisie again on Westminster Bridge. But when we examine what really happens we do not find the underlining wholly justified. Maisie 'spoils his aim' for the three months of his absorbing and hopeless wooing of her; after that he paints the Melancolia which is his masterpiece. She does not blind him intellectually, for during this time he becomes more, not less, aware of his art and its claims, and of the nature of love. She does not blind him physically, though the agitation and turbulence she wakes in him hurry on his fate. The oculist makes it clear that blindness would have come anyway; it was a hazard of his profession as a war artist.

There is, then, a gap in logic between the facts of the narrative and the striking design imposed upon them. There are other patterns, however, that do not raise such a question, for the book is full of echoes and correspondences. The yellow sea-poppy, nodding on the shore when the Boy Dick first kisses Maisie, reappears, and then is shadowed by the dried rose nodding in the garden during her sleepless night at Vitry-sur-Marne. The two kisses he gives her, as boy and man, and her tears of defeat in his arms the last time they meet, mark the stages of his love-story. Maisie's passionate 'Mine,—mine,—mine', echoes Dick's assertions and is the stamp of the likeness between them, and a barrier to his suit that he is bound by his nature to respect. Binat, the ruined genius, a powerful symbol, crops up in all sorts of contexts. Maisie hears of him, without understanding, in her artschool at Vitry-sur-Marne. The words 'payment' and 'punishment' recur strongly through the whole book, from the time when the boy and girl defy Mrs Jennett's punishments to the time when Dick, half-asleep on the camel that is taking him to the camp and to his death, mutters to himself a 'punishment hymn' of his boyhood. At times the patterns almost click. When Maisie describes the Melancolia she means to paint as a woman who suffered till she could suffer no more and then began to laugh at it all, the next sentence runs: 'The red-haired girl rose up and left the room, laughing.' An older Kipling would certainly have jettisoned some of these patterns. They were his Delilahs, and he became fully aware of their seductive and fallacious power. More than twenty years later, describing in 'Egypt of the Magicians' his first voyage up the Nile, he allowed himself to play with the fancy that the desert, wimpling and changing under the wind-scurries, is where the little devils learn to draw, and he identified their handiwork by the elaborate and purposeless detail, the heaped decoration and over-insistent design. He does not mention his own early novel as he approaches the terrain of its second and last chapters, but his mind is full of the past, and we can make what connections we will.

There is, however, one design with which the little devils had nothing to do, which holds the book together, not by the clamps of an imposed pattern but by a genuine though unmatured life that runs through all its parts. This is the question of degradation, the possible degradations of art, of love, and of life. It is from these that Dick is to be saved, by Torpenhow, by Maisie, and finally even by Bessie's spite in destroying the Melancolia, so that he cannot traffic in it to buy an inglorious physical comfort. It is this thought that controls the book's course during its last chapters, when Kipling is detached from personal experience and working on his imagination. The tragedy is over—not the loss of Maisie, but the loss of the complete artist, trained, enlightened, put through suffering and humbled until he knows what his art is, and then destroyed with his masterpiece; but something remains to be done besides getting Dick off the stage. In the verse at the head of the fourteenth chapter, in which he is to burn his sketches, will his money to Maisie and start out blind for the Sudan, Kipling evokes a captive, maimed and broken in the hands of his enemies, who at the last 'called upon Allah, and died a Believer'. What Dick in this pass believes in is not altogether clear, but what he rejects is clear enough, as is the resurgence of his essential temperament as he forces and lies his way back to the fighting. The lines of the narrative turn upward. He has 'paid for everything' and is free of self-pity. He is back among the sounds and smells of the East—a full battery of them, poured out on the last pages. The fighting men he knows go about their bloody and necessary business, and he exults to hear them. He has come out of the land of bondage, like Israel in the punishment hymn. The epigraph of the last chapter sets the mood of his departure with a verse from Kipling's favourite 'Tom a' Bedlam's Song':

> *With a heart of furious fancies,*
> *Whereof I am commander;*
> *With a burning spear and a horse of air*
> *To the wilderness I wander—*

and in Dick's last words—'Put me, I pray, in the forefront of the battle'—Kipling's excited Muse, under the cover of quotation, reached for the proud amplitude of Jacobean speech. The allusion is to Uriah, and the unspoken words are 'that I may be smitten, and die'.

The handling of some of the scenes in *The Light that Failed* has a lack of emotional reserve that brings up the question of Kipling's sentimentality. This question will not be debated here, for it cannot be discussed profitably out of its historical, social and linguistic context. The term itself, always fluctuating in meaning, seems to be stuffed just now with a more than usually variable content. At times it seems to cover all modes of treatment that are not strictly objective, so that it might be applied to the whole tradition of English fiction, except for a few recent practitioners. At the other extreme, it indicates those emotions, or that degree of them, with which the speaker is most reluctant to be assailed. We should all agree that to indulge in emotion in excess of the requirements of the subject, or to the obliteration of them, is bad and sentimental art; but to impose our own view of the requirements on the artist may be bad, and even sentimental, criticism. Yet, though our standards are mutable, though they are elemented by age, experience, sex, class and fashion, we cannot cease to apply them for we cannot cease to react to what affects us as second-rate, embarrassing, overdone or over-sweet. At present the taste in literature, as in wine, leans to the dry flavours, and these alone seem adult; but wine has been consumed hot and sweet, and so has literature.

The emotion in *The Light that Failed* is heady but it is not factitious; it is genuinely a part of the subject. The friendship of the men, the craving of the lover, the passion of the artist, the pathos of his blindness—these are not slipshod conventions. The very defiance, amounting at times to blatancy, with which they are projected on to paper, is the measure of the writer's conviction. Indeed, there are not many pages in Kipling's works of which it may fairly be said that the emotion rises from inadequate causes, or intrudes irrelevantly into its context, and most of these belong to his crowded twenties. He spoilt the grim farce of 'The Mutiny of the Mavericks' by a (to me) incredible episode with the regimental colours; but the tale is not an important one. Changing social habits throw an unsympathetic light on some passages.

Kipling tells us that, at the Grange, he was allowed to blow the big organ in the studio for his beloved Aunt Georgy, and this association with the little boy's intense relish of his too short intervals of peace and domestic affection must lie behind the hymn-playing mother in 'A Deal in Cotton'. Agnes Strickland's style is out of date, but she stands relevantly in the frame of the tale to indicate one necessary part of the breeding and training of 'The New Knighthood'. The soft, relaxed tone of this passage, the reliance on attitudes that are now—and were even then—felt to be cloying, may usefully recall some sensible remarks by Keats's friend, Richard Woodhouse, on mawkishness. 'The feeling of mawkishness', he wrote to John Taylor, 'seems to me that which comes upon us when anything of great tenderness and simplicity is met with when we are not in a sufficiently tender and simple frame of mind to hear it: when we experience a sort of revulsion or resiliency (if there be such a word) from the sentiment or expression.' This divides the responsibility for the failure in communication between writer and reader. The reader is recalcitrant and the writer has not managed him properly. The writer's response to some imagined situation has been, for personal reasons, unusually quick and warm, and he has assumed the reader's sympathy instead of creating it; or, alternatively, he has been moved to aggressiveness, to break violently through some accepted reserve, and has expected to carry his unprepared reader with him. In this last case, however, time and change are involved, since what is accepted varies from group to group and from generation to generation. Nothing chills response like the shorthand of a group to which we do not belong, or the idiom that has become stale and somewhat ridiculous. Nothing is more perturbing than the antics of a writer as he makes up to a barrier that is no longer there, or invokes a symbol that has lost its original reference. Kipling was keenly interested in codes and idioms, and often, particularly in his earlier work, he chooses to move within them, and more often still to display them. But at times these limits are too strict for him; his strong emotional nature requires the scope of explicit statement; and then, both in the outbreak and the reimposed check, there is apt to be an uneasy assertiveness as of one testifying loudly on an unsuitable occasion. The fact that the testimony is true—that parental love, the suffering of children, the comradeship of men, the devotion or the despair of the young are indeed sources of profound emotion—does not diminish the embarrassment; probably for a time it increases it. But this embarrassment itself is subject to time and change. Kipling has now, it seems, three kinds of readers. Circumstances bring back from the periphery of our culture older readers to whom such phrases as the lump in the throat and the stiff upper lip are serious expressions of the facts they indicate, and to whom the technique of strangled and diverted emotional expression, interrupted by moments of outrageous directness, is familiar and acceptable. There are others to whom these things are intensely irritating—I remember somewhere an exasperated comment that it is actually the lower lip that requires stiffening—so that they cannot accept or even listen to what is told them in this mode. And already we have the third kind, the younger readers, to whom Kipling's mannerisms of language and attitude are as much a matter of history as Lamb's puns or Dickens's dealings with Little Em'ly. In a short while it will be possible to see the critical problem fairly, as it has become possible with Thackeray's sentimentality.

Meanwhile I admit that there are passages in the earlier Kipling where the emotion is too blatant for me, and passages, early and late, where it is a little too soft. They are local inflammations, natural blemishes in the work of a writer who dealt in states of strong excitement and liked to do so in strong colours. My own reaction must, moreover, be due in part to the idols of my particular den. In *The Light that Failed* I wish that, in the scene where Torpenhow finds the half-blind Dick easing himself through the last stages of the Melancolia with drink, Kipling had not first executed his I-could-an-if-I-would manoeuvre in approaching the 'sacred and intimate' reproof of a friend, and then side-stepped into semi-jocularity with a hint at the unseemliness of Torpenhow's metaphors. The rapid succession of exposure and evasion shakes the focus of the scene, though it cannot discredit it. I can find other technical reasons for my recoil; the words 'sacred and intimate' are an intrusion of the author on his story; they are an appeal to the reader to supplement what the author should have told through his characters and his incidents. But these are all rationalizations of a personal distaste. Such blemishes diminish in the perspective of time and are taken with less perturbation, even where they are still disapproved. Let an author be a hundred years dead and they are seen as the idiom of his genius, running into temporary excess, and a variant of that of his age. Kipling's idiom, though often curt and packed, was seldom austere. He was, like so many figures in English literature—Webster, Smollett, De Quincey, Dickens, Browning—essentially an emphatic writer, and in this he went with the grain of the language and followed in a deep hereditary track. *The Light that Failed* is an emphatic work. Image, assertion, eloquence, irony are all means, direct or indirect in action, of raising the content to its highest emotional and imaginative power. It is essentially a young man's book. Later he learnt to use fewer of his heavy strokes and to apply them dramatically.

The fate in publication of this considerable effort is not without irony. It is widely known that the tale, as first published in *Lippincott's Magazine* and in the first American reprints in book form, ended happily with Maisie's surrender to Dick. It is not so widely known that it was also much shorter. The conversations about art are much reduced; we do not find the visit to Fort Keeling with the passage about the 'go-fever', or the fine description of the picture Dick painted in the lower deck of the crazy ship, 'just three colours and no chance of getting any more, and the sea outside and unlimited love-making inside, and the fear of death atop of everything else'—an achievement quite free from the thought of success, since no one saw it but the stevedores. The last half of Chapter VI, in fact, and all of Chapters VII and VIII of the standard edition are absent.[1] Professor Carrington has explained that the limits of the magazine would not have admitted the complete novel, but apparently no evidence remains to prove whether it was first written at length and afterwards shortened and deflected for the magazine market, or whether *Lippincott's* was the original finished form. The former is by far the more probable. To take only one point, Bessie's destruction of the Melancolia hangs in air in this version: nothing comes of it; Dick does not know it has happened and it is not even used to motivate Maisie's submission. When the full English edition came out with the tragic end, Kipling confined himself to writing that it

---

[1] I rely on the British Museum copy of the *Lippincott's* version, of which a few copies were issued in London to secure English copyright (c.f. Charles Carrington, *Rudyard Kipling*, p. 167). This is 61 in Miss Flora V. Livingston's *Bibliography of the Works of Rudyard Kipling* (1927), but she does not state that it is in eleven chapters, not the twelve of the first authorized American edition.

contained 'the story of *The Light that Failed* as it was originally conceived by the Writer', and of that there can be no doubt. The badness of the happy ending is quite shocking. Maisie lets down her hair and talks baby-talk, and says that, when a woman loves a man, she does not care for his work, which, whatever comfort this doubtful generalization may offer to the disabled Dick, is wholly false to Maisie, whose charm was that she understood like a man. At the end, for good measure, the assembled journalists sing 'the terrible Battle Hymn of the Republic'. Kipling was well aware of what he was doing, and it was exactly what Dick Heldar had done with 'His Last Shot' and executed with the same 'cold-blooded insolence'. Art was submerged in love, and he might hope that the magazine-reader, satisfied with the final union of man and maid, would have forgotten the stern warnings in Chapter IV about the integrity of the artist and the 'obligations of the service'. In the first authorized American edition,[1] however, all Chapter VI and Chapter VII are included (Chapter VIII did not make its appearance until the first English edition in 1891), the discussions on art and success are continued between Dick and Maisie, and the reader is enabled to measure the distance between intention and performance. 'I don't practise what I preach', Dick admits to Maisie. It is, however, disproportionate to spend much moral fervour on this episode. Other writers have dipped their colours before their publishers and their public, and the 'originally conceived' version has quite displaced that in *Lippincott's*. But it must have been with a high sense of irony that Kipling re-entered the skin of his hero in his most buccaneering phase.

'Under any circumstances,' says Dick to Maisie, 'four-fifths of everybody's work must be bad.' No doubt the recurrent pendulum-swing of humility made it easier to fadge the deplorable alternative ending, when it was called for; but only about one-fifth of *The Light that Failed* is bad. In it a young man, who was already a considerable writer, explored a wrong turning; the novel was not for him. There were other wrong turnings at about the same time, the Meredithian 'Lamentable Comedy of Willow Wood', for instance, and the stodgy blank verse of 'Evarra and his Gods', but none explored at such length or with such sincere fervour as this. Into his novel he poured his life and experience,

[1] New York. United States Book Company, successors to John W. Lovell Company. No. 25, *Westminster* Series, Dec. 5th, 1890.

his deepest concerns no less than his temporary circumstances, and it is not surprising that later, seeing its faults, he still betrayed in his tone an affection for it. Its faults were not at all those of a jerry-builder, though certainly some of the materials he used were less seasoned than he judged at the time. What it lacks is composure and the distancing that all his best work has. There is, moreover, a certain disharmony between its nature and its manner. Its nature, setting aside the ardent fabrications of the conclusion, is that of an interim report, written *in medias res;* but the manner, with its patterns and echoes, the firm outline of its detail, its ringing ironies and aphorisms, makes the opposite effect, as of something concluded, summed up, comprehended, judged. He had drawn much of his material from a part of his personality other than that displayed in the confident and worldly 'I' of the Indian tales, but it was often this 'I' that shaped his sentences.

Nothing of this kind happened with *Kim*. That book was doubly distanced in time and space. It was conceived in Vermont and finished in Sussex, some half-dozen years later, and though it is dated a little after Kipling left India—the 1887 Jubilee is over when Kim meets the old Ressaldar early in his adventures, and they cover about three years—in feeling its roots run back behind 'Seven Years Hard' to the days of his Indian childhood. Not that Kim is such a child—Lockwood Kipling's first illustration is here a little misleading, for he is thirteen when we meet him—but that he is completely at home in his rich and varied world, and has never entered the House of Desolation. His lies are for profit and gaiety; his fears are never stronger than his curiosity or his resource; he has not learnt the lesson of hatred, but, like all happy children, he has begun unconsciously to learn the lesson of love, and he learns it more fully as the book proceeds. Death is near him, as it had been near the little house on the Bombay Esplanade, where his creator's first years were spent, but it does not trouble him. He is the Friend of the Stars; the cards are dealt him, as Kipling generously said of his own hand, and he has but to play them. He is also the Little Friend of all the World, as he is first called in the Lahore ward where he grows up, a casteless waif, curious, flexible, resilient, accustomed to blows, but quite free from tyranny, and fed by the charitable gifts of the people who are always called gentle and kindly. Intrigue and murder are part of his world, but, since he is wary and spirited, they excite without oppressing his imagination. Kipling's concern in this book is not with any form of evil or terror. Kim is a limpid eye through which he looks back on 'the great and beautiful land' of Hind. The vision is romantic in that, though complex in detail, it is simplified in impact. It is a youthful, enthusiastic and acquisitive vision. It is the artist's 'loot', though Kim is no artist, but content to immerse his self-contained, ambiguous little entity in the warm and flashing stream. It is not, however, a romance of maharajahs and fabulous jewels; it is nearer to the romance that brings up the nine-fifteen; the characters are small landowners, horse-dealers, peasants, shopkeepers and clerks, and Kim has no taste at all for the heavy-footed soldiery with their red faces.

Kipling has called this book plotless, and there is no justification for going behind this description. Nevertheless, certain balances are kept and certain turning-points are marked. The book falls symmetrically into three parts, and the divisions are equal to within a page or two. The first five chapters lift the Irish-born, Indian-bred waif out of his setting in the slums of Lahore, acquaint him with one of the directive forces of his life, the Tibetan lama, bring him to the fringe of the other, the Indian Government Intelligence Service, and return him to his countrymen and his father's regiment. The middle five are devoted to his training, and the last five to the testing of the sixteen-year-old lad, now at last entered for the 'Game' on the threshold of adult life. Tests there have been all through the book, contrived and fortuitous. Lurgan tests him when he tries to hypnotize him, Hurree Babu when he slips in the disrespectful 'Old Creighton' to see if Kim will pass it, but at Shamlegh-under-the-Snows he sustains a multiple test of his intelligence, hardihood and self-control—even of his ability to jettison the desirable but incriminating equipment of the Russian agents—and that is followed by the profounder and long-drawn strain of the lama's spiritual trouble, which Kim only half comprehends, and of his physical weakness, which he supports with his own overtaxed strength. One result of this testing is that he graduates as a reliable 'chain-man' in what is euphemistically called the Government Survey. This end is an anti-climax to some readers, especially to those who disapprove of the British rule in India, but also to those who think that the spiritual progress of the lama's *chela* should have led him to some such withdrawal as that of Purun Bhagat. Kim, however, is barely seventeen when we leave him, and Purun Bhagat, who has been, in accordance with the recommendations of the Old Law, 'twenty years a youth, twenty years a fighter ... and twenty years head of a household' is on the verge of old age. Mr Edmund Wilson's expectation that Kim would throw in his lot with his mother's people should be mentioned, because it is based on a mistake; Kim's mother, as Kipling explicitly tells us, was Irish too. However the end is weighed, it is foreseen from the beginning, and there is no excuse for surprise. It is on the self-same day that Kim learns of the lama's search for the River of the Arrow, that washes away sin, and perceives that the pedigree of the white stallion, given him by Mahbub Ali for Colonel Creighton, is a matter of life and death; and henceforth the Search and the Game exercise a double attraction upon him, and he goes through the book with the lama on one hand and Mahbub Ali, to whom are soon associated Colonel Creighton, Lurgan and Hurree Babu, on the other. He understands the Game more readily than the Search, but the lama's gentle, selfless wisdom is more compulsive on him, even at first, than the fascination of having a price on his head and a number instead of a name. There is, however, no point at which a choice between the two ways of life is forced upon him, and at his age he would hardly have reached such a point. Nor is it inevitable in the future. The sympathies of the book are inclusive not exclusive, and the lama assumes that his beloved, now freed from sin by the accomplishment of the Search, will remain in the world as a 'scribe', since 'to that end he was prepared'. Kim himself is not credited with any political opinions at all. The Game to him is a 'good service', satisfying his curiosity, his adventurousness and his sense of importance, and putting into play his unique qualifications. At the end there is a pension, though Hurree Babu is more interested in this than Kim, and to both of them money is less important than the exercise of their special aptitudes. For Kipling, certainly, these aptitudes are finally directed to the welfare of India, as he conceived it, and Kim, steadied at moments by his knowledge that he is a Sahib and a boy of St Xavier's, but aware of no boundaries of caste, colour or status, is, as it were, an offering of the imagination to this welfare. History has thrown this conception out of perspective, but the book, which was written in love, is not much hurt by that. Kim remains a 'chain-man' in another sense, a bridge suspended for the passage of understanding between two territories of Kipling's heart. Kim's own welfare, moreover, requires that he should enter some service; for to Kipling the masterless man, who carries no yoke, has not come into his full manhood.

The lama has nothing to do with the Game; he is, when we meet him, wholly set on the Search; but the great world of his pilgrimage has already stirred in the one-time abbot of Such-zen a response that is faintly discordant with his ascetic rule. He has heard the singing-game of a woman with her baby and remembers it to repeat to a village-child. His heart is the more readily open to Kim, because he thinks he may be a disciple sent to guide him on his quest. His unused capacity for affection flows out to the lad who protects him and begs for him and knows his way so well in the terrible, crowded world, and this love brings him at times to moments of anxious self-scrutiny, since it plunges the devotee, who would be free from the Wheel, back into the mists of Desire. The beauty of *Kim* lies largely in the figure of the lama, which is drawn with great delicacy. Benign, courteous, humble and clean of heart, but a man of authority in his place and time, he draws Kim not to any mystical height—the boy remains firmly terrestrial and takes a very practical view of the lama's immersion in the River of the Arrow—but to a perception of these qualities in his master and a loving service of them. The childish attraction, mixed with inquisitiveness and self-importance—'He is a very holy man . . . I am his *chela*'—grows into the patience of the hungry lad in the Jain monastery, the self-command that submits to unmerited rebuke at the moment when he has made his first independent success in the Game, and to the self-forgetful fury with which he flings himself at the armed Russian who has struck the Holy One.

The special tenderness in the writing of *Kim* has much to do with the opposition of age and youth. Except Kim himself the chief characters are old, Mahbub, the Sahiba, the Ressaldar and the lama. They feel the solicitude of the aged for the young. They move in their own closed worlds of experience, which are pictures and stories to the boy. The Ressaldar quavers the song of Nikal Seyn, the Sahiba remembers the ways of mountain rajahs in her youth, and the lama the battles between the Himalayan monasteries and the novices placing the cups. A delicate humour touches

Mahbub's jealousy, the Sahiba's chiding affection, and the readiness with which the lama accepts the excuses, suggested to him by his tactful hosts in the Jain temple, for his visits to Kim; and this is blended with the general pathos of old age, the impatience of failing strength and the dependance on the vitality of the young. 'Surely,' says the lama, 'old folk are as children . . . they desire a matter—behold, it must be done at once, or they fret and weep. Many times when I was upon the road I have been ready to stamp with my feet at the hindrance of an ox-cart in the way, or a mere cloud of dust. It was not so when I was a man—a long time ago.'

In the Himalayan chapters these subjects—the Game, the Search, the love between youth and age—are more closely developed than would be expected in a 'nakedly picaresque' book. Beyond and above Kim's ordeal, like a distant, cloud-piercing peak beyond the crest of one of the lower hills, towers the lama's crisis. We see it with a double vision, humanly, as Kim does, and thereafter in the lama's stern interpretation. The old mountaineer's renewal of strength and pleasure in his prowess, the flash from under the ashes of mortified years of a moment's indignant anger, become to him, as he meditates in the little hut on the edge of the precipice, filled with mingled moonshine and lamplight, so many plunges backwards into illusion and the gross life of the senses. He is beaten back like a strayed yak; there is only a finger-nail's breadth of life left to him on the torn chart of the Wheel, and his Search is still unfulfilled. There follow the moving farewell to the hills and the panic-stricken flight back to the plains. While, however, the threads are plaited together all through the book, they cannot be said to be drawn into a masterknot. One cannot replace the missing choice of Kim by an ordeal of the lama. It is not his love for Kim that provides the crisis. The tension in that has been wholly relaxed since he has accepted his *chela* as the medium of his Search and the beneficiary of its achievement. His spiritual anguish, like his serenity, are things that Kim comes to know about, that bring him to maturity. The tale presses no further into these regions than the travellers did into the Himalayas. The great heights are beyond. Yet, because the lama's love is the most important of the things that Kim comes to know, its consummation makes the end of the book.

It is partly the absence of insistent patterns in *Kim* that makes the narrative run so smoothly; partly, no doubt, the depth of memory and delight from which it was drawn. The contrasts present themselves easily. The scene opens and shuts. We are in a shop or a crowded railway-carriage, and presently marching brow-bound against the blowing desert sands or ambling through the league-wide crops. The ground spreads into the plains or piles itself up into the heights. Much of the charm of the pictures is in the lighting, and this varies continually. The sun sets red through a mango-grove or washes across the gold-coloured grass of a hillside; the lights prick out in Simla; the Sahiba's palanquin swings round the homestead with its escort of smoky torches, and the old servitor curls his white moustaches savagely in the young moonlight; and then the dawn rises cold on the waking camps, the railway-sidings, the little villages with their temples and the cool, cut stone of the cells of the Jain monks. And from these sliding scenes there rises a babble of voices, men, women and children in gossip, abuse, advice, remonstrance, Indian, English and Indian-English, with the gong-like swell of the lama's tones to close the variations. Kipling is masterly in his appeal to the aural imagination. This gift, like his other gifts, is not flawless. The language of Mulvaney has often been attacked (though the notation should be questioned here as well as the observation. What does Kipling mean by 'sorr'?). Scots have disclaimed the talk of McPhee and Germans, no doubt, that of Muller. The child-talk of his early tales is highly questionable and it may well be—I do not know—that the language he evolves for Mahbub Ali and the lama is faulty as an impression of what they would really have said. Mr Hilton Brown declares that the feats of objurgatory description achieved by his soldiers and sailors are not at all like the usual fashion of abuse in the Services; and even at his best one may be momentarily aware of a slight check (the lama's 'thou'lt', for instance, in the first chapter of *Kim*) before his imagination has entirely appropriated the idiom it has created. But what is under consideration is not authenticity —the exactness of ear and record that makes it impossible for Trollope or Rose Macaulay to write a sentence of dialogue at which the reader boggles—but the quality that Maisie lacked— conviction. The analogy is rather with the speech of Dickens or Ben Jonson, triumphs of style and flavour, shaped on the lips of the author for the lips of the reader. In his later work he learnt to use the normal speech of contemporary educated Englishmen for his purpose, as in 'Sea Constables' and 'Dayspring Mishandled', where there is no marked local or professional colouring, but his earlier successes are chiefly in character-parts. Thus we have the exquisite fantasy of the Portuguese Governor's broken English in 'Judson and the Empire' ('Madeira she are still to us, and I have of the best she manufac') and, in *Kim*, the proverbs and puns of the Sahiba and the rich parade of Hurree Babu's English, contrasted with his sensible directness when he is speaking Hindi. But the very best of Kipling, and it is not often attained, is not in these arabesques, but in a translucent simplicity that he can reach when his eye is single. It is found when the lama comforts Kim after the descent from the Himalayas, unharmed by the faint colouring of archaism; it is found, in narrative, in the last pages of 'The Miracle of Purun Bhagat', sustained throughout, save for two sentences that are like a hot fingermark on glass, and fade in the memory as quickly. It is found in the tales he wrote for children, when the thought of his audience melted out the complexities and ecstasies of craftsmanship These passages are not show-pieces and they cannot often be lifted from their contexts without injury. It is perhaps significant that most of them deal with the simplifications of old age, the quiet retrospect and the unemphatic wisdom. Akin to them, but not the same, are the passages of grave elevation, such as the reception of the news of the death of Maximus in 'Winged Hats'. They have the ring of metal, the controlled weight of rhetoric put to its proper use, but were perhaps willed and achieved; the rarer simplicities seem to flower from the soil.

Some of the depth of perspective in *Kim* is due to the old people. The Ressaldar looks back to the Mutiny, when he rode seventy miles with an English mem-sahib and her babe on his saddle-bow, the lama to the high black seats of his mountain-monastery and, far beyond that, to the wanderings of the Blessed Feet through India. This historical distance will sometimes be given by a single sentence in Kipling, as when in 'The Tomb of his Ancestors' he writes: 'All India is full of forgotten graves.' But there is another kind of distancing in the book that grows almost imperceptibly from the lama's reiteration of 'illusion'. It is not so powerful as the treble distancing of 'The Bridge Builders', where the responsible frenzy of heavy construction-work is reduced by stages to an infinitesimal speck on the great wheels of mutability, as they swing us through historical and geological change until the solid world melts in the dream of Brahm. None the less, a vibration spreads from the word, and at times the hard edges of the multifarious bright objects quiver. Once the rich land that is Kim's playground is called 'the great, grey, formless India', and three times, at turning-points in his life, Kim, repeating his name, questions his identity. And if these three passages may seem a little patched on, though with a purpose (everything revolves round Kim, but *what* is Kim?), no such charge can be brought against the phrase, so surprising and yet so inevitable, with which the lama takes his farewell from the high hills, blessing them in detail—'the great glaciers, the naked rocks, the piled moraines and tumbled shale; dry upland, hidden salt-lake, age-old timber and fruitful water-shot valley'—and calling them 'shadows blessed above all other shadows'. During most of the book we are absorbed in brilliant detail with the definition of a miniature; the lama picks out in the photographs in the Lahore Museum 'the little door through which we bring wood before winter', the 'long-haired, strong-scented Sansis with baskets of lizards and other unclean food on their backs' travel the Great Trunk Road in 'a quick, furtive jog-trot', the Sahiba's jewelled forefinger snaps out 'little sparks of light between the embroideries' of the palanquin curtains; but at times we hear the ceaseless human knocking on the doors of mystery. 'All India is full of holy men stammering gospels in strange tongues; shaken and consumed in the fires of their own zeal; dreamers, babblers and visionaries.' Without the lama, this might be only part of the romantic plenitude of the scene, another note in the reiterated rich chord of the strange, the amazing, the mysterious; with the lama, it is perceived as the antithetical thirst for liberation. There is, however, no dwelling on this note. The distant view closes. The cheerful, active things of the world cut across the Search. The Sahiba's pet palanquin paddles up 'with a hot air of importance' to terminate the lama's ghostly comfort, which has already modulated delicately into mirth, and Kim's questioning of his identity ends with the 'almost audible click' with which he feels 'the wheels of his being lock up anew on the world without'. The play of humour over the whole book is like the sunlight sifted through branches. The bright spots slide and recoil. The lama starts to explain the Way to the Ressaldar, and both old men fall asleep. The attainment of the River is an occasion for Hurree Babu's science. ('He is afflicted with infirmity of fits. Yes, I tell you. Cataleptic, too, if not also epileptic.') Kipling rounds off his tale with the *chela* at his master's feet, 'outlined jet-black against the lemon-coloured drift of light' of the sunset, but the voices of the Many are only temporarily hushed. The lama's life is near its end; in six months the *chela* will be beyond Balkh with Mahbub Ali. The myriad lives of India, ascending and descending, turn upon the Wheel, and an old man in a dream wins salvation for his beloved.

If *Kim* is set beside Mark Twain's *Huckleberry Finn*, to which Kipling had referred in No. XXVI of *From Sea to Sea*, certain qualities are brought out in each book. There is some likeness in the broad, general plan of the two stories. They are picaresque narratives, with boys as travellers, sweeping in the characteristic scenes and figures, opinions and superstitions of a particular society at a particular time. Even here we feel a distinction, for the fullness of things seen seems, in the American book, to arise rather from deep familiarity than from delighted investigation. Beyond this, there is a gulf of difference. To juxtapose them is to juxtapose two kinds, not two specimens. *Huckleberry Finn* is the book of an older man and a less conscious artist, as the collapse of the last chapters makes clear. It is a book grown in stony soil, and, setting aside the last pages, its supreme virtue is candour. Its world is accepted, not created, and it is distanced only in time. In so far as it has a political frame of reference, it seems a consequence of memory, and it has no transcendental frame of reference at all. The author, in a preliminary note, disclaimed motive, moral and plot. A moral value must inhere in anything so truthful and, beneath its ironical humour and its forced good fortune, so sad; but the moral is without resonance and without arrangement. The boy's adventures do not fit into any sequence of training, test and triumph; things happen to him, and he meets them from what resources he has, which are often a little better than he thinks in his humble-mindedness. Huck, who tells his own story, has no confidence in himself. He enters our field of imagination as a sort of Sancho Panza to Tom Sawyer, whose whole-heartedness and *panache* in his world of fantasy are far closer to Kim than his henchman's mild acceptance. Huck is the child of his circumstances, and they have made him a waif and a fatalist. Will, intention, enterprise, of which *Kim* is so full, play little part in his life; his natural gesture is evasion, and he is left considering yet another withdrawal. He accepts without question the standards of his time and locality; unlike Kim, he has nothing to compare them with; and this gives to his untaught stirrings of compassion and honour a strongly ironic and moving quality, since, when they transgress these standards, as they do in his relations with Jim, the runaway negro, he regards them as wrong and bad and due to his not being 'started right'. 'A body that don't get *started* right when he's little, ain't got no show—when the pinch comes there ain't nothing to back him up and keep him to his work, and so he gets beat.' But the essence of Kim is that he *is* started right—uniquely right—and that he finds helpers to speed his progress. He has, moreover, an unshaken confidence in the 'two separate sides to his head' as an equipment for an interesting life. If it were not for the lama's part in the book, Kim, so exceptionally placed in relation to Hindu, Mohammedan, Sikh and Englishman, would be no more than an instrument, contacting and recording, like one of Scott's heroes, first one group and then another. As it is, though he does serve as an instrument, he is more than that and experiences his own development. Perhaps not wholly a person, he is certainly a presence and a focus of interest. Huck Finn, however, who has not the comfort of being exceptional but is what many homeless boys must have been, is a person, whose slow and hampered growth we watch with pity and warmth. It cannot be said that he was born in the House of Desolation, for the foundations of that sad place are laid in loss and Huck has never possessed anything; but he is a waif in bone, bred to the outside of the door and the edge of the circle, and he has not the temperament to turn his deprivations into advantages. The world of Huck has more rigour and crushing weight than that of Kim. The cruelty and violence that are a generalized background to Kim's adventures, but are never felt, roll their products across Huck's path in the shooting of Boggs and the feud of the Grangerfords and Shepherdsons with the slaughter of the boys. 'Kim had known all evil since he could speak', says Kipling in an explanatory tone, and we are given some substantiating detail and plenty of hints, but they are largely a decorative border to the page. Kim has absorbed his knowledge with unassailable poise and is neither aghast nor dismayed. Huck, however, is both; and, more than all his boyish delight in his adventures down the great highway of the river, the reader remembers those from which his hurt mind shies. 'I don't want to talk much about the next day. I reckon I'll cut it pretty short.'

The scenes in which we see the dim growth of the boy's mind are not very many, but they stand out in the narrative by their fundamental pathos. He does not co-operate in his development as Kim so eagerly does. Events strike him and move him on, staggering a little. He fools and agitates Jim, feels bad, and 'didn't do him no more mean tricks'. He can't understand the magnificent Tom helping a negro to escape, but works out for himself that Jim, grieving for the wife and children he thinks he will not see again, or telling how he struck his little deaf daughter, must have much the same feelings as white folk. He sees the two swindlers tarred and feathered and carried on rails, and discovers that he is sorry for the pitiful rascals, and that it was a dreadful thing to see. 'Human beings *can* be awful cruel to one another.' His involuntary perceptions bewilder him—'a person's conscience ain't got no sense'—but he lets them lead him, and has decided to go to Hell rather than give up Jim, before the story, deserting this theme, reduces him to the docile lieutenant of Tom's fantasies. Little candle-gleams of love and pity flicker in the hard world of *Huckleberry Finn*. They are hardly beacons, for they do not point out a direction. They are the natural product of human nature, like the violence and the cruelty, and they make its state tolerable. Huck does not speak of love, but he says that Buck was mighty good to him, and he feels it when Jim tells him that he is the only friend he has. He also feels the beauty and power of the river in the same undefined way, and passes a magic hour imbibing the beauty of the circus.

There is then a latent tragedy in *Huckleberry Finn* which is absent from *Kim*, and a hard realism which was no part of Kipling's intention. Both authors have moments of unlaboured pathos, blended with a humour which in one case is strongly ironical and in the other gracious and tender. There is nothing in Huck that corresponds to Kim's conscious delight in the glowing and various world, his keen intellectual interest, or his pleasure in his own faculties. Nor is there anything in Mark

Twain that corresponds at all closely to the love which is the medium through which the places and characters of *Kim* are presented. Both books are reveries, in which the beanstalk of invention flourishes out of the soil of childhood's home-plot. With the older man it runs wild, and in the end trails on the ground; the younger has trained it to clothe arcades and frame distances, and has nourished its root with a compost of learning and high and hopeful imagination. Among the leaves of one stands the earthbound Huck; up the other lightly ascends the Son of the Charm. Literature has room for both plants, and a moderately various taste can find its pastime under either.

After *Kim*, Kipling completed no more long stories. The 'plotless' nature of the book and the absence of conflict in its central character suggest that he had already begun to doubt his capacity to achieve the well-constructed novel. The unity of the narrative is one of mood and colouring. There remained over thirty years of his writing life during which the torrent of his imagination drove through the narrow channel of the short story, widening its bed as it went.

CHAPTER TWO

Laughter

In *Something of Myself* Kipling, praising the English gift for talking 'real, rich, allusive, cut-in-and-out skittles', and characterizing American conversation as too anecdotal and French as too oratorical, concludes by observing: 'And neither race delivers itself so unreservedly to mirth as we do.' This remark, which implies a conviction of the value of such self-delivery but does not define it, was made near the end of his life and it may serve as an introduction to his farces. Complex, deliberately wrought, visually rich and ringing with various voices, these astonishing structures stand along the road of his art from 'The Rout of the White Hussars' in *Plain Tales from the Hills* to 'Aunt Ellen' in *Limits and Renewals*. They are houses of boisterous and primitive mirth, 'mere farce', as the School Certificate Class, labouring towards a comprehension of critical categories, write depreciatingly, and often without any consciousness of their own natural pleasures. Sooner or later, in these tales, we reach the moment of physical disorder, the inversion of human and official dignity, surely the oldest and most proved of the sources of laughter. On the country platform below us the gigantic navvy, heaving with the operation of the unwanted emetic, clutches the philanthropic doctor in an ineluctable grip; in the village pond the pompous administrator struggles furiously with the assault of four swarms of bees; on the arterial by-pass in the dawn stands the policeman, speechless and plastered with the contents of an eiderdown quilt. Nothing has been spared in the approach to these rites. They take place against the sumptuous beauty of early summer in Wessex or after a panorama of the Sussex roads. There is nothing inartificial in the arrangement of the preliminary circumstances, where logic and chance meet in the moves of a dance to usher in the climax; and all round the arena stand recognizable English types, railwaymen, undergraduates, night-lorry drivers who are ex-service-men, expressing themselves in recognizable accents. The victim, whether select and dedicated or a ram caught in the thicket, is a gift from and to the Gods, which it would be ingratitude to waste. The question of sparing him does not arise, but he is esteemed precious, and offered up with costly accompaniments.

Close to these farces, but not quite the same, are those in which the ridiculous incidents serve some extraneous purpose as ordeals or gauges. The gaudy jest of 'The Horse Marines' reassures the retired Colonel that the spirit of his regiment has not changed since he commanded it. 'Same old game—same young beggars.' The young officer in 'The Honours of War', enraged and humiliated by the practical joke played on him by his comrades, is given an opportunity to retaliate in kind, and lets go his pride in his differentiating qualities, and his chance of making a damaging public protest, to outdo his tormentors at their own game, thereby proving that he is no Coriolanus but 'their equal and their brother'. The farce here, though elaborate in its appliances, is less so in its movement, since it is man-made and depends little on chance. The ambuscade from which the urns of mirth are emptied is not unsuspected nor the work of an unknown power. The Demon of Irresponsibility has no part to play. In fact, Stalky (now a Colonel) and his henchmen are entirely responsible; they are playing for the careers of three young men and the reputation of their regiment.

Lastly there are the punitive farces, in which killing ridicule, sometimes physical, is aimed by angry men at an offender. These are not—and were not, I think, intended to be—wholly hilarious. In 'A Friend's Friend', the earliest and simplest of them, when the drunken guest has insulted the women and dishonoured the men of the little English community at their ball, he is elaborately done up with gelatine, meringue-cream, cork and red cloth, hoisted insensible into a bullock-cart and sent out into the night. The narrator says: 'This was punishment, not play, remember. ... We were so angry that we hardly laughed at all.' Nor is there laughter during the action of *The Tie*. In fact, ridicule is so little in the mind of the youthful Mess of the Welland and Withan Rifles, in 1915, when they revert to the methods of their recent school-days to deal with the catering-contractor who is starving them, that, but for the faint flavour of Anstey's *Vice Versa*, it would have no claim to be mentioned here. Both tales belong to the tales of revenge and are expressions of psychological curiosity. They recount the spontaneous, corporate action of a group, united by the same sort of upbringing and exposed to the same conditions, against the malefactor who has injured them at a primitive level, who has shamed them before their women or starved them, for his own profit, in war. In these tales, and in 'Beauty Spots' and 'The Village that Voted the Earth was Flat', though the methods used by the avengers can be riotously comic and fantastic, the mood of the story is not wholly so. Except in 'A Friend's Friend' it is also astonished, disquieted and bitter. In 'Beauty Spots' two alarming things confront each other, the malignant country magnate, using the powers of local authorities to persecute his neighbour, and the 'mirth more dread than wrath' of the post-war generation 'that tolerates but does not pity'. At the end of 'The Village that Voted the Earth was Flat', when the whole jaded House of Commons is roaring a comic song in a sort of ferocious variation on *Iolanthe*, it is not suggested that this is simply an epiphany of the god of mirth. On the contrary, it is the climax of a deliberate stunt, closely co-ordinated through the press, the films and the music-halls by Bat Masquerier, the great man of the entertainment world, of whom the hard-bitten young journalist, Ollyett, says he is afraid, as he is the first Absolutely Amoral Soul he has met. The irresponsibility of this story is not Kipling's familiar demon; it is much less genial. As the action enters on its last phase, a violent simile compares the interval of expectation to 'a suspense of fever in which the sick man perceives the searchlights of the world's assembled navies in act to converge on one minute fragment of wreckage—one only in all the black and agony-strewn sea'; and just before the last scene, when the confederated avengers go to the House to see their quarry run down, we hear Bat Masquerier ruminating momentarily and vaguely on what he has done, and the inadequacy of his reflections is disquieting. The last sentence, when the hubbub has died away and the House has adjourned, 'some of it nearly on all fours', leaves us confronting the white faces of the victim and the implacable pursuer—who has not laughed. To be able to break even a noxious insect on so huge, glittering, vibrating and maddening a wheel as modern publicity is no simple joke; it is really not a joke at all.

It is unnecessary to take the flouting of police authority in 'Steam Tactics' so seriously. The tale is compounded rather than developed, and the ingredients are the antics of the narrator's incalculable steam-car, naval characters on leave, the Sussex countryside with its landowners, cottagers and police, and the black, twenty-four-horse Octopod, humming uphill into the future at a 'resonant fifteen an hour against the collar'. To confound the politics of the police and frustrate their knavish tricks —those who think the plain-clothes officer was merely doing his duty should look again at what is said about Agg the carrier and the measured quarter-mile—chance puts fantastic weapons into the motorists' hands; indeed, the last page reads very much like one of the Brushwood Boy's dreams. The victim is not much the worse; his quandary cannot be equated with the ruin of Major Kniveat in 'Beauty Spots' or Sir Thomas Ingell in 'The Village that Voted the Earth was Flat'; but the element of resentment and malicious triumph in his instructors brings 'Steam Tactics' nearer to ' "Brugglesmith" ' in tone than to 'Aunt Ellen', though it is much more loosely constructed. I shall write of ' "Brugglesmith" ' later in this chapter.

Further distinctions could be made. In 'The Puzzler' and 'The Vortex' the Heavenly Lark is commandeered to serve as a political allusion and this application is prepared for in the first pages of the tales, but it is no human manoeuvre that 'joins the flats of Time and Chance Behind the prey preferred'. Kipling's God of Mirth is sometimes concerned with politics, where they rest upon a broad basis of common experience (as in 'the Ties of Common Funk') and he is often concerned with ethics, especially the overthrow of vanity, but he is not devised to administer any code. He is anterior to codes, though he extends his scope both by supporting and flouting them. His original seat is in the midriff, in the physical delight of laughter, and especially, when it has been raised to a painful ecstasy, in the consequent relaxation of the whole body, the ease and well-being after the convulsed muscles have steadied from their orgasm and before they take up again the usual labours of life. When to physical pleasure is added intellectual delight the mirth-saturated man achieves a full catharsis; fears and enmities stream away from him with his tears; his lonely entity is linked in warm fellowship to those of the other laughers; and the necessary victim, even when he cannot 'take' the jest, is somehow commended to charity, since his antics have been the medium of the divine visitation. Thus even the inebriated Scotsman in '"Brugglesmith"', defeated at last in the night-long duel, is borne out of the lists with a salute to his 'magnificent mind', while Mr Lingnam becomes quite human and almost lovable when in his bee-stung frenzy he demolishes under the wheels of the car the bicycle, that was the cause of the trouble, and gleans it ruthlessly from the highway. 'Childish but necessary', as Mr Wontner says in 'The Honours of War'.

Not every lover of Kipling can love these farces. Some are repelled by the barbarousness of the occasion and some disconcerted by the imagined pain of the victim. Others share the genial contempt of Meredith for 'the great stomach laugh of the English—on which they found their possession of the sense of humour'. If the mirth-quake, towards which the story forges, does not appear to the reader to be an exquisite moment of perception and sensation, then the whole tale results for him in an anticlimax and the elaborations of the approach to it become tedious. Moreover, some who would be swept into laughter by the equivalent of such farces in the theatre or on the film find that they misfire when read in the cool solitude of a study. Considerations of this kind complicate the art of the comedian on the wireless and the television screen, for laughter spreads by infection; and it may have been with some regard to this difficulty that Kipling repeatedly stresses the physical manifestations of extreme mirth, the stamping, rolling and snatching at the ribs, and provides in most of his farces a group of spectators to suffer a convulsion almost as grotesque as that of the victim. The solitary rapture occurs in 'My Sunday at Home', but it is rare. In the last resort, however, and after repeated silent readings, the reader does not expect to be physically wrought upon by the tale. He knows the moves and surprise is absent. The success of the farce is then seen to rest upon his contemplative relish of the total event, the lightning reversal of all expectations by unimagined circumstances, the fantastic exposure of the suitable victim, and the richly-rewarded devastation of the spectators by their mirth; also on the infectious vigour and picturesqueness of the writing. The dream-like smoothness and rapidity with which incidents interlock to make an extravagant design is offset by the credibility of each incident in itself and the solidity of the English scene which provides them. The exotic bloom burgeons out of the soil of daily life. Springing from some negligible detail, the packing of a parcel or the ambiguity of the word 'taken' in a telegram about a bottle of medicine, it unfolds petal by petal till it covers the whole landscape with its monstrous glory, and then instantaneously dissolves, so that normal life can be resumed. It is in this momentary transmutation that the reader must find delight.

Kipling's own delight in these tales is manifested in the gaiety of their detail. His imagination keeps offering him more and more. Scenes, types and similes bubble up, and savoury scraps of conversation float on the confused air. Like Pyecroft's shipmate, 'Op, Kipling was 'always a fastidious joker—in his language as much as anything else'. Hinchcliffe's skill with engines is such that he can 'coax a stolen bicycle to do typewriting'. Many of these accessories to the jest are fibres that tether it to earth; such are Pyecroft, shining his uncle's boots at the beginning of 'The Horse Marines', and the atrocious and familiar architecture of the villa in 'The Puzzler'. The fantasy of the 'Archimandrite's' deck in 'The Bonds of Discipline', however, is of another kind. Here it is the absurdity that is inflated, stroke by stroke. 'Let me play', pleads the 'I' of 'The Honours of War', and meets Stalky's curt rebuke: 'You'll overdo it.'

The laughter in these tales is sometimes called primitive and sometimes hysterical. In their strict sense these terms must be left to specialists. The layman generally applies them dismissively, and often in relation to some conception of Kipling's personality. Taken colloquially, however, they do convey some truth about orgiastic laughter, though they are inadequate as labels. We know that delight in uncontrollable mirth is found among primitive peoples. Sir Arthur Grimble in *A Pattern of Islands* shows us the Gilbert Islanders, convulsed by whole villages, covering the beach or the speech-house floor with their relaxed and palpitating brown bodies at the startling eloquence of the angry old woman or his own painful efforts at shark-fishing, and afterwards offering courteous thanks in words and gifts to those who have so cheered their hardworking and dangerous lives. We have recently been told that the mountain peasantry of the Sherpas take a special pleasure in practical jokes; and many cultures, where a man's life and his closest relationships are controlled by stringent taboos, allow him a joking-cousin, in conversation with whom he may overstep all restrictions. Mrs Margaret Mead in *New Lives for Old* says of the laughter which accompanied such colloquies among the Manus of the Admiralty Islands that it had a special tone, and that the village found relief from their daily rigidities in participating in it. Comparable conditions produce comparable outbreaks among Englishmen in a primitive land. I quote from Colin Welch's comment on Lord Delamere in his *Daily Telegraph* review of the re-issue of Mrs Elspeth Huxley's *White Man's Country*:

> He shared the settlers' violent sense of fun (which has caused so much offence in advanced circles, where little is known of the background of toil and loneliness from which it springs). Dearly did he love the sound of breaking glass; oranges flew through hotel windows, and every street lamp in Government Road bore witness to his good aim with the revolver.

All these examples are linked by the fact that the laughter—the 'violent sense of fun'—is accompanied by a suspension of the pressure of daily hardship and strain. In three of the preceding cases the suspension is invited, and means are provided by the community to bring it about; in the fourth, chance provides the opportunity, and it is ecstatically welcomed. The Gilbert Islanders experience 'fulfilment'; they encourage the old woman's rage and do not dream of interfering to terminate the heaven-sent antics of their well-liked District Officer. It is plain that there is a close kinship here with the attitude of the 'I' and his companions in Kipling's farces, but it is also plain that these are not shark-fishers or mountaineers or even settlers, but members of a sophisticated civilization. What strain, then, requires to be relaxed in such boisterous abandon? Kipling is not explicit in the tales themselves, but, tucked away where one would least think of looking for it, in the Johnsonian Preface to 'The Marrèd Drives of Windsor' in the completed 'Muse Among the Motors', we find the assertion that 'those same forces of natural genius, which expatiate in splendour and passion, demand for their refreshment and sanity an abruptness of release and lawlessness of invention, proportioned to precedent constrictions'. Something, too, may be gathered from the tales themselves and their accompanying verses. Those who laugh are men who carry responsibilities and control large interests. It is a Law Lord and a famous engineer who apply themselves to find out if a monkey will climb a monkey-puzzle tree, and a Colonial Minister of State who watches their manoeuvres through a hole in the hedge. The weight of a complex civilization may be different from that of a taboo-ridden paganism but it is not necessarily less. Towards the end of 'The Vortex', which was published in August 1914, when the swarming bees have 'paralysed locomotion, wiped out trade, social intercourse, mutual trust, love, friendship, sport, music' in the village of Sumtner Barton, and are taking on, for a few lines, a distinctly allegorical appearance, it is said that they have 'small sense of humour'—and they certainly do not know how to relax. We need not, however, follow up the bees, for the Archangels present themselves. They appear in 'The Legend of Mirth' which is attached to 'The Horse Marines'. Theirs is the rigour of unresting zeal, so careful to conform to its own high standards, so anxious, so perilously near to pride, that it needs to be pierced by

> *Tales of the shop, the bed, the court, the street,*
> *Intimate, elemental, indiscreet. . . .*
> *Tales to which neither grace nor gain accrue,*
> *But only (Allah be exalted!) true,*

and Allah despatches a Seraph on this mission. The 'utter mirth' in which the Four forget 'both zeal and pride' sends them reeling through the universe, which answers to their laughter,

> *And e'en Gehenna's bondsmen understood*
> *They were not damned from human brotherhood.*

The Archangels have received new light on their tasks from frivolity, and they tell the tale roundly against themselves in Heaven. These are some of the implications that came to enrich Kipling's natural—he might have said national—addiction to farce.

Modern critical taste does not much favour mere farce, and the practical joke, which passed unquestioned for humour in Smollett's time, no longer does so. Farce today, if it is literature, is intellectual and satirical; or it deals in fantasy and symbol; and it is sometimes clad in a sobriety of utterance that enables it to dally with hints of pathos. There is none of this ambiguity and intellectual topsy-turvy in Kipling; they do not go with the exuberant laughter that is his pleasure. Here, also, he carries on a Victorian tradition that our burdened literary explorers have left to the theatre and the film. There are exceptions, however. Robert Lynd, for one, not long before his death, wrote that, if he were to take up Kipling again, he would turn to the farces; and perhaps the work most comparable to them is to be found in Ireland, in the tales of E. Œ. Somerville and Martin Ross. Discipleship may account for part of the likeness, but there is also a congenital similarity. Many of the same sources of mirth are drawn on, and a tale like 'The Pug-Nosed Fox' has a similar interplay of chance and rational consequence, leading through freshly supplied complications to a crashing and preposterous finale. The farce is seen against the landscape of the country that produced it, and speeded to its climax by the natives of that country. It begins with the mild discomfort of a Deputy MFH putting on hunting pink in August to have his photograph taken with hounds; proceeds through the contributory comedy of the photograph to his consternation when an unseasonable fox steals out of the covert and the hounds stream after it; follows him across unknown country in his efforts to come up with them, until his horse falls lame and he has to stable him at the strangely forsaken house of a newly-rich family he has been avoiding; and propels him to the appalling moment when, as he supports an inebriated best man, whom he has rescued from the inside of a feather-bed, he hears on one side the guilty pack window-crash into the wedding-breakfast and on the other the return of the bridal party from church. At this point it is a sad heart that does not rejoice.

The authors of 'The Pug-Nosed Fox' were women; but one may note that no woman shares the laughter in Kipling's farces. It may be that he thought them incapable of this form of purgation, or that their presence would have introduced self-consciousness into the masculine riot. He certainly does not think them without humour, and he concedes to them the mastery of scandalous and objurgatory language which is one of the hiding-places of that power, but they do not rejoice with aching ribs in the Heavenly Lark. Setting aside the acid housewife of 'The Puzzler' and the elderly lady of 'The Vortex', who are both injured in property by the jest, there are the Neolithic Ladies in 'How the First Letter was Written'. Like the men of the tribe, they have been unnecessarily alarmed and upset and have behaved foolishly, but when the tension of the incident dissolves in male guffaws, led by the victim of the misunderstanding himself, the ladies cannot participate. They are very polite to their husbands, and call them 'Idiot' ever so often. No doubt the presence of the helpful stranger, bruised and scratched by their attentions, with his hair full of the mud they have rubbed into it, embarrassed them; for I think it true that, while women can certainly abandon themselves to laughter to an extreme degree, the Western European woman (and the Neolithic Ladies lived near Guildford) does not like the Heavenly Lark to be too expensive in property or dignity or pain. That means that she will not pay so much for it, and consequently that she does not value it so highly. Another feminine limitation is alluded to in 'A Sea Dog'. This is the tale of Malachi, the fastidiously clean little dog on the old destroyer, shepherding mine-sweepers in the North Sea, and of how a 'Bolshie' in the crew provided lying circumstantial evidence of a misdemeanour. In the end Malachi's master tells his friends the 'name and rating' the indignant crew bestowed on the intriguer, and they 'laughed those gross laughs that women find incomprehensible'.

Looking back to the late Victorian world, in which Kipling's art evolved and of which it continued to bear so many traces, we come on *The Wrong Box* (1889) of R. L. Stevenson and Lloyd Osbourne. It is not a book that has attracted much attention lately, but it delighted Kipling. He refers to it twice in *Something of Myself*, and a quotation from one of its arabesques unites the Agent-General and the narrator in 'The Vortex'. Possibly its Gilbertian sporting with the macabre may go for something in 'Aunt Ellen', though this is a far cry. The book was first written by Stevenson's nineteen-year-old stepson, and was ready for the press before there was any question of his collaboration. Then he read it, fell in love with it, and took it in hand. Whatever it had been to the boy, to him it was a piece of wild buffoonery, but with the curious grain of morality in its intricacies, without which Stevenson could not write. The menacing irrationality of circumstance deluges, in this case, not the pompous but the inadequate, who are called upon to disembarrass themselves of an unexpected corpse. The dealings with this human residuum have an engaging innocence, which must be ascribed to the junior partner, but at least it is understood that such things are heavy. There is a comic discrepancy between the characters and the kind of problem they have to face, between their inadequate emotions and ruses and the chilling load of death. They are always juggling with an object too big for them, in a reaction of petty irritation or pathetic incredulity to find themselves in such a situation. The courage and the desperation of the weak interested Stevenson, their unexpected sticking-points and breaking-points; this was not one of Kipling's themes. The ordeal, therefore, to which we come through these astonishing exercises, is not the chastisement of the bumptious, but the summons to a mild young barrister to show himself man enough to discard conventional rectitude and deal with the thing. When he has made an effort to do this, chance comes to his assistance, and the author disencumbers himself of the corpse with insouciance. The extravaganza unfurls itself against a solid background of London and the home counties, and the exhilaration of the nightmarish parlour-game breaks out in delightfully intricate loops and twists of fancy—poor little William Dent Pitman's worship of the hairdresser's wax model, for instance, or the young carter's efforts on the penny whistle.

'"Brugglesmith"', the first of Kipling's full-size farces (which, to echo his phrase, may or may not have been stimulated by *The Wrong Box*), is also set in London; between after-dinner and dawn we accompany the narrator from the Pool of London to Brook Green, and he too is trying to get rid of an encumbrance, but not an inert one. An old man of the sea is on his back, crapulous, clinging, ingenious and maliciously aware of the advantages of the disgraced over the respectable. There are many turns in the night-long duel, but, until he plays his last counterstroke in the dawn, it is the narrator who is the victim. He has been dining soberly on board the *Breslau* with her first officer, a little stately —we hear later that he is in evening dress—and well abreast of himself and his circumstances. He has already made a name by his books, and knows his way about, and he is understandably a little pleased with himself—or, as M'Phee, the engineer, tells his drunken guest, 'vainer than a peacock'. He is thus assailable, prepared by fortune for her sport, which begins when the drunken man, who is going ashore with him in the dinghy, kicks it off from the ship's side before the lascar can get in, and they are adrift on the Thames. From this point there are, by my count, ten turns in the match. Each move of the narrator to disassociate himself from his scandalous companion is countered with a tipsy adroitness that leaves them staggering through the night indissolubly linked. The fetter that links them is the drunkard's knowledge of his companion's just-made name, that valuable name which he imparts in such unwished circumstances to the river police. 'Here he shouted my name twenty times running, and I could feel the blushes racing over my body three deep.' It is a ridiculous humiliation. The police say: 'You're a nice pair', and the narrator feels 'cut off from all respectability'. Already a little desperate, he manages to disengage himself, recovers his sense of absurdity in the momentary relief, and is laughing aloud when a hand falls on his shoulder.

'Go away,' I said; 'go home, or I'll give you in charge.'

He leaned against a lamp-post and laid his finger to his nose, his dishonourable, carnelian neb.

'I mind now that M'Phee told me ye were vainer than a peacock, an' your castin' me adrift in a boat shows ye were drunker than an owl. A good name is as a savoury bakemeat. I ha' nane.' He smacked his lips joyously.

'Well, I know that,' I said.

'Ay, but ye have. I mind now M'Phee spoke o' your reputation that you're so proud of. Laddie, if ye gie me in charge—I'm old enough to be your father—I'll bla-ast your reputation as far as my voice can carry; for I'll call you by name till the cows come hame. It's no jestin' matter to be a friend to me. If you discard my friendship, ye must come to Vine Street wi' me for stealin' the "Breslau's" dinghy.'

At St Clement Danes he is betrayed into a scuffle with two constables, and the police-court looms much nearer; but here, goaded by the 'tingling horror' of his shouted name, he becomes the aggressor and, by unscrupulous provocation and bullying, subdues his captors and his persecutor alike, and is presently 'pacing proudly a little ahead' of the ambulance in which the latter lies and speaking 'with condescension' to the former. It is a curious misreading of this tale to suppose that his mood here is one of simple triumph, or that the fun lies in the victimization of some genial old Falstaff. The narrator is watching himself quite as closely as the reader can. With a smarting sense of the ludicrous, he sees himself deprived of his dignity and security, fighting back tooth and nail, scraping his way to safety by begging a policeman to speak for him, and filled with malice against the agent of these fantastic degradations. It is the sudden downfall of an Arabian Night, and, when the night-walker in Trafalgar Square begs for money, asserting that he had been a gentleman once, ' "So have I," I said. "That was long ago".' Once before, when he had freed himself, his unwary laughter had retarded his escape and delivered him back to his nightmare; now it is malice that makes him overstep the mark. Nothing will serve but that he will wheel his tormentor, strapped in the ambulance, home to his wife for domestic retribution; and home is 'Brugglesmith'—Brook Green, Hammersmith. There follows the description of the pilgrimage. The old rascal is still strong. He can even drive his charioteer into a pub at dawn to get him whisky and stop him kicking the canvas; and when Brook Green is reached, honours are once more even, for there is no home, nothing but an empty villa with a board signifying 'To Let'. It looks as if the match will end in stalemate; and then the narrator, with a 'base' and brilliant move, tells his charge to ring the bell. After this, drink, the mechanics of the Victorian bell-pull, and the strength of copper wire do the rest, and the narrator has only to open the gate politely and summon the police to deal with the extraordinary cocoon that passes through it. It is not, however, a personal triumph, but a vengeance 'allowed'. Only drink defeats the demonic resourcefulness of the old scamp, silencing alike his stern Scottish moralities, his relishing allusions to his victim's vanity, his pathos and his fine, confused arguments. Like Hercules in frenzy, he turns his strength upon himself.

'"Brugglesmith"' stands alone among Kipling's farces. It is the only one in which the 'I' is a protagonist; and the 'I' is so close in stature, residence and circumstances to the Kipling recorded in the 'Interregnum' chapter of *Something of Myself*, that it has needed an effort of consistency to avoid using the proper name. It is at least his simulacrum that is dished up together with his persecutor in this double sacrifice to the spirits of irony and ridicule. In all the other farces he stands on the edge of the convulsion, an aide-de-camp to Chance.

Laughter, says Hardy, is always the result of blindness. 'A man would never laugh were he not to forget his situation, or were he not one who never has learnt it. . . . Laughter always means blindness—either from defect, choice, or accident.' In 'My Sunday at Home', the first tale in which Kipling examines the achievement of orgiastic laughter and begins to set it in what came to be almost mystical relations with the powers that rule life, he confronts his great senior on his own ground. As the train stops at Framlynghame Admiral in Wiltshire the devoted American doctor puts his head out of the window, sniffs the may, and says: 'And so this is about Tess's country, ain't it?' Kipling never labours these hints; they fall almost noiselessly, but in a sufficiently copious shower. Here in the rich Wessex countryside, crossed by the white road along which fateful arrivals and departures take place, a stalwart, uncomprehending son of the soil, whose 'only desire was justice', is subjected to the assaults of circumstance. His fellow-victim is a sophisticated traveller, and the situation that overwhelms them both is built up of the tiniest of unlucky chances and impulses that waste the seconds while explanation or escape is still possible. Aloft on the footbridge the narrator watches the 'machinery' working, 'foreshortened from above', abandoning himself to 'the drift of Time and Fate' and meditating on the inevitable consequences of our actions in 'the appointed scheme of things'. Even in Wessex, he seems to suggest, the artifices of chance are not always tragic or life's little ironies deadly. The hints might be followed further. At times a recognizable shadow is thrown across the style. The painstakingly literal elaboration of the postures of the navvy and the doctor, the transitions from action to evocation of the countryside, soaked in midsummer beauty, and the uplifted melancholy and stinging irony of the end, when the seven-forty-five carries the narrator 'a step nearer to Eternity, by the road that is worn and seamed and channelled with the passions, and weaknesses, and warring interests of man who is immortal and master of his fate', are by Kipling's hand but not in his calligraphy. The pace, particularly of the scene in dumb-show, is strikingly retarded, and we feel the slight jerk as he addresses himself to the next phase of his tale, which is so often felt in Hardy and never elsewhere in Kipling, who is a master of transitions. But 'My Sunday at Home' is not a parody, though it may be a counter-statement. It is even possible that it was his reaction to Hardy's tragic artistries in circumstance that made him define his own attitude to comic chance more clearly. Hitherto he had proceeded upon the traditional basis of farce without comment; 'The Rout of the

White Hussars' and 'The Arrest of Lieutenant Golightly' run their brief and boisterous course without inviting any celestial onlookers, and there is no elaboration of the gusto with which, in 'The Battle of Rupert Square', he watches the tenacious, ingenious and silent conflict between a cabby and a sailor, his would-be fare, while the horse trots round and round the square, until the hansom disintegrates and the cabby explains: 'It's mee brother.' But we cannot assume that such a stimulus was needed. Once he was free from the journalistic pressure of his youth, Kipling was a ruminative writer. If the early farces grew out of the unexamined hilarity of the schoolboy, perpetuated by the communal mirth of army messes and professional groups, he had had plenty of time since then to consider laughter. He had tried his hand at the sophisticated and ironical kind, which he afterwards rejected, and he was well aware of the laughter that is the expression of, or the release from, strain. Nevertheless, he had recently heard at the Savile Club, as he tells us, 'Hardy's grave and bitter humour', and he must have perceived that his own drew from different springs. It did not imply blindness but vision, the comic vision of the involvement of man, with his dignified and blinkered endeavours, and his enormous, ununderstood circumstances. That is why, as soon as this becomes his conscious theme, he needs the wide and solid landscape, populated by minor characters, the leisurely beginning and the ranging, allusive conversations. It is from 'My Sunday at Home' that we begin to trace the metaphysical as distinct from the psychiatric bearings of farce. The traces are not yet quite clear, for at times Kipling is walking in Hardy's footsteps, especially when he distances his actors till their conflicts look like the agitations of insects between the flowering hedgerows in the rich, absorbent calm of the countryside. But here is what he says about circumstance and the philosopher:

> I knew that so long as a man trusts himself to the current of Circumstance, reaching out for and rejecting nothing that comes his way, no harm can overtake him. It is the contriver, the schemer, who is caught by the law, never the philosopher.

This passivity while the curves of a design unfurl themselves, until the artist's intention can be identified, is a feature of all the later farces. The narrator, watching the elements of the coming orgy flash and wheel into place, holds his hand, inactive or merely following suit under the orders of a companion, until, often preluded by the round wind of dawn ('always favourable to me') the crowning moment comes. Then sometimes, but by no means always, he finds a leading card in his hand and plays it with panache. Sometimes, however, it is a less perceptive companion to whom this grace falls, as to Lettcombe in 'Aunt Ellen'; for the narrator offers his own small morifications as a minor sacrifice on the altar of the god. In 'My Sunday at Home' he trots up and down the train, eagerly but ineffectively, after the majestic guard; in '"Their Lawful Occasions"' (not strictly a farce, but enriched with farcical elements) he overhears Pyecroft's comment on his navy-talk and is dropped into a dinghy by the slack of his clothes, and in 'The Vortex' he is commanded by the irate householder to wait in the scullery. And who or what is the Power of whose mysteries he is so richly rewarded a minister? We cannot expect a categorical answer in so sportive a medium. The Demon of Irresponsibility, who prompts the narrator, is not the Daemon who sometimes controlled Kipling's art, but a recognizably human and personal impulse. In 'The Necessitarian', however, the verses prefixed to 'Steam Tactics', we meet the suggestion that, like all Kipling's ultimate powers, this Power too is outside man. Time, Chance and Circumstance are merely the instruments of the unknown Jester, the culmination of whose play is called the Sacredly Absurd, as if a manifestation so excessive, so unaccountable and so complete must, like lunacy in former ages, somehow belong to the divine. Of this Power Kipling posits only craftsmanship, but a conscious craftsmanship, not the 'rapt aesthetic rote' of Hardy's Artificer; he admits that 'no creed has dared to hail him Lord', but in the well-known last verse hazards the speculation:

> *Yet, may it be, on wayside jape*
> *The selfsame Power bestows*
> *The selfsame power as went to shape*
> *His Planet or His Rose.*

The human being, perceiving and drawn into the operations of this Power, feels the ecstasy of mirth in the full meaning of this somewhat flattened word, and the Curé of Saint Jubanus has no difficulty in acknowledging a divine intervention in the farce that heals the despair of his young parishioner.

LAUGHTER

There are later verses in which Kipling queries the mysterious nature of laughter, though no longer from a metaphysical angle but a human one. Before 'The United Idolaters', a late *Stalky* tale, he placed an appropriately Horatian ode 'To the Companions', in which he asks:

> *How comes it that at even-tide,*
> *When level beams should show most truth,*
> *Man, failing, takes unfailing pride*
> *In memories of his frolic youth?*

Love, pleasure, ambition, wealth, even fame in the end, cease to comfort as do the 'unforgotten, innocent enormities' of the 'frontless days', when they rioted in the tumultuous companionship of the God of Mirth and asked no questions.

> *Then he withdrew from sight and speech,*
> *Nor left a shrine. How comes it now,*
> *While Charon's keel grates on the beach,*
> *He calls so clear: 'Rememberest thou?'*

Lastly, before 'Aunt Ellen', he placed 'The Playmate', in which the Power, so constantly evoked, appears modestly as a genius or nymph—his special Egeria, one might say—stealing to him in the twilight to herald 'new-framed delights', in which

> *all an earnest, baffled earth*
> *Blunders and trips to make us mirth.*

She is still mysterious. He knows that she is not Folly, nor yet Wisdom,

> *but, maybe,*
> *Wiser than all the Norns is she:*
> *And more than Wisdom I prefer*
> *To wait on Her—to wait on Her.*

The power that is wiser than fate (the Norns) is perhaps the power that has the vitality to accept, or withstand, to transmute, or simply endure a decreed issue. One must not press a poem for more than it was meant to contain; but these lines will serve to introduce the laughter of defiance, which, though it is seldom consciously wiser than the Norns, is in a sense stronger, since by it man preserves himself from degradation.

The laughter of defiance is the fighting-laughter of the human race. It may include the excitement of conflict and various ironical perceptions, ranging from the cheerful belief that one can yet show the enemy a thing or two to a conviction of the minuteness and inutility of one's supreme effort. It may be bitter. But it is, before all, the laughter of affirmation, the assertion, while one stands in the jaws of fate, that one will be swallowed whole and alive. Dick Heldar's Melancolia laughs, and so does he when he realizes that his picture has been destroyed. It is not the hysterical laughter of strain and wretchedness, with which Kipling had made facile play in the early tragic tales, rounding off 'Thrown Away' and 'In the Pride of his Youth' with this natural but distressing noise. It is not the cynical laughter of defeat, nearly the mirth of the damned, like Hummil's laughter in 'At the End of the Passage' when Mottram plays an evening hymn on the worn piano. This laughter is the rallying of forces in the face of fear. Leo and the Girl, the half-gods in 'The Children of the Zodiac', learn to laugh like men when they have accepted the human necessity of death. They laugh at the House of the Crab, high above them in the darkness, knowing that the Crab will smite them at the time appointed, and life seems richer now it is known to be a precarious and wasting good. They have looked on the worst, and it has not abolished them. It is the extension of understanding that nourishes the capacity for laughter. It is because Leo has known 'all the sorrow that a man can know, including the full knowledge of his own fall who had once been a God,' that he can make men laugh, so that they go away from him 'feeling ready for any trouble in reason'. It is not, however, the laughter of mockery—as Hummil's was; that, Leo tells his audience, is 'even more cowardly than running away'.

Laughter pierces the crust of egoism. When Adam and Eve in 'The Enemies to Each Other' fall under the sway of the Peacock, the Archangel Jibrail reports: 'The last evil has fallen upon Thy creatures whom I guard. They have ceased to laugh and are made even with the ox and the ass.' The cure is to provoke their folly to extremes, until the perception of self, the inescapable human characteristic, is forced to distinguish between the real creature and the image of pride, and blindness dissolves in laughter. It is a bout of laughter that marks the convalescence of Frankwell Midmore in '"My Son's Wife"' from the infection of the Immoderate Left and the Wider Morality; indeed, it is his capacity for laughter that marks him out as worth saving. It follows on a fit of outspoken and justified anger, and arises not only from a perception of the comic aspects of the unvanquishable old reprobate he has been trouncing, but also from an acceptance of the figure that he himself cuts in his tenant's eyes. This tale is a counterpart of 'An Habitation Enforced' without the ideal elements. It is, in its way, more interesting, though less charming. The derelict estate in the earlier tale, where the young American couple find health, peace and fruitfulness, is a sort of sleeping beauty, exquisite in its appeal, which they can restore to waking life. Nothing more sordid than children with sore throats besets Sophy's steps when chance leads her back to the home of her ancestors. The elements of '"My Son's Wife"' are less refined. Frankwell Midmore, who has spent his time unprofitably in intellectual circles in 'facile Hampstead'—and they are described quite as unkindly in 1913 as similar circles had been over twenty years before—is to be restored to moral health by immersion in a life he recognizes as much the same as that described in the novels of Surtees, which he first reads, in wet and wintry weather, in the small country house of which he is the unenthusiastic inheritor. The agencies of the change are the house; a scandalous old tenant farmer; Rhoda, his dead aunt's elderly maid; the local hunt, and the quite ordinary girl who moves happily and practically through the fields and the weather. There is nothing ideal about these agencies. The house stands in a shallow and uninteresting valley. The sexual irregularities of the countryside are well represented, especially in Mr Sidney, Midmore's tenant-farmer, whose morals, according to the plumber, are those of a parish bull. This is one of the 'iceberg' stories; much of it is below the surface. Midmore is a secretive man; we hear what he does, but little of what he thinks. It is not even pointed out that all the suppositions of his 'bright' letter to his mother after his aunt's funeral are reversed by the end of the tale. Even the 'peasants who do not utter' have uttered with force and point. One phrase, the well-placed 'epicure in sensation', indicates how he makes the intermediate stages of his change acceptable to himself. For the rest, we linger among the pleasant little facts of possession and discovery, as Midmore did, the choice of baths that Rhoda offers him—"ip, foot, or sitz. . . They're all yours, you know, sir'—the gravel, pitted by the returning hunt, even the smell of wet cloaks in the hall of the lawyer's house, where the singers practise the winter cantata. But when Midmore laughs, the process breaks surface for a moment. 'For a few seconds the teachings of the Immoderate Left, whose humour is all its own, wrestled with those of Mother Earth, who has her own humours. Then Midmore laughed till he could hardly stand.' The enormous old farmer with the red eyelids is a curious and unconscious apostle of wisdom, but he has his own species of integrity, and to cheat his inexperienced landlord is 'too dam' like cheatin' a suckin' baby'. Midmore laughs again at Mr Sidney's domestic arrangements. Natural lust, taken with cheerfulness, it seems, is more wholesome than the cerebration and fornication of the Immoderate Left. It may even be called more decent, though decency is not Mr Sidney's strong suit.

Laughter is also the solvent of despair and hatred. Its impact shivers the insubstantial, impassable wall of glass between the sufferer and the reality of life. The best example of this is the late tale 'The Miracle of Saint Jubanus'. The young French countryman, Martin Ballart, has returned from the trenches 'immobilized from the soul outwards'. His priest, himself an old soldier, understands the obsession but cannot reach him; nor can the girl who loves him. But when the two acolytes, already vested for Mass, get hooked up by the split whalebone of the Curé's big umbrella, and the rotund, atheistical schoolmaster, attempting to free them, is himself caught by the beard under his chin, and the umbrella promenades like Salome's charger, 'offering to all quarters the head of the Apostle *and* of two of the Innocents', supported, with involuntary genuflections, by the writhing bodies beneath it, then the village hears the rich, fresh laugh of Martin Ballart and his whole mind comes back to him. This is one of a group of tales in Kipling's last collection on the neuroses of ex-servicemen, in which the injuries to the inmost nature are healed by different methods; this, the simplest tale, applies the physical shock of laughter to a nature inaccessible by reasons of its simplicity to the detective reasoning that solves Wollin's trouble in 'Fairy-Kist' and too numb to be moved by the stimulus of affection that saves John Marden in 'The Woman in His Life'. The same theme, however, had been handled nearly forty years earlier in a tale that was not collected until the Sussex edition included it, 'The Legs of Sister Ursula'. Like many of the early tales, it is an anecdote; no pre-history attaches to it; we are given the rich man in his fifth-story flat—the scene is American—so exhausted by a long illness and its aftermath of depression that he takes no interest in the stream of life, nearly a hundred feet below in the street, 'just the kind of over-educated, over-refined man that would drop his hold on life', as the Doctor thinks, ordering him a dose of a new medicine every twenty minutes. We are also given the young nun that nurses him, simple, kindly, very chaste and very dutiful, and her dilemma when the door of the flat clicks to behind her as she fetches the medicine from the lift. The dose is due in a few minutes, the caretaker has gone out with the keys in his pocket, and the only way into the flat is up the fire-escape from the ground floor. In the first paragraph Kipling invokes Sterne—the only time, I think, that he mentions this tightrope dancer over the gulfs of sentiment and ribaldry. The caretaker's wife prays that there will be no wind; but Sister Ursula's legs, with elegant ambiguity, appear only in the title. As she forges her way upwards, to the sound of halloos from the street, we accompany her, noting the wave of indignation that sweeps her at being 'singled out for these humiliating exercises', her distress at her battered coif and rust-flaked kerchief, the strain of the ascent, and her disturbing memories of mild youthful follies. The analysis is interesting, because Kipling seldom essayed this method; it is successful because, though we are not told the figure Sister Ursula cut to the white-faced patient at the window, we know perfectly well, and add a perception of the simple heroism that unconsciously carries up the cup of healing. The method is not, however, wholly consistent, for Kipling cannot deny himself the arabesque that enriches the jest, the portly violinist who thinks the flats are on fire and follows the nun up the fire-escape, in morning dress, holding his violin, and with the bow between his teeth; and this figure is out of her sight and not part of her interior monologue. When Sister Ursula, back in the flat, administers the medicine to a patient helpless with laughter, she is surprised to find a revolver in the bed, but he throws the cartridge out, saying: 'The dear old world is just the same as ever. . . I'm going to get well, Sister Ursula.'

Since, then, laughter to Kipling was as essential to the wellbeing of man as music to Shakespeare, a bond of union, a strong hold on sanity and health of mind, a relaxation and restoration of human temper, it was bound to appear somewhere in the tales he wrote for children. So we find the laughter of joy in 'The Butterfly that Stamped', when Suleiman-bin-Daoud forgets all about his quarrelsome queens and the danger of showing-off and makes a great and memorable magic for the sake of a butterfly. The older children, for whom *Rewards and Fairies* was written, hear Master Culpeper recall how, when his friend Jack found wife and children still alive in the plague-stricken village, they stood in the rain and gave way to an 'unreasonable gust or clap of laughter which none the less eased us'. This outbreak is incidental; but in 'The Wrong Thing' laughter is crucial. This tale is told by Hal o' the Draft, in Dan's presence, to Mr Springett, the old builder, who dredges up out of his memory parallels to every point in it; and these homely anecdotes help to clarify what Hal has to tell and bring it closer to the boy's comprehension. Even so, Dan and readers of Dan's age cannot wholly understand the emotions in which the tale deals—the anguish of the artist whose conceptions are beyond his achievement, the mortal envy of the better craftsman, the mingled flavour, bitter and comic, of the reward that is given, not for the laborious triumph of disciplined art but for the casual by-product that falls in with the patron's interested requirements. Yet this is often found to be a favourite tale. There is rich entertainment by the way in the picture of the craftsmen 'toiling like cock-angels' in Henry VII's Chapel, of the fires on the cold pavements at nights, and Torrigiano dealing out insults and priceless instructions to his young men; and a great deal of the humour, if not of the mingled humours, is accessible to young readers in that exquisite scene where the King knights Hal for saving him thirty pounds. They may not be altogether clear as to what it is in this incident that disarms the murderous rival with laughter and breaks up the old crust of hatred about his heart, but it is felt to be a satisfactory conclusion when he and Hal reel back to the Chapel with their arms about each other's necks. They perceive something of the artist's passion, and some oddity in the world's acceptance of its fruits. The irony can wait for a later day. The mature reader, meanwhile, admires the skill with which Pride, Envy, Hatred and Disillusion are passed before the boy's eyes, in their true nature, accompanied by Delight.

CHAPTER THREE

Tales for Children

It is not easy to take a dispassionate view of a book to which we have been much indebted in youth. Sometimes we are even unwilling to disturb the original associations by trying to do so, for a child's imagination can be consciously enlarged by a mediocre book. No deflating experience awaited me when, after a break of years, I came back to the books that Kipling wrote for children; yet, if this study had aimed at critical evaluation, I think I should not have dared to write this chapter. For my purpose of analysis and display, however, it is surely a positive advantage that I read and re-read the books as a child. They have of late been sometimes belittled and often ignored in criticisms of Kipling, though this is in face of the fact that he says more about them—especially about the *Puck* books—in *Something of Myself* than about any other of his works, after his beginnings. It has even been questioned whether children have ever cared for them. There should be, then, some value in the testimony of a reader who was a child of the generation for which they were first written.

I had the great advantage of being read aloud to, extremely well, by both my parents. The *Just So Stories* were on my nursery shelves. The jocular manner and the refrains ('You must *not* forget the suspenders, Best Beloved') amused me, though a young cousin complained: 'You needn't say that again.' But the charm lay in the hints of mystery and remoteness. 'The great grey-green, greasy Limpopo river, all set about with fever-trees' never sent me to the map but rolled through my imagination, and runs off my pen now without any reference to 'The Elephant's Child'. 'The Beaches of Socotra And the Pink Arabian Sea' sang in my fancy as Cotopaxi and Chimborazo did in W. J. Turner's. I was present at the creation of the world with 'The Crab that Played with the Sea' (though I perfectly understood that this was fantasy), and the prehistoric background of the Taffimai stories and 'The Cat that Walked by Himself' offered me a fascinating blend of the cosy and the infinitely distant. How thrilling to a child is a skin-curtain over a cave-door, and the thought that darkhaired Phoenicians once brought their goods to a place called Merrow Down above the River Wey—obviously in England, though not known to me. I did not know what 'racial talks' were, or 'gay shell torques' which sounded the same, and no one bothered me by explaining; they sounded satisfactory when I repeated the lines or my mother sang them. But the great joy was the pictures, with their deeply satisfying detail. I used to work through Taffimai's necklace, checking the beads off by the list helpfully supplied by the author, though the black snake-like background always puzzled me.

The two *Jungle Books* had been on the dining-room shelves for some years before my father began to read to my brother and me every evening. I do not know how many times we worked through them, or quite how old I was when we began—about eight, I think. We made no difficulty over the humanized animals; they followed on nicely after Beatrix Potter, and, being town children, we much preferred Mowgli's wolves to natural history. But it was not the playful and domestic passages in these tales that impressed me most, but the notes of elevation and melancholy. The description of Cold Lairs, the crashing salute of the elephants to Little Toomai, the secret beach where Kotick led the seals—it was certainly a happy ending; *why* did I feel so sad?—and the fighting death of old Akela moved me to the depths. We did not turn often to *The Second Jungle Book*. 'The Miracle of Purun Bhagat' was beyond me—I did not understand what was happening; 'The Undertakers' perturbed my brother in bed; I fancy the end of 'Kaa's Hunting' had to be shortened, though it was certainly read in full sometimes, the memory is so deep and clear and awesome. I cannot read 'Red Dog' now without hearing my father—he had a magnificent voice and no distaste at all for rhetoric—giving out with tragic scorn the cry: 'Howl, dogs! A wolf has died tonight', while the tears with which, when we are young, we recognize nobility, poured down my face. Won-tolla, however, meant nothing to me; I had quite forgotten him when I came back to the books in middle life; nor did I ever follow Mowgli's manoeuvres clearly, here or in '"Tiger-Tiger!"' The grip of the stories was extraordinary, and a sense of something wild and deep and old infected me as I listened. I knew most of the songs by heart, and know parts of them still. 'What of the hunting, hunter bold?' had on me the effect that I now recognize to be that of a heroic lyric.

Puck of Pook's Hill came out before these readings stopped and was read aloud to me once, I think, but the absorption of it was done by solitary reading. I read it again and again with the intensity of childhood, and I can still, when I turn to it, trace the tideline of my youthful understanding. Certain pages seized my mind and have never disappeared from it; such is that where Parnesius marches his men to the Wall, and they come to the blocked gateway with 'Finish' scratched on the plaster, where the mainroad used to run through to the lost province of Valentia; the full significance of this was developed much later, but the impact was immediate, though obscure. Other pages, especially fragments of dialogue, I puzzled over; and there are a few passages that wake no echoes, and are read now as any other printed page might be read. These I could never have taken in at all. I waited ardently for *Rewards and Fairies*. Five tales, 'Cold Iron', 'The Wrong Thing' (I never understood the title), 'The Knife and the Naked Chalk', 'The Conversion of St Wilfrid' and 'The Tree of Justice' mastered me in the way I desired. The others I remember as a little baffling and disappointing, at first; but in nearly all of them there were glowing spots, as it were, from which some sort of warmth or force proceeded, which made it worth while to re-read the tale, so that gradually some of the mists on the face of it dissolved, but never all. One of these spots was the end of 'Simple Simon', in which I felt a pathos I could not account for. The scenes were always entrancingly vivid, and the voices rang in my ears with conviction. So I was led, and many children of my generation were led, by intimations of the imagination into a sort of tactual familiarity with what the intellect could not yet clearly see. Emotions, motives, conditions—the loneliness of command, the obscurity of sacrifice, De Aquila saying to Richard and Hugh: 'Welcome, poor ghosts', Pertinax calling the young man in clean armour 'You fine and well-fed child'—such things were carried by conviction into the mind, and there they set up vibrations that increased until, many years later, all their meaning was disclosed. Kipling, like his admired Juliana Horatia Ewing, did not write down to children. His tales are about what Gray calls the

Ministers of Human Fate, though not quite the same set as Gray evokes.

I must have stopped reading the *Puck* books at about fourteen or fifteen, and *The Jungle Books* well before that. When, in my twenties, I returned to the former, very briefly, under the compelling necessity of composing a lecture on the author, I found a Rowntree's Clear Gum in 'The Knights of the Joyous Venture', and that is not an adult book-mark. This was when I first began to read Kipling as a whole, for hitherto, besides the children's books, I had read very little, so that youthful prepossessions do not colour my judgment of the rest of the work. To end this tedious detail and, I hope, account for its introduction, my early readings were so persistent, and were so completely cut off from my adult readings, that there is little risk of my confusing what I perceive now with what I perceived then. When in the following pages I say 'a child', I mean primarily myself as child, but I was not solitary in my taste, nor can it be set down to the fact that I was an Edwardian child. The *Puck* books are still listened to with delight. Even the much-attacked *Stalky & Co.* survives. A fifteen-year-old schoolboy recently volunteered to me that he had enjoyed it. On my enquiry, he said he found it quite real, though a little exaggerated in parts. He seemed to relish the exaggerations.

As a matter of convenience I will consider the *Just So Stories* first, though they were written later than *The Jungle Books*. They are fables about how things came to be as we see them, the elephant's trunk, the camel's hump, the whale's throat, the armadillo's scales, the alphabet that children learn. They are not at all misleading; the fancy and the nonsense are apparent, and the reassuringly familiar is nicely mixed in with Djinns, Afrits, and the high and far-off times on the turbid Amazon. The idiom, with its Oriental grandiloquences embedded in colloquial narrative, seems (as far as I can find evidence, which it not very far) to be a variation of Burne-Jones's playful *Arabian Nights* rigmarole—and nothing could be more likely, since Kipling was to beg the very bell-pull of 'The Grange', in order that children might pull it as his own door and enter into a similar happiness. The difference lies in the rhythmical emphasis and incisive shape of the sentences, which have none of the stumbling, trailing naïvety and clownishness of Burne-Jones's private jargon. There are manners and morals in the fables, but they are not at all oppressive. The shipwrecked mariner, a man of 'infinite-resource-and-sagacity', has 'his Mummy's leave to paddle, or else he would never have done it', but the Elephant's Child, by a joyous inversion, spanks all his dear family with his new nose. Only in the lovable tale of 'The Butterfly that Stamped', which is, we are told, 'quite different from the other stories' and is written throughout with gentle dignity, we find the most wise King, Suleiman-bin-Daoud, who never forgets how he once showed off and was made ashamed.

The fun of a fable lies in inventive and appropriate detail. There is plenty of this in the *Just so Stories*, but Kipling's high-spirited detail is best shown in the animal and machinery fables of *The Day's Work* and *Traffics and Discoveries* which were not primarily directed to children at all. They have so often been quoted to substantiate the melancholy assertion that his scope shrank from men to children, from children to animals, and from animals to machines, that it is as well to begin with one of their positive qualities. But in fact nothing can be securely established upon so faulty a chronology. Kipling found the fable a congenial form at all stages of his writing life. In verse or prose, with primeval or archetypal characters, with humour or elevation, he used it not only as a playground, but to express some of his intimate convictions about life and art. 'The Story of Ung', 'The Children of the Zodiac', 'The Legend of Mirth' and 'The Enemies to Each Other' are all making statements of importance to Kipling in an ingenious and depersonalized way. But it is against that type of fable in which the actors are animals or machines that the heaviest charge is levelled. The animal fable is a very old and recurrent literary type, which has been found strong enough in our day to carry the sardonic humour and hinted horror of Orwell's *Animal Farm*. We need select from its long tradition only two books which we know Kipling read as a boy. *Uncle Remus*, as he tells us in 'The United Idolaters', was the rage at Westward Ho! for one term, and in his holidays he had read Mrs Gatty's *Parables from Nature*. This pleasant and natural little book expresses a conviction as strong as Kipling's of the necessity of obedience, discipline and proper subordination, and on two occasions in very similar terms, though with only a shadow of his political reference. In 'Kicking' a chestnut colt is given bad advice by an old, half-bred, white Arab mare, to whose 'monotonous existence the power of lashing a young colt up to indignation was rather an amusing novelty'. He throws a young girl, and is consequently sent to a trainer, who first forces him to submit and then gentles him until he gives willing service. 'Happy the colts who learn submission without a lifetime of personal struggle', concludes Mrs Gatty firmly. The likeness in substance and method between this little tale and the more complex and amusing 'Walking Delegate' is clear enough, and, since Kipling mentions Mrs Gatty, he may have been conscious of it. But the comparison of young men to half-broken horses, with all the metaphor that can be drawn from harness and manège, is frequent in Kipling's early work. If it is now somewhat irritating in its glibness, it is because horses are no more an accepted part of our lives as they were in Kipling's India—or, for that matter, in Mandeville's England, for the same image occurs in *The Fable of the Bees*. After Kipling left Vermont, this metaphor was disused, to be recalled 'at eventide', with his school and his Horace, in 'The Centaurs' and later still in the early chapters of *Something of Myself*. The other fable that may have lingered in a cranny of that retentive mind is 'The Law of Authority and Obedience'. Mrs Gatty, like most fabulists, considers the bees (though she believes the workers to be male) and uses the subdivisions of function in a hive, and the damage done when these are neglected, as a parable against social discontent. It is not one of her best tales, and Kipling, who was a bee-keeper himself, had no need to recall this pallid sketch for his much more far-reaching and uncompromising political fable 'The Mother Hive'. So indirect are the channels of literary influence that Melissa, the faithful bee, may just as well derive from Milton's Abdiel as from Mrs Gatty's 'old relation'—rather better, in fact, for Mrs Gatty avoids the catastrophe, while Kipling presents it in terms of corruption, fire, and the 'Voice from behind a Veil' of the Bee-Master and his son. But this is trifling. The fable, however, is sinister enough, and locked closely, from the very first sentence, to the contemporary realities it purported to reflect. There is anger in it, and menace, and an element of the repulsive, and the unremitting allegory is relieved only by the ingeniousness of the parallels and Kipling's usual amusing linguistic inventions for the speech of his bees.

There are three fables in which machinery is personified; '·007' records the conversation of American locomotives in a roundhouse (Bret Harte had described their remarks

Facing on the single track,
Half a world behind each back);

in 'The Ship that Found Herself' the different parts of a ship are animated, and in 'Below the Mill Dam' the waters, the wheel, the cat and the genuine old English black rat who lives in the mill. This last fable, with 'The Walking Delegate' and 'The Mother Hive', is aimed at the unproductive, who withhold their work from the community, whether they are demagogues, like the yellow horse in 'The Walking Delegate', aesthetes, like the waxmoth in 'The Mother Hive', or sentimental and privileged conservatives like the rat. The personification of machines perhaps comes into adult literature with Samuel Butler's forecast of a happy union between two steam-locomotives with the young ones playing about the doors of the sheds. That is a tabloid fable, amusing and seriously significant. But the scholar, who wishes to trace the growth of this sort of device, will have to look at children's books and comic drawings, and allow for the extension of the sailor's personification of his ship to the other large implements with which men spend their working lives. But chiefly he should have regard to the potentialities of the English language which, largely through its verbal usages, continually hovers on the verge of personification. A visitor to Paris, footsore with walking the length of the Champs Elysées on gravel, explained: 'The motor-cars hooted me off the pavement', and was startled at her hostess's pleasure in the unstudied locution. Humorous and fanciful speakers consciously work this vein. To say that a little garden is bursting into bloom is to note a natural phenomenon; to say that it is bursting itself with bloom is to suggest a laborious and well-meaning little plot, with whose achievement we sympathize. When Hotspur complains that the Trent 'comes me cranking in' and cuts off a monstrous cantle of his third of England, the Trent is at least exasperating and perhaps intentionally inconsiderate. One can hear this sort of latent personification emerging through a sequence of sentences in daily life, and a sustained account of a struggle with a barrow-load of garden implements, with a rake on top, will end: 'And after all that, the dam' thing up and hit me'. The extension of the active mood of the verb—doors bang, trumpets blow, cups clatter, houses shake—readily indulges a native play of animistic fancy that is more congenial, I believe, to the South of England than the North. Dickens availed himself to the full of this lively ambiguity of language; and when, as in Kipling's case, the artist's quickness to take a visual suggestion is added to the writer's zest for the potentialities of words, there is no need to account for the manifestation by assuming a defeat in his more ambitious endeavours. However serious the burden of the fable, the fabulist is having fun.

Kipling had this sort of fun all through his writing life. It came on him spontaneously, without any moral afterthought, in the engine-shops at Jamalpur, which the young journalist describes in 'Among the Railway Folk'. Engines, he tells us, are the 'livest' things man ever made. 'They glare through their spectacle-plates, they tilt their noses contemptuously. . . Their fires are lighted, and they are swearing and purring and growling one at another.' The scornful stare of one reminds him of a colonel's portly wife. The likeness is quite casual; nothing is built on it; he notes it and lets it go. These evocations of human or animal shapes and behaviour by natural and constructed objects meet us all through the travel-books. They may be only hinted by a single word, or developed into a complete simile. The imaginative content may vary from caricature to myth. In 'Letters to the Family' he notes the wrecking-cars on the Canadian Pacific 'with their camel-like, sneering cranes'. The landslide that has demolished a little mining village suggests to him the mountain kneeling on it, 'as an angry elephant kneels'. Power, natural or contrived, generally stimulates the double vision. The pools and cliffs and river of the Yellowstone Park in *From Sea to Sea* are seen, largely through the verbs associated with them, as monstrous, primal creatures, dangerous and capricious. In *Brazilian Sketches* the great dynamo by São Paulo is the Hooded Devil, the Father of Lightnings, bound down under stringent conditions to the service of man; and in *With Number Three*, a piece of Kipling's Boer War journalism, the Red Cross wagons, lurching and pitching on the three-day trek with the wounded to the rail, express half-audibly the callousness of things and the fatalism of soldiers. 'This, said the wagons, is the custom with the wounded.' The personification is fully developed in 'Egypt of the Magicians', where the lateen-rigged ship, with its piratical associations, marks Kipling's return to the East.

> 'This is *not* my ancestral trade', she whispers to the accomplice sea . . . Then she tacks, disorderly but deadly quick, and shuffles past the unimaginative steam-packet with her hat over one eye and a knife, as it were, up her baggy sleeves.

Ships, personified, one supposes, since men sailed in them, invite him to pause and elaborate his images. Dan and Harvey watch the 'We're Here' 'sayin' her piece' at anchor in a swell, and the sturdy little schooner runs through a series of quick-change impersonations in one paragraph. At the end of ' "Their Lawful Occasions" ' the disreputable-looking group aboard their speckless but helpless quarry look back at their own masquerading craft.

> Precisely over the flagstaff I saw Two Six Seven astern, her black petticoat half hitched up, meekly floating on the still sea. She looked like a pious Abigail who has just spoken her mind, and, with folded hands, sits thanking Heaven among the pieces. I could almost have sworn that she wore black worsted gloves and had a little dry cough.

These are deliberate and finished studies; the associative imagination presents a complete picture which is superimposed on the ship; it is the Abigail that floats on the still sea. More idiosyncratic, however, are the semi-personifications, caught intermittently in whirling movement, as in the distracted antics of the carriages in the emporium with which 'My Lord the Elephant' makes his kittenish sport. Momentary, too, is the vivification of metal and masonry in 'The Bridge Builders' when the rising waters whirl the cribs from under the bellies of the spans and lick the throats of the piers. This is implied beast-imagery—the overhead crane has already been compared to an elephant; it is an effect of intensity, a little beside the path of a story which is to reduce the vast engineering works of men to the shifting of a little dirt. We do not gain by the slight, excited blur in focus.

All this varying play of fancy is picturesque and associative. It is often humorous, but not satiric. Kipling does not play the satirist's double game. We are not asked to think whether, if machinery is so like men, men are not rather like machinery. It is hardly an exception when, on the Nile steamer, he watches the encounter of two American winter visitors,

> each visibly suffering from congestion of information about his native city . . . They turned their backs resolutely on the River, bit and lit cigars, and for an hour and a quarter ceased not to emit statistics of the industries, commerce, manufacture, transport, and journalism of their towns. . . . It sounded like a duel between two cash-registers.

Amusement is here, and pleasure in behaviour so characteristic, but not satire.

In his fables, then, Kipling explored a spontaneous habit of his imagination for its artistic potentiality. The fleeting likeness was fixed and a congruous world elaborated round it. Since, however, it is only a small part of the appearance and behaviour of animals and things that can really be compared to those of human beings, the fun arises from a simultaneous perception of likeness and unlikeness, and the path, if not a tight-rope, is sufficiently narrow. As Goldsmith said, it is difficult to make little fishes talk like little fishes. With machines, whose 'personality' is put into them by the men who design and handle them, there are few, if any, real equivalences; the game consists in the ingenious invention of substitutes. The new engine in the round-house 'looked at the semi-circle of bold, unwinking headlights, heard the low purr and mutter of the steam mounting in the gauges—scornful hisses of contempt as a slack valve lifted a little—and would have given a month's oil for leave to crawl through his own driving-wheels into the brick ash-pit beneath him'. The 'personalities' of the engines are comically clear, and their speech is enriched with racy parallels to human modes. The switching-locomotive Poney's side-spurt of steam is 'exactly like a tough spitting'. The novice $\cdot 007$ 'put both drivers and his pilot into it, as the saying is'. The bravura-piece of $\cdot 077$'s rush to the rescue of the ditched Mogul freight, when a wet leaf sticks to the glass of his headlight and scares him with shadows on the line, almost surprises the reader into sympathy, and it is hard to see why anyone should be annoyed at the charming mock-solemnity of the Engines' Lodge at the end. The tale is an extended conceit; it does not tread, as *The Jungle Books* do, on the borderland of myth. It is a nursery-game, played by a grown-up, and raised to its highest power.

Kipling's fastidious linguistic jokes also occur in 'The Ship that Found Herself' and in his animal tales. The thrust-block in the 'Dimbula', calling for justice, gets hot under all his collars, and one polo-pony remonstrates with another: 'Just think a stride, Shiraz'. The vocabulary of abuse, whether in the world of horses or machines, is particularly rich and inventive. The language of the dog-tales, 'Thy Servant a Dog' and '"Teem"—a Treasure Hunter', however, written towards the end of his life, though closely akin, does not seem to me quite the same in intention. When an old sheep-dog bitch, jealous of her mistress's affection, growls at the newcomer: 'My bone', or when an Aberdeen terrier calls a car a 'stink-cart', there has been added to the conceit a speculation as to the working of a domesticated dog's brain. There is nothing like that in the talk between the ponies in 'The Maltese Cat'. Nevertheless, this tale provokes a reference to probability, as '·007' does not. Accepting the convention, we may yet ask if the cleverest polo-pony would avoid looking at an exciting chukka, for fear of taking it out of himself, and the question disturbs the pleasure. Over-elaboration is the danger of both types of tale, the fable and the possible incident told from the angle of a partially-humanized animal; it is the greater danger, because elaboration is a necessity.

The Jungle Books had been a different sort of achievement. André Chevrillon rightly selected for praise the beautiful passage at the beginning of 'Red Dog' where old Kaa, the rock-python, dreams slowly back into his early years, like some embodiment of geological time, while the man-child lies in his slack folds. This is, perhaps, one of the passages that a child passes over, unimpeded but impercipient. So are some of the most delicate touches in 'The Miracle of Purun Bhagat'. That tale, indeed, and 'Quiquern' seem to hold their places in *The Second Jungle Book* because they are tales in which animals play an important part. They are not particularly children's tales, and the animals do not speak. Kipling did not describe these two collections, as he did the *Puck* books, as tales for children to read until their elders had learnt that they were written for them, too, but he was as ready to stretch the young imagination as to invite the adult to play. He was, however, considerate of his childish audience and often carefully explanatory to them. He used familiar idioms in the earlier tales—'he lay as still as still'—and cut down his descriptions to the minimum—'the moon rose over the plain, making it look all milky'; in the second book the childish idioms are fewer and the descriptions expand—that of the drought-smitten jungle in 'How Fear Came', for instance; and at no time did he hold back from his young listeners the momentary glimpse of things sad and grim.

The peculiar quality of *The Jungle Books* consists in the fusion of three worlds.[1] First of all, there is the child's play-world, where all is really subject to his pastime. It is essentially a homely world, and the good beasts have prototypes in the child's daily life. The identification of the similarity in the difference is part of the pleasure. Baloo is the conscientious, solicitous, elderly schoolmaster; but what enchanting lessons he teaches! From him Mowgli learns the master-words of all the tribes in the jungle. Mother and Father Wolf live in recognizable domesticity with their four cubs—who, apparently, like grown-up Victorian sons, remain under the family roof for years—but their delightful home is a cave. The heavy Sea-Catch, with his bristling moustache, and his gentle mate, Matkah, reflect another kind of parental grouping, and it is with warm satisfaction that the child reads how Sea-Catch flings himself into the battle on Kotick's side with the shout: 'Don't tackle your father, my son; he's with you.' To this world belong, in the first instance, the pass-words and taboos of the jungle, which are entirely congenial to a child's imagination. This is the part of the books that grew from the remembered children's stories of Kipling's youth, the Freemason lions and the boy who lived with wolves.

The second world, which it is impossible to distinguish from the first by the material it is built of, is the world of the fable proper. The elements of moral instruction, which are certainly not alien to a child's world, are systematized. The beasts, without discarding pleasingly incongruous habits of their own, are plainly representative of human traits and conditions, and we are never oblivious of their counterparts in the world of men. They are grouped into arrangements that point a moral, and the moral may extend beyond a child's comprehension, though it should not lie wholly outside it. In *The Jungle Books* the fable comes and goes,

---

[1] I find I am in agreement with M. Robert Escarpit (*Rudyard Kipling: Servitudes et Grandeurs Impériales*, 1955) as to the triple nature of the Mowgli tales, and as to the nature of the first and second world. I diverge from him entirely in my third world.

and sometimes lies like a transparent glaze over the adventures. The examples are best found in the Mowgli tales, where we move, most of the time, in a self-consistent animal world; where human beings play a large part in the story, as in '"Rikki-tikki-tavi"', the conditions for fable are less good. In 'Kaa's Hunting', however, the fable and the play-world are inextricably fused. The Bandar-log, the monkey-peoples, who sympathize with Mowgli when he is under punishment and abduct him into the tree-tops, are primarily figures in a thrilling and grim story. The green roads through the trees, along which they take Mowgli, his presence of mind when he gives the master-word to Chil the Kite and bids him mark his trail—this is the stuff of the play-world, raised to an exciting pitch by wonder. But very early and easily, before the adventures begin, the Bandar-log—irresponsible, chattering, without law or shame or memory—are seen as the antithesis to jungle-righteousness, and their dangerous futility is brought out by their doings at Cold Lairs. The adult reader can find the Bandar-log elsewhere in Kipling's writings and read how Frankwell Midmore was saved from one tribe of them. He has a clue in their self-comforting cry: 'What the Bandar-log think now the Jungle will think to-morrow'; but this, in its immediate meaning, is not beyond the child, and at no time does the allegory press too hard. Baloo and Bagheera, fighting for their lives in the moonlight at Cold Lairs, are the beloved beasts in peril, the companions of the man-cub in the play-world; when they become the mouthpieces of the Law, and Mowgli has to learn that sorrow never turns aside punishment, it seems to the child a suitable law in this sort of world; the types and morals are fully absorbed into the story. In 'The King's Ankus' Kipling takes a version of a wide-spread moral apologue, which Chaucer had used for his *Pardoner's Tale*, and combines it with a tale of hidden treasure and the following of a trail. The failure of Mowgli, the fosterling of wolves, to comprehend the value of the cumbrous jewelled ankus, for which men kill each other, serves the same purpose as the Pardoner's sermon. The power of the ancient tale sends a cold breath of awe through the narrative. In '"Tiger-Tiger!"' the fable-elements are more insistent. The young wolves desert their old leader to accept Shere Khan's demoralizing advice, and, at the end, when Shere Khan's skin is pegged out on the Council Rock, they illustrate a Wordsworthian moral—'Me this uncharted freedom tires'. At times, especially near the beginning of the series, before the jungle world has grown into full imaginative authority, the human counterparts of the doings of the pack show too clearly. In the matter of the taboo against killing man the wolves are human enough to give an idealistic reason for what is a measure of plain self-interest.

More important than these two worlds, however, is what I can only call the world of the wild and strange, the ancient and the far. It includes myth, but extends beyond it. There are not very many pages of strictly mythological imagination in *The Jungle Books*. There is Hathi's tradition of how Fear came, a more mysterious *Just So* story, told in the setting of the Water-Truce; there is Kotick's search for the shore where man has never come to destroy the seals—a combination of Leif Eirikson's Wonder-Strands with the Islands of the Blest; and there is, in the later Mowgli tales, the majestic shadow of Adam, King of the Jungle. It is, however, only a shadow; for Mowgli moves in place and time, suffers the ill-temper of Buldeo and the stones of the man-pack, lets Messua comb his hair, and speeds her to the unknown English at Kanhiwara. He has drawn the milk of a woman and a wolf. Messua thinks him a wood-god; but to children he is more like a boy who is helped by kindly beasts in a fairy-tale. He has a fairy-tale extension of power, and his communion with his foster-brothers, which makes old Muller of 'In the Rukh' describe him as before the Stone Age, is to the child another magic power.

The Mowgli of 'In the Rukh' does not quite tally with the Mowgli of *The Jungle Books*. Professor Carrington tells us that the tale was written after 'Mowgli's Brothers', the first of that series; otherwise we should have guessed that it was written before, and, indeed, that is the impression that Kipling himself conveys in *Something of Myself*. It is not so much that 'In the Rukh' plays in the Doon, a far cry from the Seeonee Hills, or that this Mowgli's sketch of his history needs some humouring to fit it into what we know of the boy of *The Jungle Books*, but he speaks to Gray Brother as to a dog, in human language, and is 'very mistrustful of the firelight and ready to fly back to the thicket on the least alarm'. Yet the child Mowgli spoke to the beasts in their own tongues, and, in the first tale, showed his superiority to them by nursing the Red Flower in a fire-pot and using it as a weapon against the tiger. It is an odd inconsistency, if Professor Carrington is right; but all it signifies, perhaps, is that it took time for an imaginary world to establish its conditions. Kipling was embarked upon a different kind of creation from the brilliant selections from the known world that had made his name. 'Mowgli's Brothers' never falls upon my ear with quite the authority of the later tales; nor does 'Weland's Sword', with the first appearance of Puck; and we know that the author rejected the original tales of the *Puck* series. Muller's talk about paganism and the Stone Age does not point exactly down the road that his Daemon was to travel.

The realm of wonder extends beyond the limits of myth. The magical distance and strangeness, of which there are hints in the *Just So Stories*, are here all around us. In the midst of the jungle there is a vast ruined city, and under it an abandoned treasure-house, where a sacred white cobra still guards the jewels; there are glades, too, where the axe of the little Gond hunter flies across the clearing like a dragon-fly. Up in the Arctic the pack-ice grinds and roars round the unseen shores, and the sorcerer sings charms in his snow-hut. The wise elephants, tame and wild, in the Assamese hills, meet at night to trample out their dancing ground.[1] A Himalayan mountain-side is loosened by rain, and the animals sense the coming landslide and save the holy man who has shown them hospitality. And in all these places people live with strange skills and strange beliefs. Kotuko buckles himself into his belt for the long watch by the seal's breathing-hole; old Buldeo asserts that the Lame Tiger embodies the spirit of a dead money-lender; the seasonal round of a Himalayan village takes place at a great depth below the shrine where Purun Bhagat meditates. The refinement of human senses to meet special conditions and the intuitive knowledge of ancestral habit are often brought to notice. In the jungle Mowgli weaves little huts with sticks and creeper, like his forefathers the woodcutters, and knowledge comes to him, as to the beasts his brothers, though not so unerringly, by a taint in the air, a falling shadow, a movement of the grass, the faintest of sounds. All this wonder comes with vivid concrete detail. The world unfolds, unspeakably various and wild and old; and everywhere the family group keeps the child in touch with its own reality. Toomai's mother and Matkah the seal sing their lullabies;

---

[1] I believe that J. H. Williams (Elephant Bill) in *Bandoola* was the first to establish in print that the trodden areas are not dancing-places but maternity wards. Kipling's story, fifty years before, was based on tradition.

Big Toomai and Sea-Catch grumble; and Kotuko's little brother gnaws a nice nutty strip of blubber.

But the true *utile dulci* of the children's book is not attained unless it conveys intimations of obligations and passions outside the reach of a child's experience. *The Jungle Books* do this again and again. Sometimes, though not always, a clue may be laid in his hand, or a violent action may be attenuated for his behoof. When Mowgli's bitterness against the man-pack, who have stoned him, doubles his bitterness against the young wolves, who hate him because he has taken thorns out of their feet, he resolves: 'Now I will hunt alone', and his mood is brought nearer to a child's level by the title of his 'Song against People'. When in his revenge he lets in the jungle on the village, no human blood is shed. Nevertheless, here and in 'Kaa's Hunting' and 'The King's Ankus' and 'Red Dog', there is a strong note of the terrible, and the corpse-laden waters of the Mutiny in 'The Undertakers' are horrible enough, even when reduced by distance in the relishing memory of the gluttonous old crocodile. Here the note is macabre, but in 'Red Dog' it is heroic. The hunting-grounds of Mowgli's pack are over-run by the inferior but vastly more numerous pack of the Dholes from the Deccan, and the wolves fight to the death for their lairs and their cubs. Only the confidence that comes from moving for a long time in a powerful and coherent world of the imagination could have enabled Kipling to write this tale at this pitch. It is extraordinarily—almost blindly—bold, and courts every disaster; and yet I do not think it can be read without emotion by any except such as are unable to read these tales at all. We are presented with the ancient patterns of desperate valour—the threat of the barbarian horde, the sacrificial exploit, the fight in the narrow place, the death of the old leader—in terms which, if we stop to think, are wholly artificial. But we do not stop to think, because the patterns are too strong. The same thing happens in Professor Tolkien's *Lord of the Rings*. The spells work. It is very odd that they do, and a strong note of surprise was perceptible in the reviews of Professor Tolkien's great imaginative story. In 'Red Dog', Won-Tolla, the maimed Outlier, whose mate and cubs have been killed by the horde and who asks only to fight them and die, runs three-legged along the river bank, as his enemies come downstream, taunting them and playing 'his horrible sport'. Considering what parallels such an episode must recall, it is odd that Won-Tolla holds his place as an adequate symbol. The language of the battle is wolf-metaphor. 'The bone is cracked', says Phaon, as the Dholes give back. There is no attempt to obscure the growling, biting, worrying pack, and the tale ends with the cold requiem of Chil the Kite as his hosts drop to their feast. But before that Won-Tolla has died on his slain enemy, and Mowgli has held up Akela to sing his death-song. It is carried through with astonishing conviction and intensity, and with an elevation that does not flag. The laws of life and death have their way with Mowgli's brethren, and the child learns all this from the shelter of a fairy-tale.

The last tale, 'The Spring Running', where Mowgli goes back to his human kindred, is written with a delicate mixture of humour and pathos. At last the Time of New Talk, which sends the wild creatures singing and roving through the jungle and incites even Bagheera to undignified antics, touches the young man. 'Red Dog' could be told through bare facts; but to convey the compulsion that is driving Mowgli, which neither he nor the child who reads about him understands, Kipling has to move indirectly. Mowgli wonders if he has eaten poison; his unhappiness covers him as water covers a log, and the tears that Raksha, his wolf-mother, has told him are the signs of manhood, come to his eyes, for 'It is hard to cast the skin', says Kaa. But he has seen the young girl walk through the crops, and he goes with the favour of the jungle and—such is the reconciling nature of the fairy-tale—with the company of his four-footed foster-brothers. The young child accepts his departure as he accepts Hiawatha's, as another obscure necessity of the strange life of men, and responds to the high mournfulness of the farewell; and the acceptance of uncomprehended necessity is no bad preparation for life.

Writing for children, and often at a high imaginative pitch, has clarified Kipling's style. *The Jungle Books* have tenderness and dignity, and the playfulness of linguistic equivalents is not overdone. Kipling's strong physical sensitiveness is all in play. Mowgli's skin is in contact with the warm dust, the black deeps of the jungle pool, the brushing jungle-growths, the fur of the beasts. In the *Puck* books also Kipling's audience was a clarifying factor. The tales slip along in easy sentences of narrative and conversation. There are not many quotable set pieces. Three magnificent paragraphs give us Parnesius's march northward to the Wall, but the mode is conversational and reminiscent. There are also the two night-pieces in 'Cold Iron', which Kipling thought his best in that kind, made out of a mingling of magic and weather, and a storm-scape of the same sort, that I like better, in 'Weland's Sword'. But mostly the sentences are brief and suggestive. 'Even our Libyan cohort—the Thirds—stood up in their padded cuirasses and did not whimper.' The historical background never clots; the facts are introduced in a personal and narrative context. The legionary looking suspiciously at his helmetful of British water-ground flour is a permanent type, and his behaviour a test of the young officer's quality. The amused account of the fat old general consulting the oracle in his sword-hilt owes its effect to the naturalness of its presentation, as a familiar part of Parnesius's life. The method is thus dramatic, with Puck in reserve to elucidate, when the narrator's assumptions are too remote from an Edwardian childhood. The distance in time of the narrators, of which some of them are aware, permits a light period colouring which adds to the idiosyncrasy of the speakers without ever removing them from our elbow. The Tudor and Sussex touches in Hal o' the Draft's speech correspond to his doublet and hose, half-seen where he sits behind the planks in old Mus' Springett's loft. Unassertive archaisms in Sir Richard Dalyngridge's gentle talk recall the strangeness through the familiarity, as the clink of his helmet on the saddle-bow of the grazing war-horse lightly punctuates the golden afternoon in the horse-pasture. 'When these lands were mine,' he says, 'I never loved that mounted men should cross the brook except by the paved ford.' It is from this pitch, so very slightly removed from good contemporary English, that the dialogue can pass to the cry: "Ware Senlac arrows!' that rings explicitly out of the past. Mostly when Kipling requires dignity he draws on the 'middle' of the language, using words and constructions that do not become antiquated, but are not often heard, in daily speech, without some accompaniment of limiting idiom. This is the language which, with an intensification of rhythm and a very simple sentence structure, serves for the Flint Age man. The most various speaker is Parnesius, and the skill of Kipling's almost imperceptible transitions of tone can be illustrated from his tale. When he describes his home in Vectis he uses language entirely familiar to the children who question him, but, as he moves into the longer laps of unbroken narrative, the rhythm strengthens, and the language, without ceasing to be entirely speakable—we never question the authenticity of the narrating voice—acquires a precision and an order which is strictly outside colloquial usage. 'Red-hot in summer, freezing in winter, is that big, purple heather country of broken stone.' At the height of the story, when the Winged Hats bring the Emperor's letter to the Captains of the Wall, they show Parnesius 'a dark stain on the outer roll that my heavy heart perceived was the valiant blood of Maximus', and the deliberate, dragging cadence, the stately artifice of the words, commend themselves to the hearer as what the event requires. The descent from the intense pitch of experiences that have made grey-haired veterans of two young officers comes naturally through the unslaked curiosity of Dan and Una about the minor matters, well within their understanding.

The response of the children is used not only to control the interest of the young readers, but to elicit various effects for the older ones. They are the inheritors of their country's history, and of the general state of man. They are intelligent but young. Una's polite enquiry—she is a very polite child—if Parnesius, newly arrived on the Wall, felt happy after he had had a good meal, gives the peculiar emphasis of innocence to the indication of the young man's real state of mind. The question shows her womanly concern, for she is embryo woman as Dan is embryo man. It is to Dan that Queen Elizabeth turns for acquittal when she has told how she sacrificed her two expendable young men, trading on her charm in defiance of her genuine remorse, and carried to her purpose, when she would have relented, by the fires she has lit in them. Dan, 'young Burleigh', understands enough of the political necessity to exonerate the Queen with the words which are the *leit-motiv* of the book: 'I don't see what else she could have done'. His sister merely dislikes the woman. At times Puck and the narrator speak for a moment above the children's heads, as adults will. What follows for them is usually an explanation; for the adult it can be another dimension to the tale. When Parnesius says that he met his friend Pertinax at the Bull Killing, Puck glosses swiftly: 'That's something you wouldn't quite understand. Parnesius means he met Pertinax in church', and the adult's first reaction is amusement at the equation of the Mithraic blood-baptism with service at St Barnabas', which the children frequent, but his second is to perceive that this is the truth. This is a small example of what Kipling means when he says in *Something of Myself* that, in writing the *Puck* tales, he overlaid tint with tint, so that it showed differently according to the sex and age of the reader. The most developed example of this overlaying, however, is 'Simple Simon', for here part of the meaning of the tale remains submerged. Puck restrains Drake's friend, Simon Cheyneys, from saying what is on his mind about the hanging of Thomas Doughty by Drake's orders on the *Golden Hind*. His name comes up and is dismissed. Simon's aunt prophesies that Drake will bury his heart beside the road he will open from east to west and back again; and, before the tale begins, the children have seen Cattiwow, the woodman, lash his team-leader to get the last ounce of effort out of him, and Simon has pointed out to them that Cattiwow 'cherished his horse, but he'd ha' laid him open in that pinch'. But such knowledge is too hard for children, and the tale moves on another course, towards the Armada that Dan has been hoping for. Nonetheless they feel —I felt, when I failed to get any information about Mus' Doughty out of my family—that some unknown and cruel obligation, such as confronts at times the leaders of men, had awaited Frankie by the side of the road he opened. The tale puzzled me; the bits did not seem to come together, or, as I should say now, the pattern was incomplete. What is full in the child's vision, and very satisfactory, is the opportunity that comes at length to the modest home-keeping burgess of Rye to supply Drake's need for stores and ammunition in the middle of the fight with the Armada, and Drake courteously embracing his friend before all his great captains and causing his ship's music to play him away with honour. This is a situation full of the most reassuring moral and emotional lights. Also, in case Simple Simon should be held too cheap, there are his little models of iron ships that floated, but were given up, since what England needed of Rye was wooden ships. They were 'untimely', like the microscope of 'The Eye of Allah'.

The children meet Simon in their own woods, and his shipwright's apron and cap of sackcloth are doubles of those that the woodmen wear. The local approach to history, as must often have been said, makes Kipling of the school of Scott, and like Scott he shows the continuity of local dwellings and occupations. Hal o' the Draft was born at Little Lindens farm; Parnesius had shoulder-straps mended at the forge on the children's ground. The brook, with its ford and mill, the lie of the country, the farms in the sheltered valleys, these things have not altered much through the centuries, and only less ancient are the local names in the churchyard and the local character. Changes are noted. Hops come in, and turkeys; Hal, lying awake as a boy, hears the hammers of the Sussex iron-forges; the district nurse on her bicycle draws the children's attention from Nicholas Culpeper, and the plague-stone serves as a chickens' drinking-trough. The little islands and the seals have gone from Selsey Bill, but Pevensey is still the Gateway of England—and visitors there today can see the traces of a control-centre of the last war in one of the great bastions. Thus continuity and change are juxtaposed, and both are exemplified in a small and ancient district, where the layers of civilization lie deep, and where the children are at home.

The imaginative vitality of the tales comes in through all the senses. Parnesius's horse-hair crest rasps on his shoulder-plates; the ice glazes the lips of the black image of Weland that lies in the bows of the pirates' galley; the Bee Boy sits in 'the silver square of the great September moon that was staring into the oast-house door'. On analysis, it seems that it is often the weather and the natural reaction of men to it that give the force of conviction to these tales. Working from his own home and its surroundings, Kipling could not conceive an incident without its seasonal and climatic conditions. The continuous flow of physical existence through these pages, the intake of sight and sound and smell and touch, the weight and texture of solid objects, the changing horizon and the movements of men and animals—these owe their natural air to the completeness with which they have been imagined. This imagination attends him beyond his own district. When Parnesius and Pertinax come out of the Temple of Victory, where they have accepted the captaincy of the Wall,

> We saw great Roma Dea atop of the Wall, the frost on her helmet, and her spear pointed to the North Star. We saw the twinkle of the night-fires all along the guard towers, and the line of the black catapults growing smaller and smaller in the distance. All these things we knew till we were weary; but that night they seemed very strange to us, because the next day we knew we were to be their masters.

Kipling drew from both the past and the present, from an

inhabited landscape, from books and from experience. He tells us that when he talked over the plan of *Puck of Pook's Hill* with his father, Lockwood Kipling warned him that he would have to be careful, and years later, in the 'The Propagation of Knowledge', he tells us why, when Stalky rebukes Beetle because he is 'so dam' inaccurate'. Kipling was, I believe, as careful as it was in his creative nature to be; it is obvious that a great deal of investigation has gone to provide him with the detail that makes his stories stand up so solidly; but one does not need to be a professional historian to find doubtful patches in them. The passage of nearly half a century has worn the web thinner in places, but the blemishes were there from the beginning. When a creative artist uses historical material, he cannot for long, however hard he tries, approach it like a historian—unless, maybe, he has been trained as one in youth. His creative consciousness is looking all the while for what he can use, and in the incandescent flash, which occurs when it makes contact with its potential material, a century or two may easily be burnt up—almost without the author's knowledge. As far as dates go, Kipling had a ballad-like bent for round numbers. Scores and hundreds drip off his pen. Thirteen or fourteen hundred years ('few' can hardly mean less than three or four) intervene between Weland's landing in England as the god of Peofn's pirates, and his departure, as a wayside smith, on the eve of the Norman Conquest. We can get round this only by supposing that Weland was a god of the Belgae; but Kipling's point is simply that gods have come and gone in England, and that the unperturbed Puck could afford to give Weland 'lots of time'. Sometimes the artist requires a preciseness which has faded out of knowledge through the ages. The strong legendary theme of 'The Knife and the Naked Chalk', the sacrifice of an eye by the Flint Man as the price of iron knives for his people to use against wolves, must have been difficult to dress out in sufficient detail, and there is almost as much invention in it as in the Taffimai stories, though it is based on probable parallels; but when he wants a divine name for the Flint Men to hail their lonely 'god' by, he borrows Tyr from Nordic mythology. 'Cold Iron' is not open to the criticism of historians, but the juxtaposition of Thor and Sir Huon of Bordeaux shows how ubiquitously and with how high a hand Kipling would take what he wanted. The passage in *Something of Myself*, where he tells us about the discovery at

Pevensey Castle of the well which he had posited there—when Clio, we might say, honoured the cheque that he had boldly drawn on her account—has a pleasant triumph which betrays what the real process had been. The main imaginative source of these tales—the breath and blood of them—is experience, working through analogy.

Any historical fiction of human substance—that is, any that is not mere pageantry or fantasy—must proceed to some extent by analogy. It is the novelist's key of entry into the past, and the charm that stirs the dry bones. The political analogies in *Puck of Pook's Hill* have at times been over-emphasized, but they exist in some of the stories, though not in very many of them. These are the Roman tales and, to a less degree, 'Young Men at the Manor' and 'Old Men at Pevensey', the first and third of the tales told by the Norman knight, Sir Richard Dalyngridge. The Normans are a conquering and occupying power. De Aquila, Lord of Pevensey, the statesman who thinks for England, 'for whom neither King nor Baron thinks', envisages the blending of conquerors and conquered in one nation, and fears the pull of the old home interests on the Norman baronage. His Knight marries a Saxon lady and rules his manor by Saxon custom, and De Aquila gives her disinherited brother land. Here what happened in England in the eleventh and twelfth centuries seems to be presented by Kipling in accordance with his hopes for South Africa after the Boer War. He tells the story and sings the song of the conqueror who is taken captive by the land he conquers. In the service of the land and the people lie reconciliation and promise. What throve in England he might well hope would thrive in South Africa. Three years before, at the close of the Boer War, he had written 'The Settler', verses put into the mouth of an Englishman, turning the furrows of the land he has fought over, and now serves; and two years later 'The Prairie', written for 'Letters to the Family', an account of his tour in Canada, was to repeat part of the same tune. The new earth, the new seasons, with their unfamiliar beauty, can be trusted to take the settler and wean him from his earlier life. 'But now England hath taken me.'

The Roman stories are not built on a simple or single analogy. It is often said that Kipling sees the Wall as the North-West Frontier, and Parnesius and Pertinax as young English officers, 'taking heather' with friendly tribesmen in the peaceful spells, and meeting the assault of the invaders from the north with unbroken resolution but inadequate troops and supplies. We need not object to this, provided it is not assumed that, when Kipling writes of the sealed gateway to Valentia, he meant us to think exclusively of the Khyber Pass. From this point of view, the equivalents of the Winged Hats are doubtless the Russians, and the equivalent of Mithraism, that binds together men of different and hostile races, is Freemasonry. But Parnesius is not a Roman; he has not come overseas to man the Imperial Frontier. He tells the children that he is 'one of a good few thousands who have never seen Rome except in a picture'. He is a descendant of the first colonists, and his roots are hundreds of years deep in Britain. When he claims that the baths at Aquae Sulis are 'just as good, I'm told, as Rome', he is not speaking like an English officer of Simla, and he dislikes the overbearing ways of the Romans from Rome. He can afford to be casual about the Empire—'We split the Eagle before I was born'—but it is because he cannot conceive that Eternal Rome is near destruction, 'just because a few people had become a little large-minded'. In all this, he is nearer to the Australians, whom Kipling had seen in their own country and in South Africa, than to the young officers of the English army. The parallel is confirmed in 'A British-Roman Song', where the speaker prays that the heart of empire may beat strongly and send out fresh blood to the members. It is dated A.D. 406, exactly a millennium and a half before *Puck of Pook's Hill* came out. The analogies, then, are complex, and harmony can be established only by thinking in terms of the story itself. The traces of Roman workings near 'Bateman's' brought Parnesius, and Parnesius brought with him the well-known problems of a colonizing power, an ancient and distant colony, and a fortified land-frontier under pressure from the powers outside it. It is significant, no doubt, that he was placed not at the beginning but at the end of Roman dominion in Britain, showing how strongly the question of the change or the end of empire worked in Kipling's mind. But Parnesius also brought with him much that had no reference to contemporary affairs, much that is the result of the free working of the imagination on the past. The Wall is manned and officered by criminals and men who have lost their reputations. The ambition of Maximus, the great general, to wear the purple, and his stripping Britain of troops, is a development of historical data.

The analogies, in fact, are more general and less specific than has always been supposed. It can be said of all conquering and colonizing powers, as the Picts sang of Rome, that 'Rome never looks where she treads', and it would be very difficult and quite useless to shred out the various racial elements that made up Kipling's conception of the Little People of the Picts. They fill their place in the story with convincing likelihood. The analogies that are really important—what I have called the breath and blood of the tales—are quite general, and they live on the page without the need of commentary. They are as available to the children of today as to those of fifty years ago. I think of such passages as the Legion's marching-song, 'Rimini,' a doleful love-lyric that Parnesius sings with great cheerfulness, or of his account of leaving home to take up his post on the frontier:

> The night before I left we sacrificed to our ancestors—the usual little Home Sacrifice—but I never prayed so earnestly to all the Good Shades, and then I went with my father by boat to Regnum, and across the chalk eastwards to Anderida yonder.

Nothing could be more living or less ostentatious.

It may have some relevance that, when I first read these tales, I never once thought of the British Empire, that lay in pink patches all over my atlas, but always of Rome and the past.

Much more apparent than political analogies, even before Kipling pointed it out in *Something of Myself*, was the *leit-motiv* that runs through *Rewards and Fairies*: 'What else could I have done?' The nature of the compulsion behind this question varies. It arises from character and training, from office and circumstances. Mostly it relates to public obligation, but once or twice to a private relationship, and we may think that here it was sometimes inserted to complete the pattern. The necessity may be accepted in partial ignorance or full consciousness. The Boy in 'Cold Iron' puts Thor's slave-ring round his neck, saying only: 'Is this how it goes?' He has been bred up by Sir Huon to 'act and influence on folk in housen', but the service offered him is not that of a king or a knight or a sage. The Flint Man, on the other hand, gives his eye deliberately to save the sheep from the wolves. 'The Sheep are the People.' He becomes a god to his tribe, is excluded from the common life of man, and accepts the further and unsurmised burden of loneliness. Washington faces unpopularity because he will not lead an unprepared nation into war. The two young Elizabethans claim the right to undertake a service of which the foreseen reward is 'assured dishonour', and the Queen is compelled to concede it. It is not easy to find a description that will cover these and all the other ways in which the nature of a selected man confronts and accepts the demands of his office and the pressure of circumstance. Even Washington's 'My brothers know it is not easy to be a chief' will not cover the Boy's instinctive choice, and St Wilfrid was hardly thinking of his episcopacy when he told the pagan Meon that he would not desert his God in the middle of a gale. But we are continually aware of the cost of eminent service, and the loneliness, and even sometimes the mutilation, of the leader.

There had been no such strong, conscious theme binding together the tales of the earlier book. The spontaneity of *Puck of Pook's Hill* streams out in various directions. The children have their own moral standards. Una approves Lady Æluev a because 'she was sorry, and she said so', and Dan assures Hal o' the Draft that he knows perfectly well what comes of sinful pride; and the natural black-and-white of their ethics throws up, for the adult reader, the difficulty of judgment. Some of the values are left to reveal themselves. Pertinax, a 'man without hope', does equally good service with his more sanguine friend. Even service itself is not an unmitigated requirement. Parnesius refuses his general's command to kill a soldier of his troop, because he will not be Maximus's butcher, and his father approves. Nor should authority always be exercised; it should be capable of indulgence, as the children understood very well in regard to Old Hobden. But the burden of these first tales is not so much morals as meanings. The children see friendship and enmity, ambition and generosity, faith and treachery, and see them in action and character. They are not laid out in the least diagrammatically. Kipling is very skilful in developing more complex indications within an easily apprehensible outline. De Aquila is the most developed figure in the two books. He is displayed in three tales and not forgotten in a fourth. In two of the tales, he and his knights are old men, and the tales are shot with a natural melancholy which a child half-perceives as a sort of mysterious background. I put aside the question of his anachronistic care for 'England'. What is to be considered is how he is shown, and what is shown through him.

De Aquila is set before young readers in a number of vivid and humorous presentations. There is the yellow-eyed little man, who would ride big horses, hopping with his foot in the stirrup ('He could not abide to be helped') and casting winged words over his shoulder, or addressing the manor from a horse-block 'in what he swore was good Saxon, but no man understood it'. There is the old man in his furred gown, peering from his tower at Pevensey like a little white falcon, plotting and planning secretly and wisely, desperately bold of speech, and using any weapon that chance offers him. He delights the child, though not without some puzzlement, when he refuses to punish poor false Gilbert, because he would rather have 'a clerk, however false, that knew the manor roll, than a fool, however true, that must be taught his work afresh'. But within these vigorous outlines there are touches that give substance and particularity. There are his harsh humour and kindness, his multifarious interests, his love of craft and the cunning that avoids violence, his active mind that, even in old age, still finds waiting 'the most grievous work I know'. He lies in the straw of the little hut with his young knights, speaking in parables and tales, and yerking them in the ribs with his scabbarded sword if they do not see his meaning at once. Or he sits outside in the early morning, talking—it is a strangely convincing touch—'of holy things, and how we should govern our manors in time to come, and of hunting and of horse-breeding, and of the King's wisdom and unwisdom'. Kipling had known great men, colonizers and statesmen, and he places such a one, born out of his due time, in a 'black age' of violence, where his capacities, as he says of himself, have no play. His dealings with the traitor, Fulke, his dispassionate amusement, his dry pity when it will advance rather than hinder his schemes, are those of one whose experience of men is so wide, that now he is 'too old to judge, or to trust any man'. His is not the usual treatment of a villain to be found in a child's book, nor is Fulke the usual villain, when he rides away from Pevensey after his harrowing night in the well, showing very splendid and stately in his newly-scoured armour, and smoothing his long beard to kiss his young son farewell. The child who reads these books will not have to unlearn anything about human nature, though some of what is laid before him will be for many years outside his scope.

The last tale of each book is difficult, and both are told in autumnal settings that mark the end of the open-air days, when the children can come and go and look and know. Kipling says that he always felt 'The Treasure and the Law' somehow too heavy for its frame. As a child, I missed the presence of any attractive characters in this tale, for the Jew Kadmiel, once he has ceased to be the 'little Prince', is not attractive; and though, in a sense, I understood his reason for drowning the treasure—his paring beneath his nails for the last grains was particularly impressive—I could not reach the passion beneath his dry, bitter speech, or see the ironical fulfilment of his destiny. I seldom read it. 'The Tree of Justice' silences and bewilders Dan and Una. 'I think this tale is getting like the woods,' says Dan, 'darker and twistier every minute'; and though, as Sir Richard says, 'the end was not all black', it brings them face to face with tragedy, for the first time since Puck had given them seizin. The tale presumes that Harold Godwinson survived Hastings, and tells how, forty years later, an aged, witless beggar, with momentary flickers of his real self, he is brought into the presence of Henry I and dies there. In outline, then, the tale covers the same sort of ground as the much earlier and simpler 'The Man Who Was'. There it is the English officer, taken prisoner in the Crimea, who crawls back after half a lifetime in Siberia to his own regiment on the North-West Frontier. There are parallels in incident and treatment between the two tales. The scene and ceremonies of the Mess recall the officer's identity to him, and he answers the toast of the Queen from his place at the foot of the table, and snaps the shank of the thin glass, as was done in his young manhood. In like fashion, Henry's court stirs Harold's drowned memories and, when he has been given drink, he beckons behind him to have the cup borne away. In each case, after the partial recovery there is a lapse back into the dread and humiliation that indicate what the interim has been; and in each case, since the man could not be restored to his former self, death is a satisfying end. But the anecdote, during its submergence in the mind of the artist, has suffered a sea-change. There has grown over it an intricate web of motive and effect. 'The Man Who Was' is simple in conception. The visiting Russian general, and the group-reaction of the English officers to him, exist in order to underline the grimness and pathos of the strange event, and perhaps for extra-literary reasons. The return of Harold, on the other hand, involves separate tests for King Henry, Brother Hugh, Rahere the King's jester, and even, in a minor way, for De Aquila. It occurs at a moment of tension, when the Saxons are driving game for their Norman masters in a hunting that is itself a deliberate display of Norman *sang-froid*, and it could thus be a dangerous precipitant of the unstable situation. King Henry is not tested to the full, for Harold dies. Hugh's response is self-forgetful service and an anguish that is the measure of the tragic fall. Rahere is an enigmatic figure. Kipling has in mind the tradition that he turned monk and founded St Bartholomew's Hospital. Visually he seems to derive from a 'metagrobolized' Jack Point, and Sir Richard speaks of his 'sad priest's face, under his cockscomb cap, that he could twist like a strip of wet leather'. He became stabilized, it seems, as a figure in Kipling's imagination, and more than a dozen years later he built round him one of the poems that go with 'The Wish House'. Rahere has protected Harold, knowing who he was and keeping his secret, while he 'can make shift to bide his doom under the open sky'. Now he offers him to Henry and his court, partly under compulsion and partly in a bold game to deflect the trouble that has arisen between Norman and Saxon at the beat. But, deeper than this, we are to remember the 'half-priest', who brings his man to confession, knowing his death is near. Harold's long penance for his broken oath is over; no man in the King's court, baron or bishop, dares judge him. He takes good comfort, and dies on the breast of the truest knight of his house.

The dominant image of the tree of justice appears first as a reinforcement of the conception of Norman rule. Sir Richard finds the keeper's victims nailed to a beech, and says that in his time that sort of tree bore heavier fruit. The threat of the gallows hangs over the countryside during the King's sport. When Harold is exposed in the King's court, he too is nailed to the tree of justice, though he is not judged. Nails and the tree bring in, by more than a verbal association, the thought of crucifixion, and suggest the long crucifixion of Harold's sufferings. A tree appears again in the carol that closes the book. In the iron time of frost, sing the carollers,

> *We hear the cry of a single tree*
> *That breaks her heart in the cold—*
> *That breaks her heart in the cold, good sirs,*
> *And rendeth by the board;*

Which well must be as ye can see—
And who shall judge the Lord?

This 'Carol' first appeared in 1900, together with a tale of the Boer War, 'A Burgher of the Free State'. We can go back five years more and find in 'Leaves from a Winter Note-Book', afterwards gathered into *From Tideway to Tideway*, a note of how Kipling first heard this awesome sound, during winter in Vermont. 'At night a tree's heart will break in him with a groan', he writes. 'According to the books, the frost has split something, but it is a fearful sound, this grunt as of a man stunned.' The memory had drawn to itself a symbolic connotation by the time he linked the Carol to the tale of old Allen, the Scot who was a naturalized Burgher of the Orange Free State, and it was deepened when he used it for Harold. One must not press too far the application of the verses that accompany the tales: they have their own life. The tree of the 'Carol', for instance, is not the tree of justice; it is one on which judgment has passed. But it may be said of both Allen and Harold, men at the end of their lives, that their 'wood (was) crazed and little worth', and it may be said in both cases that the 'frost' that broke their hearts was ripening their lands for spring. 'And who shall judge the Lord?' cry the carollers. We cannot judge men for what they do under duress; nor can we judge the Lord for imposing the duress by which such actions are enforced. It is a dark lesson for the children. In 'Simple Simon' they had heard a remote echo of it; now it confronts them. Allen shows his loyalty to the country of his adoption in a way that many will take for cowardice and treachery. Drake hanged his friend. Harold loaded his soul with guilt, as he believed. A house, De Aquila says, cannot be built all of straight sticks; and a house must be built.

'The Tree of Justice', in its full meaning, is the hardest tale for children in either book. It is, however, commended by the high heroic note of Hugh's service and Harold's death, by the reappearance of young Fulke and by the fascinating figure of Rahere. To comfort little girls like Una, we end with the parable of the dormouse. If it is warmed, says Una, it will wake up and die straight off, and old Hobden answers: 'That's a heap better by my reckonin' than wakin' up and findin' himself in a cage for life.' So Rahere thought.

CHAPTER FOUR

Simplicity and Complexity

A few years ago, when it was the custom to dismiss Kipling's work as 'simple', it might have appeared of the first importance to demonstrate that the simplicity was often in the eye of the beholder. Now it is, perhaps, as important to establish the fact that this intricate craftsman was on occasion capable of true simplicity. This is a word that is used both absolutely and relatively; I have, indeed, used it both ways in the preceding sentences. The absolute sense is often discriminated by the epithets true, pure or perfect. Simplicity of this kind marks the highest pitch to which a certain kind of writing can go. There must be a maturity of substance—very likely an instantaneous or intuitive maturity—so complete that any form of uneasiness or display—any sediment, in fact—is impossible, and this must be conveyed in a translucent medium and with natural grace of form. This simplicity cannot coexist with elaborate patterning or conscious complexity of attitude; it does not thrive, therefore, with irony. It seems to be diminished by a strict control and condensation, that are felt to be consciously such. At least, I know no other reason why King Lear's

> *her voice was ever soft,*
> *Gentle and low, an excellent thing in woman*

seems to me to have this pure simplicity, and Samson's

> *Eyeless in Gaza at the mill with slaves*

not to have it, though it has many noble qualities, and in Samson's mouth is a plain statement of fact. Perhaps we hear the beat of the craftsman's hammer on the iron.

It will not be expected that we shall find many passages of this kind in so complex an artist as Kipling; but we can find some. They are easier to find in the verse than the prose. I will not propose examples from his traditional ballads, or even from the war epitaphs, though a choice might be made from either, for the reader's consciousness that the poet is following a model is dangerous to, though not necessarily destructive of, pristine simplicity. It is in the songs, especially in what I can only call the murmured songs, that Kipling sometimes reaches pure simplicity. They are very quiet poems. There is 'The Way Through the Woods', which goes with 'Marklake Witches'; it says no more than that life passes and its traces are obscured, but not perhaps wholly, and says it to a hushed hoof-beat and a faint melody. There is also 'Gethsemane', in which a soldier remembers a quiet, fresh interspace, before the renewal of the fighting, in a Picardy garden, where there was a girl.

> *The officer sat on the chair,*
> *The men lay on the grass,*
> *And all the time we halted there*
> *I prayed my cup would pass.*
> *It didn't pass, it didn't pass,*
> *It didn't pass from me—*

It sings itself in an impersonal ghostly way, out of a ghostly world.

This is a kind of writing that can easily be undervalued nowadays. I should be foolish to attempt to disprize the profit and the excitement of analysis, but it does put a premium on what requires to be analysed. I have read a set of scripts in which every candidate but one rejected outright a stately, melancholy and highly efficient piece of narrative from *The Vanity of Human Wishes* on the ground that it contained no symbols; and I have seen Jane Austen downgraded, because her novels were not written 'on several levels'. These things should make one careful.

Quintessential simplicity in prose can never be very frequent, and for a number of reasons, ranging from his youthful need to impress to the three-piled material of his later work, it is a very rare note in Kipling. It is hardly heard, I believe, except when he is writing of childhood, of old age, and of loss. I have pointed in my first and third chapters to examples in *Kim* and the children's books, and I add here 'The Story of Muhammad Din' in *Plain Tales from the Hills*. At the thought of the quaint, little, short-lived child his epigrams, jauntiness, challenge, even his dryness, melt out of his style and leave a sequence of perfect limpidity.

'Portly old Imam Din', the *khitmatgar*, who carries the little bundle of his son in his arms to the burying-ground, presents the other terms of the triple condition.

When 'simple' is used with a comparison, stated or implied, it is always a little depreciatory, though not necessarily unkindly so. 'Simple tales of action' means that they are not at all like Conrad's; there may, however, be a place in literature for their simple merits. 'Simple' here really stands for 'superficial', and Kipling goes a long way to invite this description when he writes in *Something of Myself* that he has dealt with large superficial areas of life. I am not sure what he meant here, but I often hear irony in his remarks where other critics hear naïvety and wistfulness. Some of his tales are indeed superficial; they make play with a superficial fancy as '·007' does, or they move with alacrity over the surface of a new and interesting territory as 'Little Foxes' does. The fact, however, that so many of them have been called enigmatic, while it does not prove that they are profound, does establish that they are not simple. In the following discussion I do not forget that complexity need not suppose depth. One can rubricate a nonsensical statement, and cross-hatch a surface that conveys nothing but the artist's restlessness. Some of my examples are quite shallow. The fact remains, however, that a simple writer can hardly give rise to so much misreading as Kipling does. No one, who with a competent knowledge of his work has followed the criticism of him for the last twenty years, especially the casual references in the newspapers, can have failed to notice the large amount of error in the allusions. I do not mean error in evaluation but in the stated facts and opinions of the tales and poems. Some of these errors are unimportant. It is not very serious if the 'heretical song' at the end of *The Story of the Gadsbys*, with its refrain

> *Down to Gehenna or up to the Throne,*
> *He travels the fastest who travels alone,*

is shorn of its sardonic last verse, where the advice turns on itself, and applauded as if it were desirable to be sped to Gehenna. Kipling himself grumbles that the opening line of 'The Ballad of East and West'

Oh, East is East and West is West and never the twain shall meet, is always quoted without the far-reaching exception that follows, but this may be his fault for putting the negative so emphatically. These are trifles as against the failure to recognize masterpieces, but the habit is a bad one and has had more serious results. Therefore it seems to me that I ought to try to establish that most of Kipling's work at all stages requires attentive reading. We ought to see clearly even what we reject.

He did not think of his work as simple. He admired complexity in structure—the calculated strains and means of propulsion of the 'three-decker'—and in ornament—the inlay and lacquer and glazing and damascening of the bazaars and the Lahore 'Wonder-House'. It is in terms of these minor arts that he speaks of his tales in the Introduction to the Outward Bound edition in 1897. These are sensuous analogies, satisfying to his strong physical sensitiveness. Nearly all such images are drawn from hard materials, from wood and metal and gems; their surfaces are engraved or enamelled, and often they are made by a juncture of two or more substances. He also uses the image of woven stuff, and extends the metaphor. The web is either shot or embroidered; if shot, it will show different colours in different lights —that is, as he made clear when he took up the same figure in *Something of Myself,* under the eyes of age and youth, of man and woman; if embroidered, the tightly packed bales must be shaken out before the design can be seen. Some of the stuffs show well only 'in dark places where they were made'. Some of the bales have private marks on them—a reference, in the first place, to his Masonic allusions and, in the second, to those particularities of place and condition that speak intimately to such readers as are familiar with them. Probably there is a third implication; the private marks of experience show here and there for those who can recognize them, but that is the case with all writers. None of the so-called 'enigmatic' stories had been published when the Introduction was written, except 'The Children of the Zodiac', yet it seems that to Kipling his art already appeared sufficiently complex and rich in texture to respond with fresh meaning to each approach. Years later he told in 'Regulus' how King, expounding Virgil, dwelt on the 'treble-shot texture of the ancient fabric', and, later still, he came back to the same analogies when he explained his purpose and method in writing the *Puck* books.

Against these images we have to set the obliterating paintbrush, filled with Indian ink. This was not an image, but a reality; with it, on successive revisions of his more studied tales, he deleted phrase after phrase which he thought his story could do without. This deletion, however, is not a simplifying process, but an intensifying one. The old ballads, as they have come down to us, with their gapped structure, are more intense than the smoothed and dovetailed eighteenth century imitations. They are also much more stimulating to the reader, as a rough cliff-path is more stimulating to the walker than miles of macadam. A short story writer of the early twentieth century, however, cannot rely upon the general preparation of his audience for his art, as the ballad-poet could do. He must somehow transmit to his readers a sufficient sense of the contents of the suppressed parts of his narrative, and this calls for delicate judgment. In *Something of Myself* Kipling says that what is deleted must have been honestly written for inclusion first, and in his last story, 'Proofs of Holy Writ', he shows us Shakespeare telling his stubborn old friend, Ben Jonson, that he ought to have removed cartloads from his plays. The assumption is that what has once been honestly written will leave its traces, and that the tale—or the play—will benefit from it. If what is explicit is fully explored, if the dialogue, in particular, is read with a full participation of the imagination, it will be enriched by what the author has suppressed, as we feel the personality of an acquaintance without knowing all that went to shape it.

One of the earliest and most extreme of the experiments in suppressed narrative was 'Mrs Bathurst'. It is unlike the later experiments, such as 'Dayspring Mishandled', in two ways. There is no difficulty about its theme, which is the destroying power of love; on the other hand, no analysis can establish with certainty how the destruction came about. We see the gaunt shrine and the shrivelled victims, but we cannot trace the avenues of approach. If Kipling meant us to do so, it may be held, as Professor C. S. Lewis has suggested, that he has overdone his demolitions. But he may have meant the unexplained in the action to reflect the inexplicable in the theme. How and why does a candid, generous woman, who 'never scrupled to feed a lame duck or set 'er foot on a scorpion', become the vessel of a destructive power? If we were allowed to trace too closely the stages by which Vickery is destroyed, we might make the mistake of thinking that we know. So Vickery appears in Pyecroft's 'résumé' only in the last stages of his obsession, in Cape Town, and Mrs Bathurst is seen far off in Sergeant Pritchard's memories of New Zealand or momentarily on the screen of the early biograph, 'lookin' for somebody'. 'I'm trying to say solely what transpired', Pyecroft remarks; but 'what transpired' is more than the few facts he has to recount, because the men who tell and hear have knowledge of Aphrodite. Pyecroft knows that 'it takes 'em at all ages', and mentions his shipmate, Moon, who ran after sixteen years' service. Inspector Hooper knows that 'if a man gets struck with that kind o' woman . . . he goes crazy—or just saves himself', as he, perhaps, has done. The arid shore, the parching wind, the 'seven-coloured sea' of the setting are the fit haunt of the goddess, as the grotesque lightning-charred group in the teak-forest is a fit monument to her. Even the song of the casual picnic party and Pritch's involuntary irresistibility to servant-girls point in the same direction. 'I used to think seein' and hearin' was the only regulation aids to ascertainin' facts', says Pyecroft, 'but as we get older we get more accommodatin'. The cylinders work easier, I suppose.' Still, 'Mrs Bathurst' is hard on the cylinders.[1]

'Mrs Bathurst' by itself will hardly prove the complexity of Kipling's art. In fact, it begs the question. In the same collection, however, there is a tale in which the intricacy of his imagination can be clearly seen, since it is one of the few tales in which he is forced by his subject-matter to explain. '"Wireless"' is not to my mind a very successful tale, though, like most of his comparative

[1] The facts about Vickery are that he has a fifteen-year old daughter; his wife died in childbed six weeks after he came out, so that he is free; he did not murder her: there was 'a good deal between' him and Mrs Bathurst and he has some wrong or deceit against her on his mind. He says that she was looking for him at Paddington. He sees his Captain, is sent up-country alone and deserts eighteen months before his pension is due. He is found dead with a woman after a thunderstorm. Pyecroft and Pritchard both insist that it was not Mrs Bathurst's fault. She was left a widow very young, never remarried, and had the respect of the non-commissioned and warrant officers who went to her little hotel in Hauraki. The scene *From Lyden's 'Irenius'* that precedes the tale makes the point that the groom, or clown, is caught in the same noose as kings—this may account for the grotesque stress on 'Click'; that the woman destroyed him in ignorance, for she loved him; and that the groom in the end threw life from him out of weariness and self-disgust—which suggests that Vickery stood up to attract the lightning. This is not a continuous narrative; but neither is it confusion. Rather it is like the early biograph, 'just like life . . . only when any one came down too far towards us that was watchin', they walked right out o' the picture, so to speak'.

failures, it is interesting. It is too full of crowded detail which, as it is structural, cannot be eliminated. The too assertive 'I' moves restlessly among the bric-à-brac, assembling and twitching it into position, and fairly prodding on the apocalyptic minute. The mind of the reader is over-occupied with matching clues; or it fails to match them and emerges with the impression that Shaynor, the consumptive chemist's assistant, is Kipling's conception of Keats. The difficulty here does not arise from the sparseness of the indications, as in 'Mrs Bathurst', but rather from their multiplicity, from the technical nature of the explicatory parallel, and from the laying of a false trail.

The situation presented in the tale takes place in a chemist's shop, on a bitter cold evening, in a town by the sea. (It sounds like Torquay, though Teignmouth, where Keats was then supposed to have begun 'The Eve of St Agnes', would have the closer link with the poet.) The narrator has come to watch the chemist's nephew attempt with an early wireless set to pick up Morse messages from Poole. In the shop is Shaynor, the assistant, who in his profession, his consumptive state and his infatuation for a young woman of abundant charms called Fanny Brand, is a deliberately coarsened and inaccurate reproduction of Keats. The discrepancies—he comes from the North and has no intellectual interests outside his profession—indicate the divergence. Meanwhile, with disturbing ingeniousness, the atmosphere and properties of 'The Eve of St Agnes' have been assembled within and without the shop and in the casual words of the speakers. It is intensely cold; the raging wind blows up the flix of the dead hare outside the Italian warehouse next door, and Shaynor says that he wouldn't care to be lying in his grave a night like this. Inside the shop the lights in the window, shining through the traditional jars of coloured water, throw 'warm gules' on the charms of a lady in a gold frame, advertising tooth-paste. Later, when the sick man has returned from a walk 'round by St Agnes' with his young lady, he eases his cough by burning incense-smelling pastilles, placing them below the picture. The images, as well as the properties, of the poem are taken up, and the tiger-moth is evoked by Shaynor's drugged and shining eyes. The unorthodox drink that 'I' has compounded in his absence sends him into a trance, and, when the chemist's nephew calls out from the back office that something has begun to come through, the transmission of the Morse message synchronizes with the beginning of an even stranger transmission on the hither side of the door; for from the pen of Shaynor and through his lips there begin to come, sometimes smoothly and sometimes with wrenching effort, lines and fragments of Keats's poems. Nearly all of them are imperfect, and some are slightly vulgarized with the degree of underbreeding perceptible in Shaynor himself. The trance breaks, through a violent and painful effort, called forth by the now audible sea, to 'get' the lines from the 'Ode to a Nightingale' about the magic casements and the foam of desolate seas. 'I' is able to assure himself that Shaynor is quite unconscious of what has happened, has not read Keats, and does not remember his name.

The awfulness of this experience has to be conveyed in shorthand; there is no room among the gaudy details to develop it. 'I' drips with sweat; he stands half-bent, hands on knees, 'much as one would watch a rifle-shot at the butts', and his racing mind leaps ahead of his facts to provide him with a tolerable theory, a refuge from the naked terror of mystery. It is here that the false trail is laid. 'Like causes *must* beget like effects', he reassures himself, keeping the explanation well within the bounds of human science; he even seizes analogies from the explanation just given him by the chemist's nephew and tells himself that 'it's the identical bacillus, or Hertzian wave of tuberculosis, plus Fanny Brand and the professional status which, in conjunction with the main-stream of subconscious thought common to all mankind, has thrown up temporarily an induced Keats'. The huddled and agitated jargon, so unlike young Mr Cashell's lucid exposition, should warn us that this is not the right way to use the analogy, and 'the other half of my soul refused to be comforted'. The Hertzian waves are not tuberculosis; young Mr Cashell has told him that they 'come out of space from the station that despatches 'em', and that the momentary cohering of the 'infinitesimal pinch of metallic dust' reveals 'the Powers—whatever the Powers may be—at work—through space—a long distance away'. Kipling's theory of inspiration is always external, like Blake's. Like will not beget like without the influx from the abyss, which is the true analogy of the Hertzian wave. Where, however, likeness of circumstance and nature counts is in establishing the receiving station within the magnetic field of the transmitter. Cashell explains carefully that the current of the receiving station is an induced current, and that the Hertzian waves are only strong enough to make the dust cohere momentarily, while the current from the home battery gets through to the Morse printing machine to record the dot or dash. This explanation comes just before Shaynor begins to 'record' the lines of Keats. After his trance is over, 'I' returns to the back office and listens to two men-of-war off the Isle of Wight working Marconi signals, but unable to understand each other. Cashell remarks that 'their receivers are out of order, so they only get a dot here and a dash there. Nothing clear. . . . Perhaps the induction is faulty: perhaps the receivers aren't tuned to receive just the number of vibrations per second that the transmitter sends. Only a word here and there. Just enough to tantalize.'

Shaynor is the receiver that is not rightly tuned. All the differences between him and Keats—differences of spiritual temper, such as his refusal to recognize the meaning of the blood on his handkerchief—show wherein his tuning was at fault. All he can get is 'a word here and there—no good at all'; nor is the home battery of this unliterary man in plight to record accurately what does get through. He can only go 'round by St Agnes'. In his trance, though not in his conscious life, he experiences the anguish of the imperfect artist. 'The agony . . . mounted like mercury in the tube. It lighted his face from within till I thought the visibly scourged soul must leap forth naked between his jaws, unable to endure.' In this strange and impressive moment the complete artist compassionately posits an explanation of the vain ardours of the incomplete one. He sees, to quote Mr Cashell, the 'unknown Power—kicking and fighting to be let loose . . . I never get over the strangeness of it'. It is a more far-reaching theory than that which equated the imagination with the memory of earlier lives in ' "The Finest Story in the World" ', for that dealt with only one of the artist's faculties. Shaynor says when 'I' tells him about Keats: 'I must dip into him'. It is exactly what he has done. He also says, when Mr Cashell remarks that disturbed wireless reception sometimes reminds him of a spiritualist séance, that mediums are all impostors. 'They only do it for the money they can make.' On this irony, and the exhaustion of the narrator, the tale closes.

We have no such evidence about the genesis of Kipling's tales as Henry James left behind, but we can assert with some confidence that this one was generated by the excitement of finding in the new development of wireless telegraphy parallels to his conception of the mysterious nature of inspiration. Keats and 'The Eve of St Agnes' are secondary; some poet of marked beauty and individuality had to be selected in order that the difference between his 'tuning' and Shaynor's could be perceived, and some poem rich in detail in order that the particles could be identified, before they cohere to such tremendous purpose. But the cluttered scene, the absorbed and rampant cleverness of the working-out, over-stimulate the reader's detective sense and also deflect it from the centre of the story, so that the awe and compassion do not always come through.

The laying of a false trail in a short story is a dangerous manoeuvre. The reader may follow it too far and have no time to get back. I do not think, however, that Kipling ever engages in it out of provocation or mere love of the intricate. It is intended as an effect of contrast and sometimes as a warning. This way exists, but you cannot escape by it; this explanation could be given, but it would not satisfy. The bio-sociological explanation of Shaynor's poetry does not appease the narrator's terror. Again, 'Fairy-Kist' seems to offer us a detective problem and we penetrate to the solution of it through folds of misconception. It opens as if it were the type of detective story that the 'I' of the tale wishes that he could write, with a corpse and a suspect and the investigations of amateur detectives. But this is only the outer and misdirected envelope, a layer that has to be peeled off, in a tale that reaches through false appearances and rationalizations to the real source of Wollin's obsession. The corpse was not murdered and the suspect was guiltless, and the pursuers know quite soon that they are 'not a success as man-hunters'. They are healers by profession and intention, detectors of disease not of crime. Their problem is pathological, not criminological, and their aim is not conviction but reintegration; but the start, with its swarming reporters and its shrewd, rough-handed policeman, emphasizes the inexplicable nature of Wollin's suffering and the danger in which he stands.

A false colouring is diffused throughout two tales. In 'The Gardener', of which I speak later, it is intentionally a transparent wash, an effect of irony; the language of Helen's lie is used throughout that we may assess the cost of it. In 'As Easy as ABC' the surface colouring is so thick and bright that it is only here and there that a menacing under-tint shows through. This tale is usually taken for a Wellsian excursion into a well-organized and sanitary future, and there is a great deal to support this impression. There is the strong, at times really savage, anti-democratic note, and there are the crimes of Crowd-making and Invasion of Privacy; there is also the effective, unostentatious government of the world by an international élite, the Aerial Board of Control. Moreover the tale takes on the framework of 'With the Night Mail', published seven years before, and that contains no disquieting notes. It is an orgy of entertaining detail, composing one of Kipling's minutely-imagined worlds, and the impulse to the writing of it, apart from his interest in the future of air-travel, must have lain in the delight of the fancy at play. If a further theme does run through it, it is the sameness of human nature in changed conditions. But in 'As Easy as ABC' human nature is no longer unchanged. The tale is told by the Board's Official Reporter, a 'conditioned' journalist of the period, who accepts his world and looks back with pity and amazement at the past; yet the very first sentence—always important in Kipling—should give us pause. It is slightly disgruntled. He knows that his report of the crisis in Chicago will not wake much interest in the 'tolerant, humorous, lazy little Planet', where 'easy communications nowadays, and lack of privacy in the past, have killed all curiosity among mankind'. In what follows, the dubitative note is frequently masked by the malicious brilliance and playfulness of the detail, but it recurs. The acquired longevity of the human species has brought it about that very few men have seen death—old Dragomiroff, a member of the Board of Control, collapses when he thinks he is going to do so—and to be a Mother is to be one of a small and important group. It is a world where men take no risks, and do not willingly assume public responsibility; the memory of the disorders of the preceding Democratic Age—the age of Crowds and the Plague—has led them to place their individual peace and privacy before all things, and their scientific control of their environment has enabled them to do so. Such a world may be easy to live in, but it is not good. To those who are so rich and happy and live so long, old Dragomiroff speculates, God may send nerves; and it is clear from the behaviour of the Mothers at Chicago, and of Dragomiroff himself, that He has already done so. The basic energy of life is failing in a world where men do not struggle and suffer to their full scope. Is not more 'pressure' needed to call out the characteristic virtues of created humanity? The question is rather breathed through the tale than directly posed, but it is felt even at the end, where the Official Reporter rounds off his account with an astonished and scornful display of the little band of anachronistic democrats from Chicago, who are to be herded, not into the wilderness, but on to the London stage, to get under 'the public's damned iridium-plated hide' with their nostalgic reproduction of emotions that are now disused, and to help, as their impresario claims, to keep the world soft and united. Everything in the tale is double-edged, and there is no conclusion; but it is not Kipling's blueprint for the future.

It is from the stringent demands of a short-story writer's technique, imposed upon material of growing complexity, that the difficulties—they are not mystifications—of some of his later tales arise. He had always asked questions and posed problems; now the questions reverberate more audibly and the problems are seen against a wider field of reference. Moreover, the craftsman in him, as in his great contemporary, Henry James, came to care deeply—though not 'only'—to do things in the most difficult way, which is, as has been explained to us, the way which conveys most of the subject. This, however, is not the Kipling who 'stormed Valhalla' in his twenties, with a blunt, aggressive outspokenness, a fanfare, we are told, on the trumpet, a fume of sweat and dust and blood and heat, a glitter of bayonets and Mess trophies and Eastern moonlight, and a determination to make himself heard—an 'angry young man', indeed, testifying to the work done by soldier and civilian in the India he had left, to the conditions it was done in, its value and its cost, and meeting, at times, with incredulity and, at times, with a fastidious shrinking from such violence. Distorted as it is, there is truth in this picture. Kipling did write, with an emphasis that became at times defiant, of all these things, and his colour and grouping, his contrasts, moral, racial and pictorial, his human types and their relations might, without much injustice, be called simple. They may even, on occasion, be called blatant. Looking back in 'My First Book' to his beginnings, he makes the point that much which appeared so new in England was common stock in India, a traditional approach to traditional material. He is thinking particularly of the *Departmental Ditties* and is amused at the reputation they got him for cynicism and worldly wisdom. Like Burns, he followed in the traces of his predecessors. It was the change of atmosphere, when the songs and stories came to London, that made the novelty, that, and the pen of a young, imperfect but decisive genius. We may also credit the bold and heavy strokes of his prose to his Anglo-Indian audience. They were tough and, he says, not easily startled or impressed; and it is not difficult to ascribe the showy and strident technique of some of the early tales to his determination to impress them.

It seems as if the toughness of the Anglo-Indian audience was also one of the cards that Kipling was dealt. The models of his youth were various—it is hard to say what he might not have read at Westward Ho! and in his holidays—but, if we except Bret Harte, it is not easy to put one's finger on anything that led strongly towards the 'simplicity' of *Plain Tales from the Hills*. He explored books old and new, English and foreign. His natural taste for the intricate—word-play, conceit, allegory, metrical echo and counter-echo, all the resources of invention and rhetoric to which he turned with as eager a zest as the Elizabethans—was well nourished. His masters can be traced here and there in his verses and the epigraphs to his tales. But the walls of Jericho did not fall to polyphony on lutes and virginals. The young man took his trumpet, and entered into another part of his heritage.

From this time, the time of his adult literary beginnings, the simple and the complex are found throughout his work in various manifestations and relations. Already in *Plain Tales from the Hills* there is a good deal of variety of handling and attitude, and the remaining Indian collections extend the scale. The quiet uncommented pathos of 'Little Tobrah' is different from the jerky, resentful pathos of 'In the Pride of his Youth' and 'Naboth' is not at all a straightforward comic anecdote like 'The Judgment of Dungara'. It covers four pages, begins with a cymbal-stroke ('an allegory of Empire') and passes at once to a dry, slight, comic little tune on a penny whistle. The narrator, tolerant, amused, a little vain, extends his protection to the wretched 'Naboth' and permits him to establish a pitch at the bottom of his garden for selling sweets. There follows the unfolding—

almost the biological development—of Naboth from beggar to shopkeeper, family man, money-lender, illicit-still liquor-trader, as his lean stomach rounds, week by week, and his pitch extents to a settlement. The narrator, immobilized by having received an offering of sweets from his 'feudatory', feels the irritation of a benefactor who has meant to help a poor man to an inch and finds an ell taken. At last the swelling Naboth goes too far; a horse stumbles on his trellis-work and has to be shot, and the Protector resumes the 'vineyard' and closes the episode. This ambiguous little anecdote can be taken from any end. The 'allegory' is ironical, since the parties are reversed; it is the Englishman's estate that is undermined. Behind Naboth's humility and insolence one senses a desperate scurry for life. The narrator, identifying himself with Ahab—a shamefully misrepresented man—ends on a truculent note; he has just broken out of a very false position.

If we turn through the books belonging to Kipling's middle and later periods, we find 'Judson and the Empire' next to 'The Children of the Zodiac', 'Below the Mill Dam' next to 'Mrs Bathurst', 'The Honours of War' next to 'The Dog Hervey', 'The United Idolaters' followed by 'The Wish House', and 'The Debt' and 'The Tender Achilles' in the same collection. There is change in both terms of the contrast. 'The Honours of War' has not the untroubled certainty of 'Judson and the Empire', and 'The Tender Achilles' has a more living and tormented complexity than the masque-like arrangement of 'The Children of the Zodiac'; but it will be seen that in each of the pairs he is basing his story in one case on an accepted set of ideals and the code of behaviour drawn from them, and in the other on a painful mystery and an unanswered question. The difference corresponds to the two aspects under which life shows itself to many men—especially, it may be, those who have adjusted themselves to the traditions and imperatives of a profession, by which a large and effective part of life is usefully controlled, but none of the ultimate questions answered. It is also a little like the two sides of Major George Cottar's consciousness in 'The Brushwood Boy'. It is rare to find an author's work divided in this way.

Other forms of the simple and the complex could be juxtaposed. The so-called 'plain statement' of '"Their Lawful Occasions"' is really the *opus alexandrinum* which the author pretends to have sacrificed. The naval episode is enriched, every inch of it, to the limit of what it can bear, with intricacies of action and arabesque, with Pyecroft's vocabulary, the old Devonian voices of the '*Agatha's*' crew, with a description of an attempt to go to sleep in a torpedo-boat at sea in the vein of *The English Opium-Eater*, with Pyecroft's spurs, the Brixham captain's frockcoat, and a number of superb sea-pictures—that, for instance, of 'the outflung white water at the foot of a homeward-bound Chinaman not a hundred yards away, and her shadow-slashed, rope-purfled sails bulging sidewards like insolent cheeks'. This is one narrative style. Within a few months the author is bespeaking our admiration for a diametrically opposite kind. In 'A Tour of Inspection' a drunken Welshman has brought a barge, loaded with clay, which he has adorned with the red flag from a dynamite cargo, down to the little basin by the cement-works, and sits on it, smoking and throwing fusees about, while the workmen take cover on the broiling shingle. One man sums up the situation.

'We found 'im 'ere when we come. We 'eard what he 'ad. We saw 'ow 'e was. An' we bloomin' well hooked it.'

Now I considered that almost perfect art; but the crowd growled at the baldness of it.

The plainness of *Plain Tales from the Hills*, however, is not of this kind. Here, and in his other early writings, Kipling is using large drafts of that complex medium, spoken English, the meaning of which lies often less in the words than in the assumptions, the undefined mental attitude behind them. English speech is full of a short-term irony, expressed in inversions, understatements, simulated attitudes and nonsense. The flattest *cliché* may prove on analysis to be an elaborate little linguistic manoeuvre; but to the speaker and the hearer it is direct communication and requires no analysis. It is a companionable idiom, more various and flexible than sustained irony, which is a feat, and somewhat alienating. This trait of temperament is very old in English. The monsters in the mere were 'slower in swimming' after Beowulf's men had killed them, and Mercutio said of his death-wound: ''Twill serve'. In some societies, however, it is—or was—consciously encouraged as a desirable convention. The young Kipling lived and wrote in such a society; its idiom was one of the languages he spoke, and one of the styles he explored as a writer. It never sufficed him for long. If the social justification of the understatement is to keep the lid on emotions which might prove disabling if they were allowed to develop into full expression, Kipling at that time was a kettle so furiously on the boil that the lid frequently bounced as jets of direct emotion escaped. He also provided himself with a number of other languages, notably the high-pitched dignity of the Punjabi dramatic monologues. There is, in fact, nothing in the least automatic or unconscious in his handling of this particular social idiom. He exploited its constant double pull, its emphatic repressions, its curtailed but not really obstructed pathos, its defensive amusement. Certainly he overdid it at times, particularly in what he regarded as ephemeral contributions to the *Pioneer*, now to be found in *From Sea to Sea* and *Abaft the Funnel*. The reader may well tire of such tricks as the nonsensical causal connection ('There was no view. That is why the Professor had taken his camera') which is a linguistic shrug of the shoulders, acknowledging the cussedness of things that disappoints our most innocent pleasures. 'Certain' and 'several' become tedious ('I am holding back the details; I am too much moved—you would be too much upset—the material is libellous—we both understand—you would never understand—what can language do in this case?') and the same may be said of 'naturally' when the tone is jaunty and irritable. But 'naturally' can convey melancholy and passionate scorn, and it had already reached literature in this sense in a verse of James Thomson's *City of Dreadful Night*, a poem, Kipling tells us, 'which shook me to my unformed core'. Besides borrowing the title for descriptions of Lahore in hot weather and of Calcutta, he quotes this verse in *Under the Deodars*. Thomson wrote of man:

> *And since he cannot spend nor use aright*
>   *The little time here given him in trust,*
> *But wasteth it in weary undelight*
>   *Of foolish toil and trouble, strife and lust,*
> *He naturally clamours to inherit*
>   *The Everlasting Future that his merit*
>   *May have full scope—as surely is most just.*

This 'naturally' and this 'just', weighted with the futility of man and the nullity of the gods, infected the young writer.

Kipling disused this particular style fairly early in his career, though traces of it can be found almost to the end. He never lost his interest in the colloquial speech of groups, and in 'Letters to the Family' mentions the difference between the 'half-tones and asides' in Canada and South Africa. As an artistic medium, however, he soon reached its limitations. It is, in fact, a medium of character, and continually suggests the presence, nature and experience of the narrator. This character, however, though it was a genuine part of Kipling, was never more than a part; there is little of it in *The Light that Failed*.

He delights in word-play. He translates the puns of his Indian speakers ('A man may turn the word twice, even in his trouble', says the Pathan of 'Dray Wara Yow Dee') and invents his own. Of Canadian clubs he remarks that 'tying their victims to a steak [they] bid him discourse on anything that he thinks he knows', and in the 'The Tie' he glosses *dura ilia messorum* 'the indurated intestines of the mess-caterer.' He uses the serious pun in a strictly literary and traditional way (' "Be quick", said Athira; and Suket Singh was quick; but Athira was quick no longer'.) His titles are sometimes puns, such as ' "Bread upon the Waters" ', 'The House Surgeon' and 'Beauty Spots'. *Plain Tales from the Hills* appears in its French translation as *Contes Simples des Montagnes*. 'Plain', however, means outspoken, as well as simple, and since the tales are set in the plains as well as the hills we may take it that 'from the hills' means sent from an observer in the hills—Kipling on holiday in Simla, surveying his India. I have heard the title 'Without Benefit of Clergy' described as one of Kipling's mistakes. This is true, if it is intended to mean outside the wedding-ring. But I think this is the secondary, punning meaning. The man who is executed without benefit of clergy dies because he cannot prove his 'clergy' by reading his neck-verse, and Ameera, who is entirely ignorant and entirely loving, is executed by the gods in her ignorance.

These are, I admit, superficial complexities, but they testify to a bent of mind, bound to assert itself at times against the compulsory 'black and white' of Anglo-Indian life where, he complains (if it is a complaint, for his zest in the heavy stroke was equally authentic), there is a 'want of atmosphere in the painter's sense . . . no half-tints worth noticing' and 'men stand out all crude and raw, with nothing to tone them down, and nothing to scale them against'. It asserts itself, too, in structure. The form of narrative that the conditions of his life and the limitations of the *Civil and Military Gazette* first indicated to him was the anecdote or yarn, told in a speaking voice to an implied homogeneous group, and intended to surprise or to illustrate. To this he added the dramatic monologue ('Dray Wara Yow Dee', 'At Howli Thana', 'In Flood Time') clearly derived from Browning's 'Men and Women', which 'King' literally threw at Beetle's head. As the space at his disposal was enlarged, the frame of the yarn was extended. It could be used to assist comprehension, when the yarn travelled beyond its birthplace, to indicate the area of experience out of which it grew, for contrast and for reinforcement. Some of the early tales, especially the military ones, are loosely concatenated, and the relevance of the frame is general rather than particular. Kipling had so much material in hand that the result is agglutinative rather than constructed. The pieces, however, are homogeneous and cohere. Heat and cholera and tedium and bouts of homesickness are the recurrent conditions of the lives of his soldiers. A tale may be told after a dog-fight, or during manoeuvres—which he wishes to describe—or to ease the strain of the intolerable weather to men on guard at night; it may be a distraction or an exemplum. Mostly, however, there is a special relevance. This is easily seen in '"Love o' Women"', where the brilliantly-written frame recounts the trial of 'a quiet and well-conducted sergeant' who has shot and killed the corporal who has seduced his wife. Mulvaney, who has been prisoner's guard, says that the dead man has been lucky; had he lived, his body and mind would have turned on him; and he brings out of his memory the fate of another gentleman-ranker, whom the men called 'Love-o'-Women'. In 'On Greenhow Hill' the object is to 'detonate' the reserved Yorkshireman Learoyd until he tells his friends of his murderous jealousy and the death of his girl at home. This is done by assembling various agencies, the sub-Himalayan hills that remind him of the Yorkshire moors, the shock of his own narrow escape from a bullet, Ortheris's absorption in his kill and the speculation that there might be a lass 'tewed up' with the deserter. The entry into the tale is oblique but not irrelevant; the duties and dangers of a soldier are set against the Yorkshire elder's condemnation of the enlisted man and the picture of the dying girl stroking the gay ribbons in his cap. In 'In the Presence' two, at first sight extremely different, anecdotes are linked together. The priest of a Sikh regiment tells how two of his men accomplished, at the cost of their lives, a ritual revenge; and the young corporal, returned from England, tells how the four Gurkha aides-de-camp kept their exhausting watch, with unremitted rigour of observance, at the lying-in-state of Edward VII. The unifying conception is honour, and the accepted rituals through which it is preserved. The tale begins and ends with the Regimental Chaplain's approval. 'Correct! Correct! Correct!' he says. 'In an evil age it is good to hear such things, and there is certainly no doubt that this is a very evil age.'

Mulvaney is an omniscient narrator, adequate to and appreciative of every situation and, except in Mulvaney's presence, the 'I' of the early tales does not come far behind him. Later, Kipling explored the device of the imperfect narrator. This is a difficult manoeuvre, but rewarding when it is successful, since it stimulates the reader and makes possible effects of irony and pathos. We see through a clouded medium. The narrator does not know all the facts, or he does not fully understand them, or he cannot fully express what he knows. Or again, we see above and beyond him, and then his limitations become a part of the subject as well as of the method. This is the case with Humberstall, who tells the tale of the happy little push in 'The Janeites', 'a cart-horse of a man', who has never been quite the same since 'the dump went up at Eatables'. A delicate effect of pathos is achieved in 'Marklake Witches', where the high-spirited girl who tells the story of Laennec's invention of the stethoscope is quite unaware of its purpose—she regards it with tolerant amusement as one of the ridiculous hobbies of the young French prisoner—and of her own consumptive condition, and equally blind to the fact that he and the local doctor love her, fight for her, and know that she is not for any living man. Una, who drinks in the story, suspects as little. The device is available for comic effects also. Pyecroft, who succeeded Mulvaney when Kipling turned to the Navy for material, is knowledgeable but not omniscient, and the 'I' who elicits his stories is no longer the young journalist, impressed by the craftiness and the tragic wisdom of the old soldier, but a man in middle life who sees all round his remarkable informant. Pyecroft's strictly professional lower-deck point of view in 'The Bonds of Discipline', his absorption in his one chance in life to kick a lieutenant, make a comical discrepancy with the magniloquent and sombre extracts from the account of 'M. de C.' of the events in H.M.S. 'Archimandrite'. The Pyecroft who walks round Cape Town with Vickery has extended his range.

Kipling's first full-sized experiment with the imperfect narrator was in 'The Disturber of Traffic', the tale of Dowse who went mad while tending single-handed a screw-pile light in Flores Straits. He was obsessed by the streaky tides, and his madness took the form of trying to keep all ships out of the Straits by an arrangement of wreck-buoys and warning lights, because their streaky wakes distressed him still further. It is a funny tale and, if we like, a tragic one. The partially restored Dowse, now a waterman at Portsmouth, believes he has the guilt of blood on his head. It is told in an English lighthouse on a foggy night by Fenwick, the keeper, an old friend of Dowse, from whom he has as much of the tale as the one can impart and the other receive. He tells it with astonishment, and some pity, and a high professional relish of Dowse's unorthodox proceedings with buoys and lights and of their effect on the shipping. The calling of the ships round the home light keeps in mind the importance of the service that Dowse's obsession dislocated; the cold fog is a curtain that lifts to show the hot shore where 'tigers come out of the forests to hunt for crabs and such like round about the lighthouse at low tide', and Dowse lies on the planking with his eye to a crack, watching the streaks and tongue-tied until slack water releases him. Fenwick can 'never rightly come at what it was' that ailed Dowse, but he tells his story, with its mixture of torment and farce, very methodically. Such a story could, however, have been told quite differently, and Kipling indicates this in the verses that he prefixes to the tale. They are printed over the name of Miriam Cohen, which I do not understand, but they are Kipling's, and an enlarged version appears in the Definitive Edition of the *Verse*. They are a prayer for a veil between the human soul and the Lord, a plea to be spared the sight of God's toil in the universe, and the madness that follows the vision. 'Tides', like 'pressures' later, easily took on extended meanings for Kipling. In the verses he speaks of 'the wheel and drift of Things', and the wheel recalls those 'turning wheels of vicissitude' which Bacon shrank from beholding, moving in a vaster cosmos than Bacon knew. There is nothing of this in the tale as it stands, and there could not be; but it is a latent potentiality of the subject. Let a beam fall from another angle and the undertint will show up. Kipling lets the beam fall for the length of three verses.

Before he developed his special form of a story held under the beams, as it were, of two lamps, he had fitted his tales with introductory fragments, proverb or verse, borrowed or invented. Most of these are flying chips from a busy workshop or jetsam of a full memory. The writer's pen jiggles into a snatch from a soldier's song, and the young poet indemnifies himself for the colloquial dryness of his prose by a brief outbreak of rhymed eloquence. The application of 'Pippa's Song' to 'The Record of Badalia Herodsfoot', is a heavy-handed irony; Emerson's 'If the Red Slayer thinks he slays' lifts the deluded doctor and navvy of 'My Sunday at Home' into unexpectedly lofty company. Some fragments set the key for the story that follows, others (that before 'A Friend's Friend', for instance) proclaim the theme in a strongly contrasting one. The triplet from James Thomson before 'A Conference of the Powers' introduces another dimension to the account of how the famous elderly novelist, Eustace Cleever, met three very young but experienced subalterns, and how one of them told him an anecdote of the Burmese War. They regard him with awe and gratitude, and he feels the passing envy of the writer for the young men who deal daily with power, responsibility and the peril of death. To this slight scene Kipling prefixes the lines:

> *Life liveth but in life, and doth not roam*
> *To other lands if all be well at home:*
> *'Solid as ocean foam', quoth ocean foam.*

The young men, established in their world and not in the least introspective, are those with whom all is well at home, whose solid and daylight concerns leave them no need to explore the countries of the mind. The third line, suddenly shifting focus, sees them and their achievements as no more than the foam on the vast ocean of time. All men's achievements are as evanescent as foam, but men, as they work, do not remember this. The poet, however, unappeased by action, is visited by the vision. It is the line of 'Bridge Builders' and 'Cities and Thrones and Powers'.

It was in the books for children, *The Jungle Books* and *Just So Stories*, that the tales were first systematically provided with their songs, and *The Jungle Books* have their full measure of chapter-headings as well, as if the intensely activated imagination could not cease sending up this rainbow-spray above its channel. *Traffics and Discoveries* is the first adult collection in which each tale is prefaced by a poem. In *Actions and Reactions* he tries the effect of letting the verses follow, and it is after we have finished 'The House Surgeon', in which the innocent dwellers in the house are afflicted by the idea of damnation which haunts it, that we reach 'The Rabbi's Song':

> *Let nothing linger after—*
> *No whispering ghost remain,*
> *In wall, or beam, or rafter,*
> *Of any hate or pain.*
> *Cleanse and call home thy spirit,*
> *Deny her leave to cast,*
> *On aught thy heirs inherit,*
> *The shadow of her past.*

In *Puck of Pook's Hill* some of the tales are supported on both sides by verses, and in *Rewards and Fairies* all of them are. In the last three collections the practice varies, but only two tales are without their poems. It is obvious, then, that we have to do with a considered literary form.

The relation of the verses to the tales varies very much, and an attempt to force too close an application will sometimes distort either verses or tale or both. Sometimes fancy ran along a by-way at a wide angle from the story; the fighting bulls of the Camargue in 'The Bull that Thought' reminded the author of his peaceful 'Sussex cattle feeding in the dew', and the bee-keeper who wrote 'The Vortex' amused himself by describing with heroic eloquence the loss of his own seven hives in a flood. These are light-weight, graceful rhymes; Kipling, as has been pleasantly said of Peacock, heard tunes in his head and gave way to them. But mostly the verses are significant. They are not indispensable to the tales, which in most cases were first published without them and can stand alone. We should not, therefore, I think, speak of them as keys. I have sometimes wondered whether Kipling added the explicit 'The Burden' after he found that 'The Gardener' could be misunderstood; but the directness of the statement could easily come about in another way. Here something is expressed which underlies and breathes through the whole tale, but of which the consistently external method of narration forbids the open statement; here alone Helen speaks of the weight and grief of her lie. There is something similar in the relation of 'At his Execution' to 'The Manner of Men'. We have seen Paul through the eyes of the captain and mate of the wheat-ship, his promptness, his unshaken courage, his ubiquity, his 'woman's trick', which displeases the Sidonian captain, 'of taking the tone and colour of whoever he talked to'; neither of them understands him at all. The poem does not attempt to suggest the motive-power of Paul, but it indicates the cost to him of his service. The man who has been 'made all things to all men' prays only at his death that Christ shall 'restore me my self again'. 'The Penalty' is what the unlikeable and distressed Wilkett of 'The Tender Achilles' might have said if he could have judged himself. The Star he loses through self-love is the woman who risked her reputation to mix up the slides, as Howlieglass's plan for his cure required. Wilkett's conscious mind, however, will never acknowledge his mistake or judge himself. The allusions to the woman in the tale are very brief though perfectly clear. It is as if 'The Penalty' grew from some 'honestly written' but later deleted part of Wilkett's story, for it falls perfectly into place in it.

Sometimes the verses link stories together and show them to be strung on one thread of thought, as is the case with those which accompany 'The Eye of Allah' and 'Unprofessional'. Sometimes a subsidiary part of the subject is brought out for inspection. After the two sufferers of 'The Dog Hervey' have been restored to happiness, 'The Comforters' tells us with bitter wit how not to console, and an elegant Horatian ode before 'The Janeites' wonders that, while wars and kings are forgotten, 'mere flutes that breathe at eve' survive. 'The Press', which follows 'The Village that Voted the Earth was Flat' is of this tangential kind. It is gay and vigorous, and does not echo the tone of that disquieting story, but it picks up and accounts for the reminiscent enjoyment with which Kipling, remembering his days as a journalist, contrives the passages about 'The Bun' and 'The Cake'.

> *As the war-horse smelleth the battle afar,*
> *The entered Soul, no less,*
> *He saith: 'Ha! Ha!' where the trumpets are*
> *And the thunders of the Press.*

'The Honours of War' and 'The Edge of the Evening', both written in the years before the 1914-18 war, have poems that were written after it had broken out. The misgivings that Stalky had felt about the new generation of subalterns, 'brought up on lemon-squash and mobilisation text-books', had been refuted more completely and tragically than by Wontner's 'common or bear-garden rag', and the poem begins with sudden anguish:

> *These were our children who died for our lands: they were dear in our sight.*

'The Edge of the Evening' is a sinister tale; the light is fading, and 'life in England is like settin' in the front row at the theatre and never knowin' when the whole blame drama won't spill itself in your lap'. It does spill itself, and the American helps the three English notabilities round a dangerous corner, indicative of a bad stretch ahead, for 'you British are settin' in kimonoes on dynamite kegs'. The prospect is all forwards to darkness and the sea and the flight of the soundless aeroplane. In 'Rebirth'. the poem that accompanies the tale, the prospect is backward to the world of yesterday, 'the far show of unbelievable years'; but the men who moved in that world have been changed and reborn, 'broke to blood and the strict works of war', and though they look back with yearning, they would not, if they could, and could not, if they would, go back on their tracks. 'For we are what we are.' It was this sense of total change 'in soul and substance' that filled the crannies of his later stories with men who had been through the war and with their memories.

There are one or two difficult cases where the link between verse and tale is, to my understanding, almost entirely submerged. We have, however, in view of the different kinds of linking exemplified in his work, no justification for assuming that it is not there. I am still baffled by 'Kaspar's Song from "Varda"', which precedes '"Wireless"', both by its title and its relevance to the tale. It seems to say that the spiritual is apprehended only if we accept the whole process of nature, as we learn to know it, and that to reject that is spiritual death. If this is so, it may be a development of one aspect of Keats's 'Beauty is truth, truth beauty', which Shaynor does not quote, but all readers know, and thus have both a general and an incidental bearing on the tale. But I am not sure, and the attempt to relate it too closely to Shaynor's state seems to throw the tale off its centre. Much clearer are those cases where the poem lifts the subject of the tale on to another level by means of parallel or metaphor or symbol. This is well shown by the first example of the linking of a complete poem to a tale, the lines that precede 'To be Filed for Reference', the last of *Plain Tales from the Hills*, and ask the question that the 'I' who tells of the degradation of McIntosh Jellaludin does not ask. The hoof of the Wild Goat strikes the Stone from the Cliff into the Tarn, where it sinks from sight. The fall was ordained from the first by God who created Goat and Stone and Tarn.

> *Judge Thou*
> *The sin of the Stone.*

'The Captive' has been strangely enough called anti-American. There are, I suppose, some pinpricks, there may be some mistakes, and there is much amusement, but the upshot is an admiration so strong that Kipling is not content until he has brought Laughton O. Zigler more than halfway to understanding his British 'enemies'. He is the necessary ally, and he plays the same part twelve years later in 'The Edge of the Evening'. This may not be acceptable to all his countrymen, but it is certainly not in English eyes anti-American. In the poem, the amusement—all but the faintest trace—drops away, and what is admirable stands out in the simplicity of a heroic parallel.

> *Not with an outcry to Allah nor any complaining*
> *He answered his name at the muster and stood to the chaining.*
> *When the twin anklets were nipped on the leg-bars that held them*
> *He brotherly greeted the armourers stooping to weld them . . .*
> *Nowise abashed but contented to drink of the potion awarded.*

Fortitude, brotherliness, undefeated hope, essential dignity, it does not seem a niggardly list of virtues; and the poet concludes:

> *But on him be the Peace and the Blessing: for he was great-hearted.*

The 'extract' from 'Lyden's "Irenius"' that accompanies 'Mrs Bathurst' and that from 'Gow's Watch' with 'A Madonna of the Trenches' are of this type, and so is 'The Centaurs', in which the masters and boys of 'The United Idolaters' are transmuted into Chiron and the colts he trains. The intensity and dignity of 'The Wish House' and 'Dayspring Mishandled' are such that they cannot be enhanced. What the poems here offer us is the stripped statement of the theme. The packed detail falls away. The grave voice declares:

> *That which is marred at birth Time shall not mend,*
> *Nor water out of bitter well make clean;*
> *All evil thing returneth at the end,*
> *Or elseway walketh in our blood unseen.*

Even the archaisms of Manallace's forgery (the note 'Modernized from the "Chaucer" of Manallace' exempts us from checking mistakes) help to generalize the statement, as does the symbolic action of the God and the Woman in ' "Late Came the God" '.

Kipling's use of symbols in his poems is not often subtle; in his prose it is more so. Moreover, the symbols are so closely integrated into the story, especially in his later work, they are so indispensably part of the action or its setting, so natural in their place and so little emphasized, that they do not call attention to themselves. In the earlier work didactic vigour and the love of pattern sometimes lead to a heavy emphasis, and in the fables both qualities combine in the deliberate process of 'working it out', and symbol gives way to allegory. There is nothing particularly complex here, though there is a multiplicity of detail. In 'The Man who Would be King' the symbols are well chosen and well used. The child's paper whirligig in Dravot's hand as he follows his troop of furious fancies over the border of the civilized world, the narrow and perilous rope-bridges of the Hindu-Kush, Dravot and Carnehan sitting on ammunition-boxes in the wilderness, gambling with cartridges, these are all illustrative of the nature of their undertaking. At Dravot's death the first two are conjoined, and when the bridge is cut he falls 'turning and twisting in the air like a penny whirligig'. These are good symbols, because their content is not exhausted at one glance, nor do they themselves exhaust the content of the story. The child's toy is not trifling; it can be the focus of the tremendous force of the child's imagination; and there is more to Carnehan and Dravot than irresponsible gamblers. These symbols are not aggressive, but some of the latest ones are introduced almost stealthily. How quietly we learn in 'The Gardener' that Helen's nephew's grave in Hagenzeele Third Military Cemetery is not yet planted out. The array of dark, raw graves, the few already planted, are the inevitable scene of Helen's pilgrimage. What the naked black cross on Helen's grave tells us is that her stony grief has borne no fruit and has no hope, and we remember that her effort to respond to the other woman's need was a failure. The discovery of Sergeant John Godsoe's body 'frozen stiff between two braziers' in 'A Madonna of the Trenches' may be a symbol of the fleshly abstinence of his and Bella Armine's love, but the primary function of the braziers, nevertheless, is to be taken literally as providing, with the old dressing-station and the wedged door, a less exceptionable way for a 'first-class Non. Com.' to 'go on leave' than the rifle which, for a second, he was tempted to use. In any event, this symbol (if it is one) is limited in its bearing. The total meaning of the tale is not frustration. We must weigh the other indications: Godsoe's quotations from Swinburne's 'Les Noyades' and the Burial Service; his expression when he gets Bella Armine's message that her death is near—'different all of a sudden—as if 'e'd got shaved'; the last excited outburst of the narrator, his young nephew, before the sedative takes hold of him, about the love that '*begins* at death'; and the confirmation of all these in the passage from 'Gow's Watch' that follows, where, after all the 'barren, unyoked years' Gow sees the spirit of Lady Frances and cries: 'What can the Grave against us, O my Heart?' In '"They"', when the narrator first runs his car up to the edge of the 'great still lawn', set with clipped yews, of the house where he sees the spirit of his dead child, he stops with the green spear of one of the horsemen laid to his breast, and this foreshows the meaning of the whole story; that way is not for him. The lightning that chars Vickery and Mrs Bathurst is a startling symbol, but Mrs Bathurst's 'blindish look', the look which marks her as the victim and the innocent agent of fate, is natural enough as she comes forward on the screen of the early cinema that Vickery and Pyecroft go to see; but then we remember that Pritchard had noticed it years before in New Zealand, and see its significance.

These symbols are all particular to the tales they occur in, and others could be found, Castorley's disease in 'Dayspring Mishandled', for instance, which disarms Manallace but also represents the concealed sense of guilt that has been eating for years at Castorley's mind. There are others, notably darkness, pressures and tides, that came to symbolize for Kipling the conditions of human life.

It seems therefore that the view which is sometimes taken that Kipling's work was simple in his youth and complex in his age needs qualification. He was never a very simple writer, though he could use a blunt instrument when he thought it most fit to strike the blow he planned. But certainly there is a difference between the early and the later work in the importance of the complexities, in the tale and to the reader. In the early work, if the reader misses the patterns, the allusions, the subtler touches of absorbed craftsmanship, he will not be much impeded, if at all. The energetic and picturesque action of the tale will not be obscured; the narrative grip will not be loosened. There is, for instance, more in 'The Man who Would be King' than a good fantastic yarn, built on the contemporary interest in Káfiristan and the information that had come to hand from Colonel Lockhart's mission, and crossed by Kipling's strong recent interest in Masonry. There is a combination of wild dignity and even delicacy of feeling in the two adventurers with the marks of commonness and unscrupulousness. There is the gradual emergence of the modest Horatio, Carnehan—who draws his breath in pain to tell Dravot's story—as the better man of the two. There are the shifting planes and illogical sequences of his delirious tale, and the sudden weighting of the phantasmagoria by the physical presence of the killers as they close round their quarry. 'I tell you their furs stunk.' There is also Carnehan's confused identification of his own fate with the death of the man he loved and admired. 'Slap from the bridge fell old Peachey.' But it is perhaps only a student or a devotee who would talk in this way of this tale. All the finer points of conception and craftsmanship could be missed, and the incandescent imagination, the blazing excitement, the manly pathos of it would still be entirely accessible and commanding. In many of the later tales, however, this is not the case. The baffled and divergent remarks of critics about 'Mary Postgate', 'Sea Constables', 'The Gardener', 'Dayspring Mishandled', 'The Tender Achilles', even 'The Wish House' prove that here complexities of substance and especially of method do obstruct the reader's approach to the sense of the story. They cannot be left on one side. One must thread the maze to reach the heart of the matter. In most of them there is an element of hidden narrative. There are always sufficient directions but they do not spring to the eye; they must be looked and listened for. It will seem a far cry and an odd comparison, but in fact Kipling's method of hidden narrative does seem to me comparable, on its much larger scale, to Jane Austen's in her later books. The submerged relations between Frank Churchill and Jane Fairfax, so beautifully analysed by Miss Mary Lascelles in her study *Jane Austen and her Art*, and so clearly imparted to us once we know how to listen; the miniature example of the new technique in Mary Musgrove's self-absorbed gossip in *Persuasion*, in which we can see the consolable Captain Benwick trying to feed his interest in Anne by attentions to her sister, drawing a blank and falling back on the available Louisa—these may not be the actual patterns for the telling of Helen Turrell's and Manallace's stories, but they are earlier examples of the same sort of craftsmanship. Miss Austen, however, is more sparing and more prudent with her new method. One can read *Emma* with pleasure, and be as surprised as Emma is when the truth about Frank Churchill comes to light.

Such intricate, exacting work is not written without cost. Many of Kipling's older readers could not keep pace with him, and the newer generation, put off for other reasons, did not make the effort. Something of what he thought about this failure in perception of his larger public may be playfully indicated in the late tale '"Teem"—a Treasure-Hunter'. 'Teem' is a genial—indeed, a sentimental—tale about a very French little dog, a trained and self-respecting truffle-hunter, and something of a sentimentalist himself, as dogs are. Transported to England and adopted by a countryman, whom he calls a peasant and 'my humble', he finds truffles in the Sussex Weald but, when he noses them to his master's hand, they are unrecognized.

> My Art he could by no means comprehend. For, naturally, I followed my Art as every Artist must, even when he is misunderstood. If not, he comes to preoccupy himself mournfully with his proper fleas.

The treasure found in 'English earth' by his specialized faculties is treated as a plaything, and thrown for him to retrieve. 'What more could I do? The scent over that ground was lost.' But the cost was not confined to Kipling's diminished reputation; there was also something to pay on the score of art. His new hunting-grounds, 'Teem' remarks, had necessitated 'changes and adjustments of my technique'. These later tales have lost much of the free sweeping movement of such earlier achievements as *Kim*, 'The Tomb of his Ancestors', '"The Finest Story in the World"' and 'On Greenhow Hill'. The long stride of the sentence is still at command, but the seven-league boot is put down carefully, and the reader, following from pitch to pitch, has to make sure that he has missed none of the waymarks. He is not borne along, rapt in the movement and the prospect. There is intellectual intensity, but not that incandescence of the imagination that saw the light slipping through the oar-holes of the galley's lower deck, or Dravot walking among the pines, like a big red devil, with the sun on his crown and his beard. These sudden glories, however, are what mark the work of young writers. They delight and astonish because the illumination is so unheralded and so strong. Youthful genius, working below the level of consciousness, sheds such a light. Its effect is immediate and lasting, but not progressive. We see at once, with deep satisfaction, all that there is. Beetle was ravished to find Mad Tom's song.

> *With a heart of furious fancies,*
> *Whereof I am commander,*
> *With a burning spear and a horse of air*
> *To the wilderness I wander;*

and in 'Cold Iron' the figure is embodied in the Boy, as Puck remembers him, before he accepted and wore the iron slave-ring and entered the common life of men, filling the valley with the whirling wildfire of his dreams and his shadowy knights and hounds and horses. 'I never guessed he had such magic at his command; but it's often that way with boys.' This is the prime and blossom of the imagination. There has been no 'burrowing' for these treasures, and there is no mistaking their quality, though it is often associated with less precious matter. Even had Kipling's art not developed in the way it did, he could not have commanded these furious flashes in later life. With what virtuosity he charges and directs the first sentence of 'The Manner of Men':

> Her cinnabar-tinted topsail, nicking the hot blue horizon, showed she was a Spanish wheat-boat hours before she reached Marseilles mole.

Colour, weather, movement, place, even (roughly) period are

given in twenty words, and in the swing of the first phrase there is the light dip of the summer sea. The rest of the tale has the same rich substantiality of the imagination, the same economy of statement. The interest is strong and various. But the wild-fire never blazes; all is passed through the intellect.

The reader who turns straight from 'Without Benefit of Clergy' to 'The Gardener' can see very clearly what has been gained and lost. Both are tales of love and secrecy, a secrecy that is imposed by social conditions; and there the resemblance stops. 'Without Benefit of Clergy' covers some three years, during which the Mohammedan girl, whom John Holden has bought and now loves as his wife, bears him a son in the little house over the city, loses the child and finally dies of cholera. The narrative moves smoothly from scene to scene, making unhurried use of dialogue and joining the incidents with explicit narration and occasional comment. The scene lies before us, as it were, in concentric circles. At the centre is the native house; all the pictorial details, the colours, the little homely sounds belong to this centre; here we listen to the language of love and grief. Outside, continuously indicated but never described, is John Holden's official life, the Club, the Office, the 'unlovely' bungalow, open to any visitor, the unsparing short phrases of order and criticism, edged with irony by the unseen facts of the native house. It is in this circle that we get the sarcasm—'cheap' sarcasm, since it is what any man's mind and tongue will produce under the pressure of circumstances and the infection of sympathy. Here, too, we get an unwished, though not quite irrelevant, appearance of the obsessive Member for Lower Tooting. Enclosing everything is the India of swarming life and terrifying epidemics, generating the menace and finally the certainty of separation. The ties that penetrate all three circles meet in Ameera's room. Most of the scenes in the little house are night-pieces. This is natural, and it emphasizes the dichotomy of Holden's life; it also shows up the radiant beauty of Ameera as Juliet's is shown when she 'hangs upon the cheek of night like a rich jewel'. It is only at the end, when the hostility of nature has broken into the house, that we see its desolation in the daylight. The tragic forces in the tale are impersonal; no malice or even callousness is involved, though John Holden, in his anguish, calls himself a brute. The brief and beleaguered tenure of human happiness is made more apparent by the difference between the lovers, and the secrecy and irony that arise from it. They themselves are only sufficiently developed for the purposes of lyrical emotion, which requires figures and attitudes rather than characters. The tenderness of the hidden household reaches outside, and John Holden, in his first dealings with love and death, has brothers in Ahmed Khan, his butler, and his portly Indian landlord, who closes the tale. Holden's life is not concluded, but this episode is, —concluded, abolished, leaving nothing but the lacquer bed that Pir Khan, the old gate-keeper, warns him will be to him a knife turning in a green wound.

There are imperfections in this tale. Kipling's insatiable appetite for fact and strong excitement makes him divert our gaze too long towards the cholera-stricken multitudes, with a blurring of focus; and some readers may find the 'ordinary' quality of the sarcasm disturbing, as if Romeo, instead of 'Then I defy you, stars', had said 'Just what *would* happen'. But flawlessness is not what we can expect from the strongly creative writer in his copious youth, but that he shall convey his vision memorably. This Kipling does, and the flaws are no obstruction to our perception of beauty, death, and the hard necessities of daily work.

'The Gardener' is fifteen pages long, half the length of 'Without Benefit of Clergy', and it covers twenty years. It is concerned with consequences. We know nothing of Helen Turrell's secret lover, except that her son has inherited his mouth (and that we know because she is so previous—and so ambiguous—in claiming it as a Turrell feature). When we meet her, she has shut away that episode and come back to the home where she has always been 'accepted', to live her life under the old forms with wary but unsuccessful strategy. There is no lyricism in the tale; the relaxation of full expression never occurs. Helen never expresses herself, though she betrays some things. The author makes no overt comment, but confines himself to what could be seen or heard and to what Helen, who was 'open as the day', said to her friends. The narrative, then, is strictly ironic; it speaks through a mask, the candid-seeming mask that Helen had designed and that her friends co-operated with her in respecting. The skill lies in imparting to us what was under Helen's mask. This must be done at the very beginning of the tale, by the quietest means; we are not to be bounced or impressed, but sensitized.

'Everyone in the village knew' are the first words of the tale, and it is to be conveyed to us, but never stated, that what everyone in the village knew was that the 'nephew' Helen brought back from the South of France was her son. But this is no case for sarcasm or the slightest jerk of the thumb. We are embarking upon a prolonged tragedy of silence, and we are among friendly people who have known and 'accepted' Helen and her family for a long time and, though distressed by 'the whole disgraceful affair', believe that she is doing her 'duty' in assuming responsibility for the child. They carefully accept her careful fiction and use her words. What conveys the unacknowledged truth is the slant of the sentences and the slightly disproportionate emphasis with which they approve the adoption of a nephew and refer—such is the fiction—to the misalliance of Helen's dead brother, George. 'Most honourably', 'most nobly' Helen has taken charge (we can hear the ladies of the village, though there are no inverted commas); she is 'justified—her friends agreed with her—. . . [in] giving the child every advantage'. 'Mercifully' (it comes at the beginning of a sentence) George's parents (her parents) are dead. And there is Helen, who has survived the threat of lung trouble which had driven her to the South of France, nursed the baby through infantile dysentery 'due to the carelessness of the nurse, whom she had had to dismiss', and returned at last to her Hampshire home, 'thin, worn but triumphant'. It is by this slight over-emphasis, secured by the placing of quite ordinary words, that each speaker reassures the other of her regret, her approval and her solidarity in the general kind conspiracy. There is nothing like this in the earlier work, though there are plenty of sarcastic inversions, grim and jocular hints, and blazing understatements. Here the tone is that of gentlefolk and people of good will. All is set to make the best of a bad job by respecting the saving surface. The concern, the genuine sympathy have to pour, with a slightly inappropriate strength, through the channels of the fiction. This is a form of irony beside which that practised in *Jonathan Wild* and even in *Barry Lyndon* is simple, because the inversions are diagrammatically plain in the first place and not very complex in the second. If Barry's vanity risks obscuring the real facts of his life, Thackeray can always make his autobiographer record with resentment that 'some people said' something to his discredit. But Kipling has no such easy devices at hand. He must also avoid, and does avoid, kindling our detective excitement. We are to know what was kept back, but always with quiet recognition and sympathy. It is marvellously done, with simple words but with the most delicate and minute adjustment. It is, however, an exacting style. Its transparency is partly delusive, for it reaches only a little way down. We have to read on slowly, picking our way, and listening for what is beneath the broken and inconclusive conversations between Helen and her growing son. We learn to see in two sentences her abortive attempt to lift the barrier between them at last, and his awkward, chivalrous refusal to let his mother's protective lie be suspended. Truth is now out of her power, and all that was most real in her life sealed in silence. After Michael's death, the inaccessible solitude of grief which she has constructed round herself cannot be assuaged by the normal human agencies that lie in wait for John Holden's sorrow. It can yield only to a miraculous moment, and then only in part.

It will be clear from the different ways in which I have had to handle these two tales how widely their conceptions and methods diverge. The earlier tale needs only to be displayed, the later must be interpreted. There is a charm in 'Without Benefit of Clergy', a pathos, an unhurried dwelling on simple events that can have no parallel in the condensed analysis of development in 'The Gardener'. On the other hand, the cumulative impression of what Helen withholds makes an effect beyond the reach of the younger Kipling. We approach the end of the tale under the weight and awe of human suffering. The quiet, limited sentences are like the shallow breaths of a man mortally wounded.

CHAPTER FIVE

Hatred and Revenge

In *Something of Myself* Kipling sums up the emotional results of his sojourn as a child in the House of Desolation in the words: 'In the long run these things, (*sc.* the unjust punishments and humiliations he has described) and many more of the like, drained me of any capacity for real, personal hate for the rest of my days. So close must any life-filling passion lie to its opposite.' It is more helpful to accept than dismiss this piece of self-knowledge. For one thing, it draws attention to the pervasiveness of the 'opposite'—love—in his work, especially family love and the friendship between men. Sustaining and stable love is very seldom at the centre of his tales; it is at the edge or in the frame; it is the condition in which his valuable men are rooted, from which they go forth and to which they return, whether it is found in the country estate that bred and welcomes back the Brushwood Boy or in the childless home by the docks where Janet McPhee makes her husband comfortable. Secondly, the limits of the statement are interesting. What is disclaimed is the capacity for personal hate. This leaves a large field open. The emotion is further qualified as 'real', and for the explanation of this we must probably turn to 'Dayspring Mishandled'; for the imagination can permit itself to indulge in a hate that is illusory, inasmuch as it would never support the proof of action.

Much earlier, at the end of 'Baa Baa, Black Sheep', the tale based on his childish passions and sufferings, he had written: 'When young lips have drunk deep of the bitter water of Hate, Suspicion and Despair, all the Love in the world will not wholly take away that knowledge.' Of these three lessons, thus early learnt, suspicion is not important to him as an artist; rather we find again the 'opposite'—proved reliance. Despair is part of his world, but seldom at the centre of a tale. It is more often in the wings or caught by a slant of memory. Findlayson, watching in fierce anxiety the flood assail the stability of his unfinished bridge, remembers how 'Lockhart's big water-works burst and broke down in brick heaps and sludge, and Lockhart's spirit broke in him and he died'. The black hours that the soul endures, abjectly or with some relics of fortitude, are conveyed by action or image, sometimes curtly, sometimes with a nightmarish suggestion of abysses, but never, except in '"Love-o'-Women"' and in the very early 'Phantom 'Rickshaw', in detail. If it is necessary to look at the sufferer, the gauge of his agony is some slight physical sign that breaks the surface. If he is to be forced, or to thrust himself, out of life, we are told the conditions that bring this about, but we are not asked to watch the process. 'Thrown Away', a sad little cautionary tale about a young officer bred under the 'sheltered life system', who takes things too seriously, and kills himself after an ordinary 'Colonel's wigging', is told entirely from outside. His follies are indicated and belittled; we hear that he has put in for two days' leave and says that he is 'going to shoot big game'; and the rest of the tale, in which the young author fully indemnifies himself for the initial restrictions, describes the discovery of his body and the actions and emotions of the discoverers. Here and elsewhere there is a mixture of reticence and violence in the handling of the subject.

The third injury that the Black Sheep suffers is the early knowledge of hate. Most children experience it in brief blazes; it is connected with their conscious impotence in an adult world, and is part of their necessary growing pains. But Punch has to live with his hate for years, and he takes pleasure in revengeful imaginings because it is one of the few pleasures left to him. Thus the natural vindictiveness of the human being plays a large part in Kipling's work. He was sensitized by early experience to the emotions it involves, and deeply interested in it as an expression of human force and conviction. It is one of the points in which he is in spontaneous sympathy with the Elizabethan dramatists, and when, like them, he looked in his work for subjects under the influence of strong excitement, revenge was one of the themes ready to his hand. He does not take it at its simplest level, as a necessity of self-preservation, except in '"Tiger-Tiger!"', but he considers it in its relation to self-respect and in its intricate connexion with that sense of 'wild justice' which seeks to even the scales and to deal blow for blow and humiliation for humiliation.

His early tales include many anecdotes of revenge. There are malicious and farcical counterstrokes in 'The Judgement of Dungara' and 'The Sending of Dana Da' and there is the effective retaliation of the harassed subaltern in 'His Wedded Wife'. There is no strong excitement here; the skill and oddity of the return-match make the story. But in *In Black and White* and *Life's Handicap* he shows us two primitive minds, wholly possessed by the thirst for vengeance. 'Dray Wara Yow Dee' is one of his dramatic monologues, pitched in a key of dignity and feverish anguish. The elderly Pathan horse-dealer, resting in the Englishman's compound, tells him how he has killed his young, false wife, and is pursuing her lover through deserts, cities and flooded rivers, in weariness, starvation and delusions, unable to sleep until his honour shall be cleansed, but borne on by the assurance that he shall taste the fulfilment of his desire. 'What love so deep as hate?' 'The Limitations of Pambé Serang' are such that his story is told from outside, drily, with a glitter of rapid detail. The Malay serang—and a Malay 'does not forget anything'—has been casually insulted and wounded, three years before, by a drunk Zanzibar stoker. His attempts to pay his score while they are both on the ship miscarry. He follows his foe to England, misses him, and waits at the docks, month by month, ill and miserably poor, until the guileless African is delivered into his hands. What we have in each of these anecdotes is a mind completely flooded by a thirst for revenge so imperative that all other considerations are abolished. The obstructions to assuagement are all external; no question is raised within the man. His code permits or enjoins revenge, and all his faculties are set to achieve it. Behind each man is a public opinion, and when the Pathan mutilates his wife's body 'that the men of Little Malikand might know the crime', he indicates an accepted form of procedure. Kipling came back to the social organization of revenge in the first story in 'In the Presence', many years later. The subject here is not primarily the passion itself but the forms provided for it to flow into and the strict ritual observance of them by the Sikh brothers, who see no way to end their oppression by their kinsfolk but by massacre and suicide. The act is controlled in all its stages by inherited modes of thought and behaviour. 'There was neither heat, nor haste, nor abuse in the matter from end to end', says the Sikh Regimental Chaplain. Rutton Singh waited to drill the recruits before asking for leave; the revolver that Attar Singh borrowed was returned with the money for the ammunition expended; the elder brother waited three days on the house-top for a warrior's death, before abandoning the body. They were 'well-conducted men of nine years' service apiece' and they 'did all things correctly as Sikhs should'. The villagers recognized their virtue and sent food to the house-top where they waited. 'I am well pleased with Rutton Singh and Attar Singh,' says their chaplain. 'They have gathered the fruit of their lives.' From this the tale passes to the four elderly Gurkha orderlies keeping guard at the coffin of Edward VII, who will not even ease the tight stocks beneath their bent chins, since on the exact performance of their duty depends, they believe, the honour of the armies in Hind. 'We are in the Presence. Moreover *He* knew every button and braid and hook of every uniform in all his armies.' Kipling believed profoundly in the steadying and ennobling effect of ritual on men. 'All Ritual is fortifying', says Brother Burges in '"In the Interests of the Brethren"'. 'Ritual's a natural necessity for mankind. The more things are upset, the more they fly to it.' The selfless beauty of the offering made by the four Gurkhas in an impersonal cause is underlined by the case of the personal passion of the Sikh brothers, controlled in its final desperation into form and order, and approved by society.

For the Englishman, however, there are no such sanctifying forms in extreme need, though in matters short of death a homogeneous group may spontaneously avenge an injury in the ruffian forms of their common boyhood. This is what happens in 'A Friend's Friend' and again, on a more fantastic scale, in the war-tale, 'The Tie'. As I have said in the chapter on Laughter, these tales cannot be classified simply as farces, though it is part of their psychological curiosity that they use farcical elements. In 'A Friend's Friend' there is some gusto in the release of resentment; in 'The Tie' this is checked by passing the tale through the mind of a reflective man, a second lieutenant of over thirty, 'anciently a schoolmaster of an ancient foundation'. 'The Tie' has been called a silly and incredible tale. It would be unlike Kipling not to have had some nucleus of reality to build round, though we need not suppose that what we are offered are literally 'the undraped facts'. It was first published in 1923 and not collected until 1932 in *Limits and Renewals*. It is presented as a tale of 1915 and this brings it close to 'Sea Constables', which was published in that year. Both of them illustrate, in quite different ways, the remark with which 'The Tie' begins: 'Men, in war, will instinctively act as they have been taught to do in peace—for a certain time.' Both show a breaking-point, a point of departure from peace-time behaviour, and the pressure that brought it about. In 'The Tie' this is something barbarous and fundamental, the primitive need of men in hard work for food, and their primitive emotions when they are cheated of it by a profiteer. Mervyn, the ex-schoolmaster, says he was 'savage, though not murderous, from semi-starvation and indigestion', when the 'unjust caterer' fell into the hands of the young officers. He claims fellowship as a school-mate of a very few years ago, and they deal with him after the fashion of their boyhood until 'all the grown-man dropped from him'. He is wearing an Old EHW school tie on his 'false bosom' and Mervyn sticks to it that 'that flaming Old EHW tie saved us and steadied us'. He means that it suggested to them the methods of the prefects' study and, availing themselves of these, they avoided more serious violence. For most of them it was only a short step back. Mervyn, who participates in the 'little affair', says that he has dug up the remnants of his civilian conscience and finds it quite impenitent, surprised at, but temperately justifying, what he finds in himself and in the youngsters, his seniors. When they carry their castigation of Haylock to the point of making him eat a full meal of the food his firm has provided for the Mess, Mervyn ascribes this action to 'the necessary cruelty' of the young, and adds that it is 'a wise provision of nature'. What this means can be found in 'Regulus', one of the later *Stalky* stories, written fifteen years before, in which we meet Pat Mullins, captain of the games, who was 'old enough to pity' and 'did not believe in letting boys wait through the night till the chill of the next morning for their punishments', and watch him deal briskly but mercifully with a miserable and misled little Lower School boy. I think the gaps in the argument can be filled in. The context is educational, judicial and punitive. Pity, bred in the adult mind by experience, introduces a reserve in the payments we exact. Therefore, some of the world's work must be done by those who are still untroubled by the knowledge of their own human condition, or are temporarily driven beyond it. This is the 'wise provision of nature'. To build this out further would be to run at once into an untenable position. The bearing of the remark is limited by the nature of the tale in which it occurs; but it does indicate one of the angles from which Kipling saw the complex of resentment—hate—ruthlessness—retribution which so much commanded his attention.

There are other group-revenges in Kipling. Stalky and Co manoeuvre elaborately against direct and delegated authority, and, though they cannot put down the mighty from their seats, they do succeed in making them look silly. They do not question their impulses, but relish the payment and overpayment of the debts they consider they owe. Hatred is not an emotion they feel; rather distaste, natural rebelliousness and a complacent conviction of superior cunning. Kipling, moving in a boys' world of the hyperbolical based on the real, does not question their values. In 'The Moral Reformers', however, when the gang subject two overgrown bullies to the techniques they have learnt as victims some years before, he drops one of his uncommented observations, which should not be overlooked. Beetle has undertaken to 'jape a bit' with one of the bullies '*á la* "Molly" Fairbairn'—his former tyrant—and involves him in a bewildering sequence of questions and penalties, until the dispassionate Stalky remarks, without understanding: 'What a bait you're in. . . . Keep your hair on, Beetle.' The answer is: 'I've had it done to me'; and, when Sefton makes unconditional surrender, which by their code terminates the inflictions, the executioner has to be restrained with a 'Shut up, Beetle.' They are all 'dripping with excitement and exertion', and Stalky says: 'This moral suasion biznai takes it out of a chap.' The text is not elaborated, but the facts are set down. The young who, for all their swagger, are essentially innocent, do not perceive the gulfs they skirt and, like sleep-walkers, pass safely.

The integration of the groups in '"Bread upon the Waters"' and 'The Devil and the Deep Sea' is much less instinctive, and so is their behaviour. It is with cool calculation that McRimmon, the ship-owner, 'cuts the liver out o' Holdock, Steiner, Chase, and Company, Limited', that mean and dishonest firm of shippers. His willing and entirely honest instrument is the First Engineer McPhee, sacked after twenty years' service because he says the new time-tables are impossible to run to, and will not cheat on them; and they have unavowed collaborators in the disgusted and underfed employees of the firm. There are motives at all levels here, from simple hunger to McPhee's injured self-respect and McRimmon's destestation of shabby dealing. The word 'hate' is not used, and the word 'revenged' only after a large mixed intake of champagne and whisky. They are all self-contained Scots. McPhee, telling the tale months after, admits to irritation. 'It's irritatin', Janet, it's just irritatin'. I ha' been justified from first to last, as the world knows, but—but I canna forgie 'em.' Hunger and humiliation are the motives that lead the pearl-poachers of 'The Devil and the Deep Sea' to sink the ship they have recovered and repaired with such enormous and frenzied labour where she will break the back of the gunboat that arrested them. This tale clanks on its way with such a riot of bedevilled machinery that the casual reader may be forgiven for failing to notice what course is laid. The machinery is necessary to the narrative, though it gets badly out of hand; the cataract of technicalities is meant to impress on the reader the magnitude of the crew's effort and of the over-ruling resentment to which they sacrifice their achievement. The Chief Engineer, who has re-established his proper pride by the wild ingeniousness of his professional performance and wants to run the ship to Singapore and show her to his brethren in the craft, is borne down by the others. 'They had not yet recovered their self-respect.' At the end, when the hubbub has died down, we see in the mouth of the world-abandoned harbour, that is the turning-point of a pearling sea-patrol, 'a little proa rocking in the warm rain . . . whose crew watched with hungry eyes the smoke of a gunboat on the horizon'. The meat they hunger for is revenge, and they are about to be fed. But it has been a noisy passage.

The twenty-two men in the proa are an extreme type and the product of extreme conditions. Except for the Chief Engineer, they constitute an undifferentiated human block, propelled by savage resentment into savage action. It is impossible to tell whether this tale was first devised to exhibit the force of revenge-ful hatred, or whether that emotion was injected into its astounding scenes as the motive most able to account for them. In either case, the significance for the study of Kipling's work is much the same. The injury the crew have received, like the injuries that incite the Pathan, the Malay and the Sikh brothers, is of the kind that pierces to the quick of personal existence and affects the terms on which men have pleasure in living with themselves.

That they are toughs and law-breakers, without, in the first instance, a shadow of right on their side, makes no difference to this; nor are we asked to sympathize or admire—except in the original sense of the word. Not all the tales of revenge, however, present extremities. Already in one of his early anecdotes Kipling had introduced the unexpected avenger in civilized circumstances.

'Watches of the Night' is a hard little farce, with too much moral underlining, but it sketches an interesting kind of avenger. Everyone accepts Mrs Larkyn as 'an amusing, honest little body'; but when chance puts it into her power to afflict the Colonel's wife with a suspicion of her husband's fidelity—the same sort of suspicion that that lady, in her zeal against sin, has sown in the minds of others—she remembers her friends who have suffered, and strikes to punish. 'I think it will do her good', she says, and will not permit the suspicion to be dispelled. She goes home, when her husband's tour of service ends, leaving the Colonel's wife still miserable and unenlightened. 'Now Mrs Larkyn was a frivolous woman, in whom none would have suspected deep hate.' The tale is treated as a curiosity, though the narrator registers some disquiet at the outcome. Half a lifetime later, in 'Mary Postgate', Kipling was to treat the unsuspected capacities for hatred in a middle-aged woman at a deeper level. 'Pig', also, is a curiosity. An Assistant-Commissioner, a Devon man, sticks a Yorkshireman with a dangerous horse, and laughs at him when he is thrown. 'Now, a Dalesman from beyond Skipton will forgive an injury when the Strid lets a man live.' Nafferton evolves a relishing, ingenious and prolonged revenge on Pinecoffin. 'He was a peculiar man, and his notions of humour were cruel. He taught me a new and fascinating form of *shikar*.' This *shikar* is the hunting of a man. It is done by involving Pinecoffin in endless official correspondence, playing up his enthusiasm and self-importance till the thing becomes a deadly load and he slips into careless error and can be accused to his superiors, shown up in a down-country paper and exposed to the chaff of his friends. Then Nafferton enlightens him and asks him to dinner. The tale is written in short sentences, packed with detail. The pages of correspondence pile up under our eyes, and Pinecoffin progresses from gratification to wonder and to desperation, until the story shuts off with a click. Payment has been made in kind, and Nafferton crosses off the account. He has made his point and enjoyed doing it, and he bears no more malice. This the narrator finds fascinating but peculiar. Nafferton is not in the least like Pambé Serang. He is not at all passionate or obsessed, but he is a naturally vindictive man. The type is rare in England, as steady, cherished hate is rare. Kipling says that Yorkshire produces it (he was half a Yorkshireman himself, and he was to make Manallace a northerner, and Jemmy Gravell in 'Beauty Spots'). So, he thinks, does Australia. In 'A Friend of the Family' Bevin says to Orton the Australian: 'I'd hate to have one of your crowd have it in for me for anything. . . . You're a trifle—what's the word?—vindictive?—spiteful? At least, that's what *I've* found.' There follows the tale of the wordless Queensland drover, who has listened at the Front to his English friend's local grievances and, after the friend is killed, comes to his Buckinghamshire village and neatly rectifies all injustices with three Mills bombs, camouflaging his actions as an air-raid. Bevin admits with placid irony that he himself is a spiteful man; he had wanted to re-bury the corpse that the enemy crumped before it was fairly under ground; but this is outside his range. 'Mark *you*, I don't say there's anything *wrong* with you Australians, Brother Orton. I only say they ain't like us or anyone else I know.' These are men, in fact, who, like Nafferton, regard a grudge seriously and carry it far, and will do as much for a friend who can no longer discharge this responsibility.

The story of 'A Friend of the Family' is a comedy, but it is linked in the minds of teller and listeners, all ex-service men, with memories that are serious enough. Wherever possible, however, these are tilted a little towards the ridiculous or, at least, the odd, and the injustice of the exemption tribunal and its effects are made more tolerable by being seen, philosophically, as 'the usual'. This is a more spontaneous and sensitively observed language than the idiom of the early Anglo-Indian tales, which was a class codification of the same self-protective habit. As Peacock said, the worst thing is good enough to be laughed at; and Bevin, thinking of the Queensland drover and the Buckinghamshire market-gardener in his platoon, discussing sheep and blacks and glass and exemption tribunals, with 'the men's teeth chatterin' behind their masks between rum-issue an' zero', exclaims: 'Oh, there was fun in Hell those days, wasn't there, boys?' This habit of thought and speech makes the occasional absolutely 'straight' sentences more impressive, and these no longer carry the unmixed emotional overcharge we find in the early tales, but are cast in a more reflective mode. Before Bevin tells his tale, an allusion in talk to a bombed hollow near Thiepval causes him to remark that, the last time he saw the place, 'I thought it 'ud be that way till Judgment Day', and the great word Judgment, vibrating in the mind of the other speaker, diverts the conversation.

'Ye-es,' said Pole. 'The trouble is there hasn't been any judgment taken or executed. That's why the world is where it is now. We didn't need anything but justice—afterwards. Not gettin' that, the bottom fell out of things, naturally.'

'That's how I look at it too,' Bevin replied. 'We didn't want all that talk afterwards—we only wanted justice. What *I* say is, there *must* be a right and a wrong to things. It can't all be kiss-an'-make-friends, no matter what you do.'

This is the wide background for the retributory manoeuvres of Hickmot, the drover. They are a small queer, limited, marginal illustration of something fundamental in human nature, standing out uncompromisingly in the solitary man from the sheep station.

It might seem at first sight that the Great War renewed and intensified Kipling's interest in this theme. The tales 'Mary Postgate' and 'Sea Constables' would uphold this supposition, together with several sets of verses belonging to this period, in which he cries for judgment and expiation. Moreover, by contrast with these, the collections published during the ten years up to 1914—the *Puck* books and *Actions and Reactions*—seem to represent a halcyon period in his art. In the *Puck* books revengeful hatred, when it is presented at all, as it is in 'The Wrong Thing', is presented to be exorcized. The lesson is taught with some particularity. Hal's enemy, Benedetto, was a good craftsman, 'but his hate spoiled his eye and hand'; Kadmiel, the Jew, says that he found no learned man in the darkness and cruelty of Bury in England ('How can a man be wise if he hate?') and one of the conditions of manhood, set forth in 'If—' is that, being hated, one does not give way to hating. We cannot, moreover, dismiss these remarks on the ground that this will inevitably be the view expressed in a book for children, for we find a different emphasis in *The Jungle Books*. In the jungle all respectable people pay their debts. When Mowgli takes a knife from a dead man, killed by a boar, he scrupulously tracks and kills the boar. He lets in the jungle to destroy the village that stoned him and would have put his foster-mother to death, and he enjoys in consequence 'the good conscience that comes from paying a just debt'. He knows hate and he exercises retaliation, which is part of the righteousness of the wild boy in his wild life. There is also to be an explanation of the working of hatred, surprising in its context of a boy's tale, in 'His Gift', which was published in 1923 in *Land and Sea Tales for Scouts and Guides*. This is not a very good tale—the Daemon was absent from that collection—though it has a pleasant idea, the discovery by an awkward, unawakened boy of fifteen, the most incompetent scout in the troop, of the gift for cooking which alters his world. His chance comes when a passer-by criticizes the methods of a much-badged, too-virtuous fellow-scout with the stew-pot, and William, who has spent some hot hours trotting about as orderly for the superior Prawn, receives a strong positive stimulus from his unrealized hatred of him. For the first time in his life he takes cover properly to listen to the rebuke, and he thinks up a way of ingratiating himself with the critic, who is the local baker and an enthusiast in his art. At this point Kipling launches into an elaborate simile in which he compares the boy to a large blunt shell, that needs a 'mere graze on the fuse to spread itself all over the landscape'. William tries his prentice hand with success, and begins to dream of keeping crews from mutiny by his eggs and bacon, and sustaining his unsympathetic uncle and the Prawn from the door of an enormous restaurant. The hatred, having done its work, disappears—as it must do, or it would 'spoil his hand'—and he feels nothing but pity for the benighted Prawn, and gratitude to him. If proof were needed of Kipling's unexhausted curiosity about the passion of hatred, it could be found in this careful and—having regard to the nature of the tale—unexpected analysis. In the same collection he reprinted the old 'Son of his Father', a quite incredible story of how little Adam Strickland, so small that he sits at table in a high chair, clears his honour and subtly avenges himself on his father for beating him in front of his ayah. It is not, then, simply the fact that the *Puck* books were written for children that accounts for the author's attitude.

In *Actions and Reactions* there is no tale of revenge at all. The air of the book is genial and untroubled; only in 'The Mother Hive' do we hear those notes of apprehension and contempt that were to sound so strongly in *A Diversity of Creatures*, the first collection to be published after 1914. The motive of healing, of which I write elsewhere, emerging with strength, has spread a hard-won serenity round it. In 'The House Surgeon' the grim conception of damnation by a vindictive God and the consequent blackness of despair are evoked precisely in order that they may be melted, dispersed, dissolved utterly out of the lives, not only of those who have suffered innocently under the curse, but of those who with passionate stern grief have imposed it. When Kipling fused his experience in the unhappy house at Torquay, of which he has told us, with the still living experience of the spiritual climate of the House of Desolation and cleansed the site, not as by fire but as by the water of grace, he performed an act of imaginative charity. Moreover, he put the 'I' into the story, subjected him to the reflected agony of despair, and used him to remove the barriers that obstructed the renewal of love and hope. The tale, which is the last in the book, ends with a young girl singing in the redeemed house, and the book ends with 'The Rabbi's Song', with its summons to 'cleanse and call home' the spirit,

> *For fear the desolation*
> *And darkness of thy mind*
> *Perplex an habitation*
> *That thou hast left behind.*

'People ought to forgive and forget', says Baxter, in the tale.

The abstention, if it was more than accidental, did not last long, however. Tales of hatred and revenge reappear in *A Diversity of Creatures*, published in 1917, during the War, and two of them preceded its outbreak. As the name suggests, *A Diversity of Creatures* is not a unified book. It contains two tales of healing, 'In the Same Boat' and 'The Dog Hervey'—three, if we include ' "My Son's Wife" '—and those are not concerned at all with hatred; two of them deal with the 'opposite', the agency of love in the exorcism of despair and suffering, and the third with moral regeneration. It also contains two tales in which revenge is taken, the elaborate 'Village that Voted the Earth was Flat' and the dreadful 'Mary Postgate', and one, 'Friendly Brook', which includes an unperforming hatred. The book as a whole seems to be poised between apprehension and anxious self-reassurance.

Kipling seems to be asking whither the modern world is tending, with a disquieting far view in the much misunderstood 'As Easy as ABC' and an alarming near one in 'The Edge of the Evening'. To these tales he juxtaposes the slightly older 'Regulus' ('You see. It sticks. A little of it sticks among the barbarians'), 'The Horse Marines' ('There's nothing wrong with the Service. . . . Same old game—same young beggars'), 'The Honours of War', in which Stalky is reassured as to the quality of the younger generation, and 'In the Presence', which establishes that strict and selfless standards of honour are still observed in the Indian Army. All these tales, contrary to his usual custom, are carefully dated by their appearance in magazines or, in the case of three hitherto unpublished, by the years in which they were written. The dates range from 1908 to 1915; the only two written after the outbreak of war are ' "Swept and Garnished" ' and 'Mary Postgate'. It is obvious then, that we cannot ascribe the reappearance of the theme of revenge solely to the intensification of political passion, anguished pity, and the will to survive, brought on by the war. Indeed, biographical deductions from the order of Kipling's works are very uncertain, until we know—if we ever can—when each of his sometimes long-incubated tales was written and—even more unlikely—when it was conceived. Yet, even if we had this information, it would not be easy to interpret. The mind of a creative artist can work almost simultaneously in different fields and to different purposes. 'The Village that Voted the Earth was Flat' and ' "My Son's Wife" ', with their opposed and complementary tendencies, were both written in 1913. Also it is to be considered that in the denser tales it is not always possible to know what were the growing-points of the composition. My own opinion is that 'The Village that Voted the Earth was Flat' grew out of a conviction, at once zestful and misgiving, of the enormous power of the modern Press and the other publicizing industries and arts, especially the Music Hall, that were linked with it. The old journalist in Kipling kindled to the power, and the craftsman rejoiced in the technique of 'the widest game that all of a man can play'. With these resources almost anything could be done, and almost anything, on so vast a scale, could get out of hand, even if the wielders of the power were fully responsible, which they are not. The submerged alarm breaks surface through Ollyett, the tough young journalist, who is designed for this purpose. Twice he says seriously that he is afraid of Bat Masquerier, the impresario, a generous man, master of enormous power, and 'the Absolutely Amoral Soul'. What this very clever young man, moulded by harsh experiences, fears must be formidable. This power is mobilized for the hunting of a man—'the chase of the Human, the search for the Soul to its ruin', as Kipling had written in *Plain Tales from the Hills* in an epigraph too drastic for 'Pig' but exactly suiting the destruction of Sir Thomas Ingell. This is *shikar* on a grand scale. The avengers are selected for their ability to bring into play the resources of their different professions. The initial insult is laid on with a trowel and with Kipling's peculiar capacity, even better shown in 'Beauty Spots', to make—there is really nothing that describes the immediate, unexamined, fermenting response of the reader to the shock except the stale old *cliché*—the blood boil. Kipling, however, does not use this *cliché*; he is more apt to say that anger makes his character sick. Sir Thomas, nevertheless, is hardly real, though his villagers are. He is the clown who starts the train of consequences, and fresh iniquities have to be devised for him, at regular intervals, lest the avengers should drop the chase. The methods of the chase are precise and fascinating; it is there that the curiosity lies, not in the characters or the motive. Indeed, by confecting a series of offences that might rouse any man, Kipling seems to have wished to dismiss psychological curiosity. Ollyett and the narrator watch the piling-up of the nation-wide ridicule of Sir Thomas and his village till it is beyond control, and they see, with some consternation, that they need no longer lift a finger. The avalanche cannot be contained. 'The thing roared and pulverized and swept beyond eyesight all by itself—all by itself.' Even the great and blind Bat Masquerier—this is one of Kipling's nominal clues—wonders a little and is glad that he always believed in God and Providence and all those things. 'Else I should lose my nerve.' The last stage of the campaign falls fortuitously into a monstrous hilarity, but this is not the true—or, at least, not the complete—ecstasy of mirth. The pursuer does not relax, and the victim is not commended to charity.

The two country tales are indirectly but powerfully reassuring. I have written of '"My Son's Wife"' in the chapter on Laughter. 'Friendly Brook' comes in here. Its main theme is the survival in the mind of a countryman of a vague animistic conception of the brook that has flooded and drowned his enemy for him. The kind of hate he suffers helps to explain his kind of gratitude. This atavism is, as so often in Kipling, an extreme case. What reassures is the country life and the characters of the narrator and the listener. The country life, growing from the permanent basis of the nature and service of the land, accepts without disorder the tarred roads, the road-engines, the Barnardo children and the 'week-end money' they bring. The self-contained, honourable life of the skilled agricultural worker goes on, generous with his toil, secretive over his money, wary towards authority, looking with unobtrusive interest and tolerant malice at the affairs of his neighbour. In the November fog two elderly hedgers, carefully respectful of each other's skill, tackle a neglected hedge running down to the brook. The sound of the rising water leads Jesse to satisfy Jabez's curiosity about Jim Wickenden's placing of his haystack within reach of the flood. Jim has said: 'The Brook's been good friends to me, and if she be minded . . . to take a snatch at my hay, *I* ain't setting out to withstand her.' This piece of paganism is quietly accepted by the two men, to whom the brook is 'she', and a power in their valley; what interests them is the nature of the debt Jim is paying. The brook has indeed been a good friend to Jim. It has drowned his enemy, the blackmailer who was extorting money by threatening to reclaim the Wickendens' adopted child. If Jim, in fact, offered the brook its chance, it was a half-hearted action, and this fits his nature. He is a quiet, careful man; he does not smoke, looks after his money, and is a good workman on his own lines, though without the virtuosity of Jesse and Jabez. He is not impulsive, and nothing less than fierce. He knows that, as the girl's father, the man has the law on his side, and once in his life he has been in trouble with the law, and got six months in Lewes gaol. Anxiety makes him sweat, and he loathes scenes. When the last postcard comes from the blackmailing parent, he 'fair cried dunghill an' run'. He is downstream, helping Jesse clear the alders which are blocking the current, when the man's body comes down the brook. In this scene we get the full measure of the hatred that would never have driven him into aggressive action. It is revealed negatively, in what is not there, the common feeling of decency for a dead human body. He has been bled of his money for months, his peace has been broken, and his tenacious affections—adhesions is, perhaps, the word—have been threatened. When he pulls in the body, he identifies it, removes the money from the pocket, and laughs to to think that his masterful old mother has paid more for blackmail than he has ever done. 'An' now we'll pook him back again, for I've done with him', he says. Jesse does not protest, and the corpse rolls down the brook. Jim's hatred has been impotent and unprogressive as nowhere else in Kipling; the man has no resources; he does not even give words to his feeling. The oppression and the relief are almost physical. For this gratitude chance is no fit recipient. Something very old stirs in Jim's unexamined mind, and in the last sentence of the tale the brook, whose changes of note are immediately interpreted by the hedgers, sounds 'as though she were mumbling something soft'.

When Kipling assembled these tales in 1917, the world had changed, and the last two tales in the book, '"Swept and Garnished"' and 'Mary Postgate', bear witness to it. These two dreadful tales assault the mind. They are the utterances of deep outrage. Both have, at times, if read quickly, the quality of a hardly suppressed scream. This, though painful, is integral to both, since both describe a repressed horror that in the end breaks out. '"Swept and Garnished"', first published in January 1915, has the nature of an immediate—almost a headlong—act of reprisal. 'Mary Postgate' is much more deeply considered and on a different level of art. In the former, which is barely a dozen pages long, old Frau Ebermann, in her fanatically tidy Berlin flat, submits to a feverish cold with a high temperature. With the relaxation of control, there emerge the images and apprehensions she has kept at rigid arm's length, clinging—for though unamiable, she is a mother—to the explanations her son has written to her. In her delirium she sees the slaughtered children of the invaded countries spot her floor with blood. She is left on her knees, trying to wipe it up with the lace cover, whose mathematically exact disposition had seemed so important to her, and praying 'that Our dear Lord when He came might find everything as it should be'. The swept and garnished flat recalls the orderly home of the German nation, cleansed of many imps that trouble other peoples, but occupied by seven devils worse than the first. So much is plain. Plain, too, is Frau Ebermann's conviction of guilt, when the defences of the conscious mind are down. But, as Kipling turned the knife that had first been turned in him, the children acquired a naturalness and pathos, a grave composure of bearing, that hardly sort with delirium, though their evasive speech continues to reflect Frau Ebermann's quailing refusal to know. We can dismiss any suggestion that this was meant to be a supernatural story. The public missile should vibrate with the public conviction. Moreover, those of his characters who touch the supernatural, with the not very significant exception of Hummil in 'At the End of the Passage', do so in health and in their right minds. But the suffering of children was a dangerous incentive to Kipling, and at times it looks as if the ghostly company, who are waiting in the enemy's capital city till their people come for them, were rather an inflamed vision of his own than a likely hallucination of the old lady.

No such doubts arise in the case of 'Mary Postgate'. Step by foreseen step, the tale marches to its end, when Miss Fowler's plain, conscientious, ladylike, middle-aged companion refuses to help the young German airman, and stands by exulting until he dies. It is one of the very few tales in which Kipling follows out in full detail a psychological development. Mary is the unexpected avenger. Hers is not a typical case, but a very special one. She has been prepared for her act and betrayed to it, quite beyond her knowledge, by her whole life, by its emptiness and deprivation, by its one passionate affection for her employer's young nephew, and lastly by a series of violent shocks and strains, beginning with his death in a flying accident, early in the war. The detached facts about her are dropped into their logical places, where they will illumine her actions. We hear of the deaths of her family, of her nine years' devoted service as butt and slave of the boy, and of her position as 'a sort of public aunt' to the village children. She is competent and colourless. Wynn tells her that she has no mind; but every word he says sinks into the texture of her nature, and it is his youthful brutalities, made horrific by passing over her lips, that come from her, 'quite smoothly and naturally', when the convulsion of her being tears through her control. She is not in the least introspective. She has been taught not to dwell on things—a key phrase that comes four times—and she is proud of her training. This self-restraint has its physical counterpart. 'Nothing makes me perspire', she remarks, and when Wynn is killed she cannot cry. 'It only makes me angry with the Germans', she says in her flat phrase. To this unresolved tension are added, stroke by stroke, fresh exactions on mind and body. The clearing-out of Wynn's possessions the day after the funeral, and the preparations, which she lets no one else share, for burning them in the open-air furnace; the smothered shock when the bomb falls behind the inn, and her boots are soaked with the blood of the inn-keeper's little girl; the further check, when the doctor, anxious not to stir people up, queries the bomb and puts the blame on the rotten beams of the stable; the renewed toil at the furnace, until—it is the one fully expressive phrase—'she lit the match that would burn her heart to ashes',—these bring her to the moment when the pyre (the word is deliberately chosen) flares up, and in its light she sees the crippled airman. He is at once the proof that it was indeed a bomb that killed Edna Gerritt and the enemy that Wynn did not live to kill. Her first feeling is one of physical loathing at the 'disgusting pinky skin' showing on his cropped head, The rest is a methodical frenzy—she has always been methodical—and a luxurious self-abandonment to the antithetical passion of hate. She shouts and stamps; she glows with violent stoking; she fetches Wynn's revolver instead of the water the young German craves; and she hums to herself while she waits for his death. For a little while her mind gropes for and finds a justification of her actions. This, too, is a woman's work, since no man would do it, and a woman who has missed other things can still be useful. But already her thought is little more than a sensation, a 'secret thrill', and soon 'an increasing rapture' lays hold of her, and she ceases to think and gives herself up to feel. The force and horror of the last lines are extreme.

> Her long pleasure was broken by a sound that she had waited for in agony several times in her life. She leaned forward and listened, smiling. There could be no mistake. She closed her eyes and drank it in. Once it ceased abruptly.
> 'Go on,' she murmured, half aloud. 'That isn't the end.'
> The end came, very distinctly in a lull between two rain-gusts. Mary Postgate drew her breath short between her teeth and shivered from head to foot. 'That's all right', said she contentedly, and went up to the house, where she scandalized the whole routine by taking a luxurious hot bath before tea,

and came down looking, as Miss Fowler said when she saw her lying all relaxed on the other sofa, 'quite handsome'.

Some three hours before, watching her labouring with the loaded wheel-barrow, Miss Fowler had said to herself: 'Mary's an old woman. I never realized it before', and her handsomeness is appalling. We have watched a moral casualty, a monstrous ebullition of passion which is at once a sensual enjoyment and an outraging of self and sex. Kipling wrote nothing else like this. To show the naked action of revenge, he put before us a woman, starved in her instinctive nature and shocked temporarily out of civilization, which can do no more for her than wave a pitiful transparency of argument over her deed and her profound ignorance of herself. As Dr Johnson said of Desdemona's death: 'I am glad I have ended the revisal of this dreadful scene. It is not to be endured.'

'Sea Constables', like 'The Tie', is 'a tale of '15' and it was completed and published in that year. It is quite unlike 'Mary Postgate' in design. The difference may be loosely compared to that between a Rembrandt canvas and a seventeenth century Dutch winter-scene—or, to take a subject more germane to that of the tale, Richard Eurich's picture of Dunkirk sands in 1940. We never take our eyes off Mary Postgate, with whose name and guaranteed virtues the tale begins. In memory we see her standing by the furnace in the dark winter afternoon, bathed in the harsh light and exulting like a Maenad. In 'Sea Constables' the design is strong, and there is nothing in it that does not relate to the central group, but it is full to the corners of interesting and clearly defined detail. There is Jarrett, the Quaker, mine-sweeping in his family-cruiser; there is the mixed 'fishing-party' in the Scottish bay, with mines piled like lobster-pots in the cutter's stern-sheets; there is the 'Culana', once the pleasure-ship 'Goneril', which went down 'off the same old Irish corner', with Portson's cousin and one of the Raikes boys aboard. In the restaurant where the tale is told we find the younger waiter with his provisional false hand, 'good to hold plates only'—the original one went at Bethisy-sur-Oise—and 'the latest thing in imported patriotic piece-goods', the actress whose beauty young Winchmore unperturbedly admires, as she lets the whole restaurant know, in a carrying voice, that in her opinion the tired RNVR men, solacing their short leave with a good meal and professional talk, 'ain't *alive* to the war, yet'.

For the purpose of comparison I have classed 'Sea Constables' with the tales of hatred and revenge, but this is rather misleading, and it would be better to class it with tales of breaking-strain, had it been at all necessary to go over again what Professor Bonamy Dobrée has said so well. It is, in fact, what Kipling calls it, a tale of '15. Like some of the early soldier-tales, it covers a wide area, a much wider one, in fact, than they do; for in India he was dealing only with a professional army and, though the private lives and hopes of officers and men were a small part of his material, there was nothing to parallel the abrupt change-over from civil life to war-service of middle-aged men, shaped and finished, it would seem, by their trades and professions, as well as of flexible youth. He had been moved to wondering pride by the volunteers of the South African Wars, 'not the Army that you and I know, but the Army of the People. . . . Blacksmiths, gardeners, club porters and small shopkeepers', but that was a slender anticipation of what 1915 was to show. A whole cross-section of national life was heaved up, as if by volcanic fires, into a rarer, more perilous air. A new landscape was forged. He never forgot this astonishing transmutation, and it fills his war tales with young men who hardly have time to observe, under the pressure of their new experiences, the startling discontinuity of their lives or the success of their adaptation. The civilian life of each one attends him like a shadow, and for a time it is almost as insubstantial. The older men, however, sometimes marvel a little at themselves, as Mervyn does in 'The Tie' and Maddingham and Portson in this tale. Maddingham breaks off his account of how he ordered into port the neutral he was convoying, and threatened to sink him if he disobeyed:

> 'Isn't it extraordinary how natural it all seems after a few weeks? If anyone had told me when I commissioned *Hilarity* last summer what I'd be doing this spring I'd—I'd . . .God! It *is* mad, isn't it?'
>
> 'Quite,' said Portson. 'But not bad fun.'
>
> 'Not at all, but that's what makes it all the madder.'

Certainly there is a kind of hatred in the tale, hatred of the neutral who, thinking 'your side's bound to win anyway', sees an opportunity to fish with profit in our stormy waters by trading petrol to the enemy, and keeps the middle-aged volunteers in their converted pleasure-yachts chasing him up and down the black seas in filthy weather, infuriated by the restraint of observing 'existing political relations', and 'new to this business', as Maddingham the banker says 'pleadingly' to the Navy man, Tegg,—with no allusion to his seamanship. He has convoyed his neutral up and down the Irish Sea for five days and four nights—three of which he has spent on the bridge; the winter weather has stirred up his sciatica; he has been humiliated at an Inquiry ashore, where the representative of the Admiralty, his young friend Tegg, has supported the neutral and hauled Maddingham over the coals, and by the neutral himself, who reminds him of his blood-pressure and describes his patriotism as 'uric acid and rotten spite'. Then, when he has harried him into handing over his oil to an Admiralty agent in Ireland, the neutral, seriously ill with bronchial pneumonia, asks to be run across to London to his doctor and lawyer, and Maddingham refuses. The neutral, to whom the conflict is an individual duel, has relied on 'proper treatment', if he surrendered. Maddingham retails the conversation, stressing—he is still sore from the Inquiry—his politeness and his strict observance of regulations. He describes himself as carefully explanatory. He might have stretched a point for a wounded belligerent, but a neutral is 'altogether outside the game', and, when he is appealed to on the grounds of common humanity (' "Why, if you leave me now, Mr Maddingham," he said, "you condemn me to death as surely as if you hanged me" '), he maintains his position, saying first: 'This is war', and then, to bring the matter within their common experience: 'This is business. I can do nothing for you.' In the end, '*he* saw what I was driving at. . . . I saw his flag half-masted next morning'. Portson, the stockbroker, who alone can gauge the upheaval of established life behind the tale—the others, conditioned professionally or by youthful adaptability to the times, are silent—goes behind the question of saving life, to ask, in the terms of their peace-time occupations: 'But why didn't you lend him a hand to settle his private affairs?' The first half of the answer is legal, a prompt reference to regulations, such as Maddingham had been chidden for breaking. Something else follows: 'I'd been on the bridge for three nights.' He pulls out his watch, sees his time is over, and leaves the question unanswered.

There is no need to labour the differences between this tale and 'Mary Postgate'. Maddingham's attitude to law and regulations —he may be angry, but he is not in the least ironical—is the direct product of his training and career in peace, and appears essentially masculine beside the contempt for 'law' in all its connotations with which a personal cause, as Kipling believed, fills the formidable female of the species. He is moving responsibly in harness. Ecstasy and brutality are equally remote from him. He will, if he lives, revert to the manners of peace and show professional courtesies to defeated rivals. But, under the pressure of conditions that are normal or abnormal as we interpret history and human nature, but of which his generation had had little experience, he comes on potentialities in himself that he had not expected. 'I was surprised at myself—'give you my word', he says.

The aftermath of the War is in nearly all of Kipling's tales of contemporary life after 1918. This is not obsession but integrity. He wrote of men whose age ensured that they had been through it, and to omit all reference to it would have injured the completeness of his imagination. This is not only the case with the tales of war-injuries and with the war-time memories of old soldiers and sailors, exchanged when they meet in Lodge or elsewhere; it also occurs in tales that have nothing to do with the War, but take place in a world that has recently endured it. The French ex-Colonial Administrator who tells the tale of 'The Bull that Thought' has 'supervized Chinese woodcutters who, with axe and dynamite, deforested the centre of France for trench-props'. The part of Lettcombe in 'Aunt Ellen' requires that he shall be able to apply some of the resources of Hollywood to the penultimate scene of the farce; but besides this he is an OBE and was a Colonel of Territorials, so that he and a passing lorry-driver can exchange terms from the same 'gory lexicon', in fellowship. 'In lots of ways,' says the taxi-driver in 'The Janeites', 'this war has been a public noosance, as one might say, but there's no denyin' it 'elps you slip through life easier.' It is not always this aspect, however, that comes to light. There are the feelings, mixed past extrication, with which the men, settled down in civil life, remember their war-service; the scars, physical and mental, that they carry; the little habits, such as the movement to tighten the belt, which revive when they meet and talk together; and the notes of bitterness and disquietude that break briefly across the flow of a tale. Over his champagne the ex-Colonial Administrator recounts the exceptional qualities of the cattle of the Camargue:

> 'After the War,' said I spaciously, 'everything is credible.'
> 'That is true! Everything inconceivable has happened; but still we learn nothing and we believe nothing.'

The tone changes immediately, as he passes smoothly to his boyhood among the 'big farms like castles' and the 'well-loved, wicked white and yellow cattle of the Camargue and the Crau'.

It is not possible on the basis of the publication dates of the tales to work out any consistent development in Kipling's attitude. The material, even when it is distilled for the purposes of art, is still too complex. His verses are sometimes more immediate in their nature, and the speeches of *A Book of Words* more topical and explicit. It is possible to find in these speeches remarks that are a vehement underlining of those expressions of distaste and anxiety at the state of his country, which are to be found, on occasion, in his tales. It is also possible to find remarks with a more hopeful bearing. We have no right, however, to resolve his considered art back into the fiercer, more transitory colouring of the speeches. The tales mean what they are and say, and they are and say different things; their method is dramatic, and sometimes subtle and indirect. Moreover, though their subjects are embedded in topical detail, they concern the permanent moral nature of man. Some of the tales were long meditated, or laid aside for a time; thus the same year may see the publication of tales rooted in different layers of observation, coloured by different moods, and perhaps grown in times far apart. 'The Tender Achilles' and 'Aunt Ellen' both appeared in 1929. The genial 'Miracle of St Jubanus', saw the light in 1932, and so did 'Beauty Spots', his last tale of revenge, in which the heat and sourness of some pages gets the overhand, in the total effect, of the fun of the petted sow, Angélique, and the affection of Mr Gravell and his son.

The heat and sourness in this tale do not arise from the feelings of the avenger, who is a peaceable young man. Jemmy Gravell and his father have been restored to each other with nothing worse than blood-pressure on one side and the after-effects of gas, which need watching, on the other. The young man takes up his career again and the old man is able to lapse into a happy and busy retirement in the country. They are not country people, and all they ask is that the 'natives' shall leave them in peace. But they are not left in peace; the country turns its unlovely side towards them, and Major Kniveat, retired, ambitious for local importance and jealous of competition, works up a pretty persecution of them through the channels of local government. Again, as in 'The Village that Voted the Earth was Flat', it is a question of setting a force in motion, and this time a lazy force. Jemmy has had all the trouble he wants. So the malignant offensiveness of the Major and its nauseating results have to be worked up through nearly half the tale. This is the cost of the subject, whether it was paid zestfully or not. Nafferton could be set in action at the expense of three sentences, but Nafferton was originally a vindictive man and had not Jemmy's reasons for loving quiet. There are in Jemmy, nevertheless, latent capacities for ingenious and callous dealings, learnt in a hard school and generally submerged in the satisfaction of the return to normal life; he has also a beloved father to protect from worry; and in the end it is to a ready and expert hand that Chance offers her weapons. The Great Idea is carried through by Jemmy and his 'all-but-brother', Kit, who has 'done time as an Army doctor', with unsparing farce and devastating results. They have no qualms.

> The generation that tolerates but does not pity went away. They did not even turn round when they heard the first dry sob of one from whom all hope of office, influence and authority was stripped for ever.

Jemmy and Kit are Kipling's subject; the Major is a necessity. Kipling accounts for him rather more fully than for Sir Thomas Ingell and treats him with a touch of dry ruthfulness at the end. Unlike Sir Francis Maddingham, Jemmy is not surprised at himself. He was taken young and thoroughly conditioned to his work, and his aggressive skill, gladly laid aside, is still at his disposal. The temper in which he 'wipes the nuisance from his path' is described in 'The Expert' as 'mirth more dread than wrath'. Jemmy's dayspring has been mishandled, also, though in a different fashion from Manallace's and we can, if we like, regard this tale as another instance of Kipling's concern with war-injuries. Its tone, however, is quite different from the other tales on this subject. The author does not compassionate Jemmy; he is cool and interested. No doubt, his emphatic generalization about the generation that tolerates but does not pity is as untrustworthy as Shakespeare's about the unmusical man. Neither writer cared to jeopardize the effectiveness of a strong statement by scholarly qualification.

Revenge, however elemented, is not always accomplished in Kipling's stories. Learoyd's onset of murderous jealousy in 'On Greenhow Hill' is not strictly revenge. It was not premeditated, when he undertook to show his rival, the Reverend Amos Barraclough, the lead-mine where he worked—neither, for that matter, was Mary Postgate's action premeditated—and even at the crisis, when he holds him over the underground swallow-hole of the beck, his purpose—so far as he knows it—is blackmail, not murder. But he is possessed, as Mary Postgate was to be; and Kipling is as careful, in this early tale, to assemble the causes of the possession as he was to be in the later one. Learoyd's physical strength and rough experience, the unnatural repression of the weeks while he tried earnestly to become a Primitive Methodist for 'Liza Roantree's sake, his diffidence, the distracting mixture of liking and hatred for the man who has converted him and is his rival, lay him open to the seizure. The most memorable passage in this fine tale is where Learoyd begins to feel his power in the darkness underground:

> He began to sing a hymn in his thin voice, and I came out wi' a chorus that was all cussin' an' swearin' at my horses, an' I began to know how I hated him. He were such a little chap, too.

There follows the uprush of violent and evil imaginings and the exacerbation of knowing that the preacher is not afraid. 'It's none so easy to kill a man like yon.' He does not kill him. In *Kim*, also, the lama, insulted and struck, forbids the bearers to avenge him, but he has 'come near a great evil'. He has been 'tempted to loose the bullet', and later, in the mountain hut, he passes judgment on himself for having suffered the shadow of the lust to kill to pass over his soul and into the world. The lesson is too high for Kim; he is glad he hurt the man. It is the lama's wisdom that is reaffirmed in 'The Rabbi's Song' after 'The House Surgeon'. Earlier in the book, in the Jâtaka that he tells to the Jain priests, we hear that it is not till the 'hate and frenzy' of the elephant's heart have been abated by acts of love that he is freed from the fetter that cuts into his flesh.

These fragments constitute a very small area of print to set against the many tales of achieved revenge, but their substance is greater than their size, for, to the reader of Kipling, they are loaded with the recollected weight of those other stories. To abstain from revenge is not easy. Twice, however, at long intervals, he wrote with elevation, tales in which the renunciation of revenge is not incidental but culminating, and once a tale in which the planned retaliation is first obstructed and finally shown to be a self-delusion. In the first two cases the moral action is simple, in the last very complex. 'A Sahibs' War' is a tale of the Boer War, vibrant with anger and with exasperation at the way the war is being waged. These emotions are expressed by Umr Singh, an officer of the 141st Punjab Cavalry, a Sikh, and they are the more vehement for being poured through the narrow channels of his comprehension and his code. This story is the last and longest of the unframed dramatic monologues, and it is told after Kurban (Corbyn) Sahib, the young Captain, whom Umr Singh has loved from childhood and who called him father when they were alone, has been shot by treachery. Kurban Sahib comes before us, 'young—of a reddish face—with blue eyes . . . keen, jestful and careless' and 'a Sikh at heart', and all that he says is said to Umr Singh and in the language that they both understand. He says: 'There is but one fault in this war, and that is that the Government have not employed *us*, but have made it altogether a Sahibs' war. Very many men will thus be killed, and no vengenace will be taken.' To Umr Singh and the Pathan groom, who serves as Kurban Sahib's cook, it is a fools' war. Treachery is on all hands, under a white flag, and the villages are not burned, and the new soldiers from England walk into high grass and are ambushed. Only the Ustrelyahs—the Australians—wage war *as* war. Yet Kurban Sahib strikes Sikandar Khan when he proposes to lie out beyond the pickets with his knife and show them how it is worked on the Border, though he cannot, in half one march, make clear to him anything that lies behind the reiterated: 'It is a Sahibs' war. That is the order.' He is shot from a house where he has been given coffee and shown permits, certifying that the old minister, his wife and idiot son were people of peace and goodwill, and he confirms the order as he dies. When the two men, sworn to the vengeance they regard as a duty, already have the noose round the idiot's neck and the end over a branch, he comes again, 'riding, as it were, upon my eyes', and angrily forbids them. They obey; they will neither save nor slay, but content themselves, when the returning Australians shell the house, by holding the inmates. 'It is a Sahibs' war. Let them wait the Sahibs' mercy.' Setting aside the passion of grief that moves, and moves us, through this tale, Kipling may be felt to have had it both ways at once. He has illustrated under what provocation and at what cost the war was maintained as a Sahibs' war, and by the help of the Australians whose mercy appears, from the memorial inscription on the face of the rock over Corbyn's grave, to have been less than complete, he has assuaged the passions he has raised and satisfied Umr Singh's conception of justice. Umr Singh is the uncomprehending narrator, bewildered by the irrational obligation of mercy. The device of the monologue sets this obligation in contrast to the instincts of the natural man, but, by its limitations, it involves some ambiguity in the nature of the mercy, and this is increased by the reader's awareness of the topical incentives to the tale. Mercy is presented as a mistaken policy, and yet we feel it as a moral imperative. Corbyn, forbidding vengeance as he dies, is not merely obeying orders, but acting according to a law of his nature, of which Umr Singh, who believes him 'at heart a Sikh', is not aware. His appearance after death is also ambiguous, but this does not hurt the tale. It is, to my mind, the only one of Kipling's tales touching the supernatural in which the question of its actuality is left completely open. The men are superstitious. They have been sleepless, waterless and foodless, except for a little opium, for more than twenty-four hours. The gestures and words of the apparition repeat what they have recently seen and heard. Ghost or hallucination, it makes no odds, since, in one way or another, the spirit of Kurban Sahib controls them.

The situation of the young officer's death was repeated, without any ambiguities, nearly a generation later in 'The Church that was in Antioch'. This is one of the tales in which many themes are woven together. It presents a picture of the duties of a young Roman police-officer in Antioch, in the first century, and the spirit in which they are performed; also of his uncle, Lucius Sergius, the experienced and tolerant Prefect of Police, to whom the religions of the Mediterranean and the East, including 'hellicat Judaea', are all 'part of [his] office-work'. From this administrative angle it focuses the disputes of the early Christian

Church and the figures of Peter and Paul. Then, against the debated question of the relation of Greek and Jew in the Church, there emerges unargued the fellowship in the Spirit of all men of good will. 'Gods do not make laws,' says Valens, the worshipper of Mithras. 'They change men's hearts. The rest is the Spirit'; and Paul accepts the young man's words as 'the utter Doctrine itself'. Valens is stabbed in revenge by a Cilician, whose brother he has killed in a brush with brigands outside Tarsus, and pleads with his dying breath to his uncle for the Cilician and his friends. 'Don't be hard on them. . . . They get worked up. . . . They don't know what they are doing.' He does not speak under orders, or tolerantly, like his uncle and Gallio; it is a spontaneous grace of the Spirit. The centrality of this conception in the tale may perhaps be obscured at first reading by Paul, who fills the scene at the Prefect's entertainment, as he might have done in life, with his brilliance and foresight, his authority, his profound and eloquent sincerity, and his unremitting struggle with his own instinctive vanity. But behind him, sparingly indicated and partly submerged, we become aware of the vital experience concealed in Peter's inert bulk, his empty gaze, his uncertain touchiness, his slow and provincial speech. He has seen such a wound and heard such words before. He has needed mercy and received it. He stands by Valens, 'vast and commanding', and rebukes Paul's busy suggestion that the young man should even now be baptized, with: 'Think you that one who has spoken Those Words needs such as *we* are to certify him to any God?'

It can be said of Kipling's revenge-tales, as it is said of Swinburne's love-poems, that the object of the emotion is not really there; that is, he is there as an inflammatory presence, a detested source of effects, but not as a person. Since the action of hatred is to sharpen the vision as to details but to obliterate the total personality of its object, this is no ground of complaint against a writer of short stories, but it is true that there is no genuine interrelation of hater and hated in any of the tales I have mentioned. They are never in prolonged proximity to each other, except in 'The Wrong Thing', where the obsession is all on one side and is to be resolved in the end. Once only, in the superb 'Dayspring Mishandled', did he undertake this aspect of his theme, and here only he makes his avenger a man of letters. The tale may perhaps be read, with due reserve, as a comment on the imagination that had conceived all the other tales of revenge, but this must be done 'In Feare and Decencie', as Kipling said his father had taught him to portray 'that Rare and Terrible Mystery . . . Man', when he dedicated *In Black and White* to him.

The tale is very tightly written. There are no flourishes in it; every sentence tells and matters. The writing is of that 'infolded' sort which, at first reading, may seem to present a crumpled mass, but which gradually fills and spreads and tightens with the fullness and tension of its meanings, until it is a House of Life itself, a tent covering the erring and suffering spirit of man. The title offers us two handles. It is a phrase from the Chaucerian fragment that Manallace forges, as an instrument of his revenge on Castorley, the Chaucer specialist; it is also the condition of Manallace which has nourished that revenge. He is the oak-spray of 'Gertrude's Prayer', bruised and knotted and twisted on itself in youth through his unhappy love, which brings him nothing but the opportunity of nursing and supporting a deserted and paralysed woman, whose eyes look always for the husband who has left her. Thus his 'dawning goth amiss', and when she dies, after many years, his life is emptied, until it is filled by his secret hate for Castorley.

The structure of the tale does not declare itself till half-way through. We seem to wander in various directions. The beginning looks back with desiderium to 'the days beyond compare and before the Judgments', and recreates Grayson and the young men of his Fictional Supply Syndicate at supper at Neminaka's, where Manallace—'a darkish, slow northerner of the type that does not ignite, but must be detonated'—fails to come up to scratch with his consignment because it has 'turned into poetry on his hands', and Castorley, who 'had gifts of waking dislike', announces that he has inherited money and is withdrawing from 'hackwork' to follow 'literature'. A glance at the older Manallace, bogged down in remunerative Wardour Street romances 'that exactly met, but never exceeded, every expectation', covers the years to the War and the death of the unnamed woman. A satiric sketch of Castorley, who has nursed himself into the position of an international Chaucer expert—Kipling is quite clear that the scholarship is genuine; it can even at times break through his obsession with himself and 'prove how a man's work will try to save the soul of him'—brings us to the point when he and Manallace meet again as temporary Civil Servants, and to the short and unexplained scene when, waiting together for a big air-raid, 'the two men talked humanly', and Manallace mentions the woman. Castorley, too, had loved her 'for a time . . . in his own way', and his proposal had been refused. Now 'he said something in reply, and from that hour—as was learned several years later—Manallace's real life-work and interests began'. But the tale turns away from this cryptic sign-post and seems to lose itself in detail about fifteenth century scribes and Manallace's 'forlorn fancy' for trifles like a mediaeval recipe for ink, a Shetland quern and a battered Vulgate with rubricated initials. Then comes Castorley's great opportunity in the discovery of an unknown Chaucer fragment; and during the run of his excited volubility all that has preceded falls into place. Point by point, as he describes the contents of the fragment and the tests he has applied to it, Manallace's patient, deadly, year-long plotting comes to light; the 'trifles' are seen as the necessary elements of his design, and the poem to derive from the Neminaka days of unspoilt hope. It is as if we had walked in a circle through high and pleasant brushwood, and, coming suddenly to an opening in it, find that we have all the time been circling the black and bitter pool of Manallace's hidden hate.

Castorley himself has provided the material with which the trap has been baited, for Manallace, who never denies his scholarship though he lures it on to treacherous ground, has sat at his feet for years, quietly provoking the display of the information he needs. The plan is to raise the expert to the height of celebrity and honour, and then—Manallace is not sure if it shall be public exposure, which may send him 'off his veray parfit gentil nut' and shorten the revenge, or private blackmail, compelling him to uphold the forgery as long as he lives. At this point the unobtrusive 'I', whose chief value has hitherto been to support Manallace morally by confirming the odiousness of his victim, asks: 'What about your own position?' Manallace answers: 'Oh—my position? I've been dead since—April, Fourteen,[1] it was.' He

---

[1] It was April, Fifteen, 'April of the first year of the War'. Kipling is never safe with dates. He complicates the dating of this tale by calling the woman Manallace loved 'Vidal's mother'. I can only suppose that he did this because names with him convey personality strongly, and she was to remain an impersonal object of devotion, particularized only through her sufferings. Vidal Benzaguen is a music-hall star in 'The Village that Voted the Earth was Flat' (published 1913). The *terminus a quo* is April 1891 when Dowson's 'Non sum qualis eram', which Manallace quotes, came out. Manallace was then 'the boy' of the Neminaka group—say, twenty-two—and

thinks that his real life ended when the woman he loved died. But the true answer comes some pages later in the two verbs 'groaned' and 'shuddered', of which Manallace is the subject. He is not dead, as he thought. His soul is alive, and the 'evil thing' begins to turn back on it. The plot is ripe and his desire within his grasp, when two shadows appear, which thicken rapidly into obstructions he cannot pass. Castorley's wife, it seems, is indicating, as if it were 'a sort of joke' between them, that she sees through Manallace's plot and would like to see it accomplished; and Castorley falls ill. That a man should hesitate to strike a foe who is already marked for death needs no explanation. The motive of Lady Castorley's hints appears gradually. She is the mistress of Gleeag, the surgeon who has operated on Castorley, and she is impatient for her husband's death. It is she, not Manallace, who has the really murderous mind, which is the reason that the last sentence of the tale is given over to her satisfaction. Worry is bad for Castorley, and she sees to it that he is worried, urging the sick man on against time with the book on which he and Manallace, now his 'most valued assistant', are collaborating. Manallace has explicitly intended to kill his enemy, by disgrace and the ruin of his ambition; but to revenge is one thing and to be the tool of a disloyal woman's callous impatience is quite another. Moreover, though this is never explicitly stated, there is, in effect though not in intention, the bond of shared work to hold him back. He postpones and evades. He goes abroad; he mislays some essential material; he lures Castorley up by-paths of interest. He is now driven into the position of protecting him; but there is no way out of the trap in which he has caught himself.

Manallace shuddered. 'If I stay abroad, I'm helping to kill him. If I help him to hurry up the book, I'm expected to kill him. *She* knows. . . . I'm not going to have him killed, though.'

Vidal's mother was unmarried, since Castorley proposed to her. This makes Vidal a star at twenty and Manallace about forty-nine at the end of the War. We must allow some years after that for the development of his plot and his holidays in the Shetlands and Faroes and the Low Countries. This fits Manallace very well, but makes Vidal a very youthful success in her arduous profession. I doubt, however, if Kipling worked all this out, any more than he worked out the connection between 'Mowgli's Brothers' and 'In the Rukh'. He thought of his own London years (1890–91) and then of a non-committal sobriquet for the woman.

He draws out their discussions; and Castorley grows worse. The atmosphere of the sick-room closes round us, and begins to vibrate with the apprehensions of the sick. It is clear that Castorley is being kept under drugs, and that his trouble is incurable. The last scene comes suddenly 'in steam perfumed with Friar's Balsam'. Castorley's confused mind, rambling through all the layers of past and present, throws up with acute distress the misgivings his wife has implanted in him, his complete distrust of her, and, from very deep down, the hidden, denied sense of guilt and remorse about the woman who rejected him.

> There was an urgent matter to be set right, and now that he had The Title and knew his own mind it would all end happily and he would be well again. Please would we let him go out, just to speak to—he named her; he named her by her 'little' name out of the old Neminaka days.

Again and again he appeals to Manallace, and Manallace, shaken, answers the appeals with reassurances. Then 'his pain broke through all the drugs, and the outcry filled the room'. Gleeag, telephoning the news of his patient's death to the narrator next morning, says: 'Perhaps it's just as well. . . . We might have come across something we couldn't have coped with. . . . We let him through as easily as possible.' This is exactly what Manallace has done, in both respects. Our last sight of him is at the Crematorium, taking out his black gloves. He has bound on his own shoulders the burden meant for Castorley's, by insisting to Lady Castorley that the book must be published. 'She is going to be known as his widow—for a while, at any rate', he says with spleen against the human hand that has helped to disarm him.

The question arises—and was meant to arise, I think—whether Manallace, even if his course had remained uncomplicated, could ever have 'pull[ed] the string of the shower-bath'. He is not one of Kipling's prompt young men. During the War he was of age to be assigned to the Office of Co-ordinated Supervisals, and by the end of the tale he is in his fifties. His reaction to his first suspicions of Castorley's wife is not to get his blow in first, but to evolve refinements of his plan. 'He wrapped himself lovingly and leisurely round his new task.' Moreover he is a man of letters. It is naturally in the realm of the imagination that he constructs, and he can find satisfaction there. All the more is he subject to the reprisals of the spirit he has raised, a spirit ironic and deadly. He has not accomplished his revenge, except in thought, or forgiven Castorley. It has been his 'interest'. He has let the Poison-tree root in his heart, and has nourished it with his grief and his deceit. But the enemy is not dead beneath the tree, as in Blake's poem; he is struck down by another agency, outside the circle of the branches. The upas crumbles, and Manallace is left 'emptied out' by hate, as he had been by his sacrificial love. It is a Limit, but there is no sign of another Renewal.

This view finds support if we follow Nodier's song of the mandragora, at the head of the tale, to its source in his fairy-story 'La Fée aux Miettes'.[1] In his preface to this story, Nodier tells us that he thinks the only way in which a fantastic tale can gain sufficient credence to be enjoyed in a sceptical age is to cause it to be told by a lunatic to a melancholic. This surprising recipe results in an introductory passage in which the melancholic, visiting the botanic gardens attached to a madhouse, finds a bed of mandragoras, largely uprooted and withered. He recalls that the mandragora is a powerful narcotic, 'propre à endormir les douleurs des misérables qui végètent sous ces murailles', and, plucking one, he addresses it as a power that carries into suffering souls a forgetfulness sweeter than sleep and almost as impassible as death. At this a young man rises from the ground, begging to know if the mandragora has spoken, if it has sung the song of the mandragora, whose single verse he repeats:

> *C'est moi, c'est moi, c'est moi!*
> *Je suis la Mandragore!*
> *La fille des beaux jours qui s'éveille a l'aurore—*
> *Et qui chante pour toi!*

When he is told that it is voiceless, like all other mandragoras, he takes it and drops it on the ground, saying: 'Then this is not yet the one.' We need not consider the tale he tells, for to Nodier the mandragora symbolizes poetical delusion, not hatred, and this has no bearing on Kipling's work. At the end, however, the melancholic, leaving the madhouse, meets a doctor who discourses with repellent pedantry on the nature of the plant. It is somniferous and poisonous. Its narcotic, anodyne, refrigerative and hypnotic properties have been known since the time of

---

[1] I owe this reference to my colleague, Miss G. E. Brereton.

Hippocrates. It can be used with success in cases of melancholy, and the juice of its root and rind is a powerful emeto-cathartic, which, however, more often occasions death than a cure.

This symbolism, appropriate to poetical delusion, becomes immensely more powerful when it is applied to revenge. This is the narcotic that Manallace finds for his empty and aching life. Since its origin is in the 'dayspring' and good days of his youth, it is indeed 'la fille des beaux jours'. It is anodyne, refrigerative, hypnotic. It cradles him in delusions for a while. But it is not the right mandragora and he lets it fall. Even the words of the doctor fit this meaning. Revengeful hatred is a powerful cathartic that can empty the mind of other pains, but it is more often deadly than sanative to the mind that entertains it.

We have, then a double reversal in our attitude to Manallace's quietly absorbed activity. His disconnected occupations, before we understand their object, are 'forlorn fancies'. When we understand it, they are suddenly seen to be purposive and part of a formidable intention. In the last stage, the whole scheme becomes again a 'forlorn fancy', a self-delusion, a narcotic that has lost its power. Nothing of the black dream is realized. One may say that it has had no effect on Castorley's life or death, except the ironically inverted effects of procuring him the recognition he thirsted for, putting Manallace into close relations with him and turning him into Castorley's defender. By this means he becomes aware at last of the strangled guilt and regret at the bottom of Castorley's mind, which, if he had known it earlier, would have prevented him from conceiving his purpose. Not even devils, but only delusions, have filled the empty house. It is Manallace alone who is poisoned by the mandragora; and it is not the right one.

The force of this conception is much increased by the nature of the man who yields to this deadly indulgence. The tale is written with such drastic and sober economy that the reader is sometimes put to it to trace a strong impression to its source; but the suggestion of charm that hangs about Manallace seems to derive from one or two pleasant turns of phrase, such as 'a day's gadzooking and vital-stapping', and from the conviction we receive of the narrator's unexpressed affection for him. All the emotions are kept battened down through the tale, except Castorley's which are liberally displayed. His skinless irritability, his overt malice and mean revenges, his craving appetite for importance are fully lighted. Manallace's long, agonizing service to the woman he loves is indicated only by her living eyes in her paralysed body, looking away from him, and by his renunciation of his literary ambitions; and this last is manifest only if we compare his cheerfully gruff refusal to 'write a real book'—'I've got my label and I'm not going to chew it off'—with the Neminaka days, long ago, when he was possessed, and 'was' Chaucer for a week. He gives away very little, while we watch him, and for pages he is removed from us. It follows, then, that an occasional adverb—'weakly', 'unsteadily',—attached to something he says, has a condensed, informative power beyond the usual force of the word, and that 'groaned' and 'shuddered' reverberate like thunder in an abyss. I cannot explain the effect of the black gloves at the end; it is like the occulting of a personality. Kipling, on the last page of a highly intellectualized tale, regains for a moment his spontaneous imaginative stroke.

Nothing hangs loose or is dropped. The 'something unpleasant' that Castorley wanted to say at Neminaka's, but was suppressed, breaks out during his delirium in a 'full, high, affected voice, unheard for a generation'. The negress in yellow satin outside the old Empire, who seems, when she is mentioned, a mere decorative blob of colour, is locked into the pattern when we learn, much later, that what the young and tipsy Manallace had said to her was that he had been faithful, Cynara, in his fashion. The grave and responsible irony in which the tale is drenched fills the key-sentences brimful. One of these comes in a couplet of Manallace's forgery:

Let all men change as Fortune may send,
But Knighthood beareth service to the end.

Castorley praises this as a 'splendid appeal for the spirit of chivalry', approving in literature what he denies in life; and by this time Manallace's service to the dead woman has taken strange shapes. A sort of refrain is introduced when Manallace says casually about his 'jocundly-sentimental' romances: 'If you save people thinking, you can do anything with them.' It is redirected as a comment on Castorley's rising reputation, and finally, weighted now with its full meaning, launched by Lady Castorley to its quivering target in her husband's self-esteem. This detail becomes tedious; but the tale has been much undervalued and misunderstood. It has even been called a structural tangle. It seems to me one of Kipling's great achievements. To analyse its patterns, as I have done, may give a false suggestion of rigidity and echoing emphasis. This is far from the case; all the exactly articulated detail is carried on a flowing and natural movement, and largely by the entirely convincing voices of the two men. There is in this tale, as Voiron says of Apis's performance in the bull-ring at Arles, 'a breadth of technique that comes of reasoned art, and, above all, the passion that arrives after experience'. The passion, however, and the compassion are implied, not expressed. It is, I suppose, an elderly tale, with its long retrospects and its quiet acceptance of human error and wastage, but it is certainly not cold, and very far from enfeebled. When it has once been fairly read, it is unforgettable. All its details are instinct with life, and, like seeds, throw up fresh growth as the years pass. The process does not stop with the solution of the 'enigma', any more than our sense of the strangeness of a particular fate stops when we know what happened to a man and what he did.

This tale can be treated as a pendant to 'The Wish House', though I do not suggest—I do not know—that the correspondences were conscious. Grace Ashcroft's passion—love—is active from the beginning to the end, in the world that is offered her. It progresses from plane to plane, seeking its proper nourishment, and at last feeds on the bread of sacrifice, for which it is ready; so that when she shows the leg that has 'turned' to Liz Fettley, in token that this is goodbye, her nature has been exercised in its deepest qualities, and she is fulfilled. One might say of her, as Kipling in *Souvenirs of France* says of the peasant-women who 'sold butter and eggs to our searchers for the dead, and religiously cheated them at every small turn' and then gave up half a day to 'walk five miles with flowers to lay on some grave of our people': 'After all, mankind is but made of earth and water; and our hearts, like muddy streams, cleanse themselves as they go forward.' But in 'Gertrude's Prayer' it is said that 'water out of bitter well' does not cleanse. The quality of the devotion that has filled Manallace's mind—extreme, self-abnegating, essentially unreturned—has brought him to middle life in a state of spiritual exhaustion—'dead', he says, and he becomes the prey of the antithetical passion of hatred, partly because he needs a new centre for his thought and partly because it seems a continuation of his former 'service' to revenge the injuries of the beloved dead woman. He is 'detonated', and his hatred burns with the same stubborn flame as his love. But his activity is delusive, and his intention and passion quail before the complexities of the real case, when he is forced to consider them. He is fulfilled in nothing, his art, his hatred, or even his embittered love.

The substance of 'Dayspring Mishandled' is subtle. It might—had the feminine element been stronger—have provided a theme for Henry James, or—had the evil been blacker and the setting less sophisticated—for Conrad. These subtleties Kipling chose to indicate by a method that is close to that of the sagas and not very far removed from the narratives of the Book of Kings. The tale is handled with a more conscious and relentless artistry than that of Naaman or that of Njál, and the 'inlay' is more intricate. It is a dramatic method, and yields its contents most readily to the reader who will 'act' the dialogue and respond to its shifts of tone. This generation is used to the exhausting exercises that are required of those who would follow out the last fine shade of meaning in James's scrupulous, voluble and highly personal style. The ear must be kept open to all that is poured into it, and the brain alert to sort and record it. But Kipling's work is full of deliberate gaps and abstentions. We are brought to the outside of the shut door or the edge of the gulf, and, if we have used our human understanding and our keenest attention, we have sufficient knowledge of what is going on behind the one or in the depth of the other. It is a method that relies silently on the reader, and it leaves him, if he does his part, as much aware of the profundities of the human spirit as *The Golden Bowl*. It is not surprising, however, that those who have trained their responses to the anxious delicacies of the one do not easily answer the proud and stringent demands of the other.

There is a brief coda to this chapter. It will surprise no-one that I have chosen to consider the prevalence of revenge in Kipling's tales; but this prevalence, and a growing attention to his later work, has led to the rash generalization, which is being blindly repeated, that Kipling learnt pity at about the time that he began to concentrate on the theme of healing. This is a great mistake. The concern with hatred and vengeance is closely connected, all through his work, with their 'opposites'. It is sometimes—I do not at all assert that it is always—the outrage to pity and tenderness that generates them, as a wound generates poison and is healed by purging it. It should be impossible to read 'Baa Baa, Black Sheep' without seeing this. But, before this tale was written, pity was to be read, clear enough, even in the worldly-wise *Plain Tales* and other stories deriving from his life in India. I will name a few examples rapidly, and they will not be taken from such obvious examples of pathos, direct and oblique, as 'Only a Subaltern' or 'Thrown Away'. The pity of 'In the Pride of his Youth' is given curtly by the facts, which are detailed and remorseless, and the over-heavy strokes of irony do not essentially injure the sadness of the tale of the young man who married secretly and too early, toiled and saved inordinately in India for the family in England, lost his baby by death and his wife by desertion, and threw up the promotion that came too late, because he was tired of work and an old man now. In the same book comes the delicately-touched, pitifully short history of little Muhammad Din, the *khitmatgar's* son. In *Under the Deodars*, though the title of 'A Wayside Comedy' is cynical enough as a description of the painful or guilty relations of the five isolated English people, yet the little hell at Kashima is terrifying, not because of the cynicism, but because of the helplessness of the prisoners, and to the young author they are 'the poor souls who are now lying there in torment'. In *Life's Handicap* the dry pity persists in 'Little Tobrah'. The first sentence of the tale is: 'Prisoner's head did not reach to the top of the dock', and it is enough to control the attitude of the four pages in which little Tobrah's life-history is set out, dispassionately and without surprise, by himself. It needs no reinforcement and no irony; it is to such little children that such grim necessities can come in India; and, though the grooms' wives wail in chorus, nobody, is astonished. Lastly there is in the gay and wicked fantasy of 'Namgay Doola' the figure of the tributary King, with a Kingdom four miles square and eleven thousand feet above the sea on the road to Tibet, and a revenue of some four hundred pounds, expended on the maintenance of an elephant and a standing army of five men; and from this comic-opera set-up, when the narrator suggests that the King shall send the recalcitrant Namgay Doola to jail, rises unexpectedly the pity of experience.

'Sahib,' the King answered, shifting a little on the cushions, 'once and only once in these forty years sickness came upon me so that I was not able to go abroad. In that hour I made a vow to my God that I would never again cut man or woman from the light of the sun and the air of God; for I perceived the nature of the punishment.'

It was on the same note, in the 'Half-Ballade of Waterval', that Kipling closed the blotted account of the Boer War.

CHAPTER SIX

Healing

The theme of healing is not, like that of revenge, one of Kipling's original themes. It emerges strongly in what I have called the halcyon period of his art, the tales that were collected in *Actions and Reactions* and *Rewards and Fairies*, and continues to act as a powerful focus of his imagination until in *Limits and Renewals* half the tales are, in one way or another, concerned with it. It is not, therefore, a development due to the War, though the War gave it a special colouring and stimulated its growth. In so far as it appears at all in his earlier work, it is incidental or consequential. The famine in 'William the Conqueror' is the test of Scott's quality and the setting of his love for a girl who shares his work and his allegiance. When she sees him in the sunset, 'a young man, beautiful as Paris, a god in a halo of golden dust, walking slowly at the head of his flocks, while at his knee ran small naked cupids'—the children he has saved by his 'absurd' performances with goats—Kipling can use the simile of the god, not only because of the pastoral grouping, but because Scott has been indeed the preserver of life and restorer of hope. The stress of the tale, however, lies on work and service and the kind of woman who understands their claims, not specifically on healing. Elsewhere the string is slightly touched now and again. Thus Kim, 'overborne by strain, fatigue, and the weight beyond his years', is drenched, massaged and fed back into life by the Sahiba, in a packed page in which the sense of wonder, so strong all through the book, sweeps in the ancient curative methods of the East; while, when the little boy of 'Baa Baa, Black Sheep' returns from the House of Desolation to the security of his mother's love, we see a sample of her dealings with him.

It is significant that *Actions and Reactions* begins and ends with a tale of healing. It is the new theme. In the collections of his middle and later life, Kipling seems to have intended the first and last tales to serve as the pillars of an archway, corresponding to each other in some part of their meaning, and framing the section of life we see between them. This refinement in arrangement begins with *Many Inventions*, but it is not apparent unless we take the 'tides' that overset poor Dowse's mind in 'The Disturber of Traffic' in the sense that they bear in the introductory poem, as 'the wheel and drift of things', the terrible 'toil' of the Lord, which must be veiled from man lest he should see too clearly for his sanity. If we do this, the connection with 'The Children of the Zodiac' is sufficiently clear, though the modes of the two tales are entirely different. In the allegory we have the 'trampling stars'—the Heavenly Houses that destroy men at the appointed time—and the 'veil' of daily life and necessary labour that hangs between men and the mystery of their fate and enables them to support it. In *The Day's Work* the two visionary tales, 'The Bridge Builders' and 'The Brushwood Boy', frame the concrete, busy, limited world between them and give it another dimension. I should not care to make too much of the correspondences between 'The Captive' and 'Below the Mill Dam' in *Traffics and Discoveries*, but Zigler's half-amused, half disconcerted experience of British phlegm in South Africa is confronted by a demand that Britain shall be brought up to date. There is substance in Zigler's criticism, and the lessons of the Boer War have not all been well learnt. *A Diversity of Creatures* has an ironic opposition of first and last tales. The far view of the world of the future, when war is unthinkable and few men see death, is answered by 'Mary Postgate' In *Debits and Credits* there are no substantial links between 'The Enemies to Each Other and 'The Gardener'. *Limits and Renewals*, however, beginning with the reduction to nullity of Manallace's life—a limit that cannot be passed—ends with the ultimate renewals of 'Uncovenanted Mercies'.

In the first tale of *Actions and Reactions*, 'An Habitation Enforced', the healing is already at all levels, physical, intellectual and spiritual. George Chapin, broken by the pace and strain of the American financial world, and his wife Sophie find health and satisfaction in the ancient, composed, fruitful life of the English countryside. When Kipling made his first acquaintance with country life in Vermont, ten years before, he wrote in 'From Tideway to Tideway' that there the visitor 'is set down to listen to the normal beat of his own heart—a sound that very few men have ever heard'. This was in the New England winter, and the conditions and his own sensitiveness exaggerated the rarity of the discovery. 'An Habitation Enforced' is soaked in summer air, and the heart-beat that steadies the Chapins is the pulse of nature, of rural society and, to quote Mr Eliot, of the past in the present. Sophie, delighted and growing daily into closer comradeship with her husband, thrusts her roots at once into the good soil; George, more uncertain of himself and suspicious of his surroundings, takes longer to yield to acclimatization, but the birth of his son and the restoration of the derelict estate he buys in the Weald combine to fix him. These agencies are the magical elements of 'A Charm', with which Kipling introduced *Rewards and Fairies*. We are told to take a double handful of English earth, praying meanwhile for the 'mere uncounted folk' that lie beneath it, and lay it upon the heart.

> *It shall sweeten and make whole*
> *Fevered breath and festered soul;*
> *It shall mightily restrain*
> *Over-busy hand and brain,*

(as it did with George Chapin) while the English flowers, sought through their seasons,

> *Shall restore a failing sight.*
> *These shall cleanse and purify*
> *Webbed and inward-turning eye;*
> *These shall show thee treasures hid,*
> *Thy familiar fields amid,*

(as they were to do to Frankwell Midmore in '"My Son's Wife"'). The bodily terms of the verses are seen to be metaphors; the inward-turning eye is the eye of the self-absorbed, misdirected by melancholy or vanity; and in most of the tales of healing both body and mind are involved. The two aspects are found apart in *Rewards and Fairies*. 'Marklake Witches' is built round the invention of the stethoscope and 'A Doctor of Medicine' round an outbreak of plague, while in 'The Wrong Thing' a disease of the mind, an obsession of inferiority and hatred, is dissolved. This separation, however, is rare, and hardly found outside the children's books. Often Kipling takes pains to relate or juxtapose the healing of the flesh and of the soul, as he does in 'The Eye of

Allah'. It is when the Abbot of St Illod's, himself a physician, is storing the opium from Spain in the cell behind the hospital kitchen-chimney, that he speaks to the young artist, whose mistress is dead, of the pain of the soul for which 'there is, outside God's Grace, but one drug; and that is a man's craft, learning, or other helpful motion of his own mind'. The tales that turn on the ills of the soul sometimes employ fantasy; for the healing of an aching imagination Kipling in 'On the Gate' and 'Uncovenanted Mercies' uses the salves the imagination itself can provide. It is the comprehensiveness of the theme, at many levels and in many connections, that makes the classification of these tales as tales of disease or of neurosis inadequate. It is as if we called Shakespeare's Romances plays of error and loss. They are so; but the description is insufficient. It is against the pervasiveness of the conception of healing in the later books that we see, in strong relief, the tragedies of those who are not healed, Manallace's mistakes in diagnosis and Helen's erroneous treatment of her hurt. Even within the tales of restoration there are marginal figures who are not so lucky. In 'Fairy-Kist' Wollin is saved, and the interest of the tale is focused on his saving, but Jimmy Tigner, standing unsteadily in the surf, is casually washed back to sea. 'He'd been tried too high—too high', says Keede. 'I had to sign his certificate a few weeks later. No! he won't get better.' And this fleeting touch recalls the verses that precede the tale, in which the returned soldier in the mental home speaks with sad detachment of himself:

> *And it was not disease and crime*
> *Which got him landed there,*
> *But because they laid on My Mother's Son*
> *More than a man could bear.*
> *What with noise, and fear of death,*
> *Waking, and wounds and cold,*
> *They filled the Cup for My Mother's Son*
> *Fuller than it could hold.*

The wide black sea of human misery washes round these green islets of healing and throws its spray ashore, and the writer looks out over it with compassion and spiritual hunger.

'The House Surgeon', the last tale in *Actions and Reactions*, leads us into shadows and uncertainties. The house of the title, open and sunny like Friar's Pardon in 'An Habitation Enforced', is not, like that, a healing presence but requires to have its own evil excised. This is a bodiless oppression of despair and horror, directed on it at times 'like a burning glass', and followed, when it is shut off, by a 'live grief beyond words', as if it were a dumb thing's helpless desire to explain. The evil is diagnosed when 'I' traces the former owner, a rigid, elderly, unlovely Evangelical spinster, who is convinced that her younger sister's fall from a window was suicide and consigned her to damnation. The house and its innocent inmates are filled with the reflection of her obsessed brooding. When, after a narrow escape from a similar fall herself, Miss Moultrie is persuaded to revisit the house and examine the window, the house is cleansed. We do not enter the room with her or know what intimations she received, but the burden of the double anguish is lifted.

This tale is closely related in subject and treatment to two in Kipling's next book, 'In the Same Boat' and 'The Dog Hervey'. The first of these is straightforward; it is also the only one of the three in which the mysterious and painful manifestations are completely rationalized, leaving no residue of the preternatural. The horrific recurrent dreams that afflict Conroy and Miss Henschil, hanging between them and natural life, are ascribed in the end to pre-natal shock; the images in them—the accident at sea, the encounter with lepers on the sandy, windy island—derive from the experiences of their mothers before they were born. 'The Dog Hervey' is to me Kipling's most difficult tale, but it is the details that are difficult, not the theme. This can be defined without misgiving. The desolate longing of a woman makes a vehicle for itself out of the little sickly dog she cherishes, and projects its wraith into the hallucinations of the drunkard who, years before, was kind to her. This, then, is a tale of sorcery, of such a 'sending' as we might read of in a northern folk-tale or find paralleled in the beliefs of a savage people. The scene, however, is contemporary, and the unhappy plight of the young 'witch' is carefully accounted for. It is not unlike that of Conrad's Flora de Barral, though Moira Sichliffe has no comeliness and no romantic love to cloak her, but is everyway ungainly and embarrassing, though courageous. The 'mid-Victorian mansion of peculiar villainy', where she lives, was the home where her father, a retired doctor, received 'stormy' young men, patched them up, insured them heavily, and 'let them out into the world again—with an appetite!' One man, Shend, saved her from the insults to which she was exposed, but he has effaced himself, for honourable reasons. Moira is not aware of her power, and is troubled by the behaviour of the dog on whom she discharges her anguished love and deprivation. Harvey's sickliness, like Shend's drunken illusions, is a state penetrable by the psychic force. The dog is bewildered and suffers; he sits outside one particular door in the corridor where the young men used to be kept, and he fixes the narrator with 'an intense, lop-sided stare', as if trying to attain some object through him. The function of 'I' in this tale is much what it was in 'The House Surgeon'; he does not here deliberately explore the strange currents that flow past him, but he is sensitive to them; perhaps in some measure they work through him, too, but this is to me the obscurest part of the story, and I am not sure how Kipling conceived the psychic mechanism that made the shadow perceptible beside the closed door and convinced Shend that the squinting dog in his delusions knew his fellow-traveller, or whether, indeed, we are to understand that the dog's appearances began, or grew more frequent, after he met the narrator. At all events, 'I' acts as liaison, bridges the separation of the lovers, and removes the obstructions to the healing exercise of love. In so doing he also returns Harvey, 'cowering beneath some unfair burden', to natural doghood, and the joyous flurry of a normal dog-fight brings the tale momentarily into full daylight. At the end, 'I' declining to attempt an explanation, calls the strange sequence of events 'all woman-work', and says it scared him horribly.

It is hard to find direct evidence in Kipling's work for what is sometimes said, that his attitude to women retained something of primitive awe, yet it carries conviction; it provides the counterweight to his belief that she should not attempt to play a man's part in a man's world. In 'The Pleasure-Cruise' one of the returned dead of the Great War, disquieted to find that 'the Island now stands again with shut eyes on the brink of fate', and that this is largely the responsibility of the women, wonders why they seek political power, since 'the power of women in themselves is dreadfully sufficient'. This is the power of Mrs Bathurst and of the frivolous little girl who destroyed Wressley of the Foreign Office. But beyond this, it seems, the unassuaged anguish or desire of a woman, not mitigated by the daily practical compromises of a man's life, can generate a psychic force like that exerted by Miss Moultrie or Moira Sichliffe, and this fits her to make contact, more readily than a man, with powers or existences outside human life. In Western civilization these powers are overlaid and forgotten. Miss Moultrie and Moira Sichliffe are ignorant of what they have done; they are unconscious 'witches'. When Kipling, therefore, deals with these borderlands of consciousness, setting his tales in a concrete, substantial modern world, with tennis-parties, hydropathic establishments, and the 10.8 train from Waterloo rolling out milk-cans at every stop, he creates extreme types to enable the intrusion of the preternatural into it, the fanatic Miss Moultrie, the blind, craving woman in '"They"', the lonely, contorted Moira Sichliffe and the archetypal peasant-woman, Grace Ashcroft. Like so many of his deep convictions, this leaves its traces, under carefully controlled conditions, in the children's books. There are Priestesses in 'The Knife and the Naked Chalk', who make prayers to the Old Dead in the Barrows, ask questions of the Gods and answer on their behalf, and hold in their hands the spiritual life of their tribes; nor does the woman in 'The Cat that Walked by Himself', even earlier in the history of man, require any instruction before she lets down her hair beside the fire and makes a Magic. She is a mother, and so is the Priestess of the Flint Men, and perhaps the figure of the Mother in Kipling, obscured as it often is with period draperies, holds some remnant of this ancient awe.

These three tales, then, are built with folk-lore material, a haunting, a sending and—to stretch the point a little—a curse. Since these influences are not willed but imposed in ignorance, all three tales illustrate the lines in 'The Rabbi's Song', that follows 'The House Surgeon' and closes *Actions and Reactions*:

> *The arrows of our anguish*
> *Fly farther than we guess.*

The victims who are stuck by the arrows are innocent and, in two tales, entirely ignorant of their source. Their world fills with a mysterious pain and darkness as the 'shadow of [the] past' moves over them, and the imaginative diversity and infectious force with which these sufferings are conveyed should of themselves suggest that we have to do with more than particular queer cases. When

Nurse Blaber in 'In the Same Boat' is able to confirm her patient's recovery by telling her how her dream originated, she says: 'You never imagined the thing. It was laid on you.' These tales are about the burdens that are laid on men, without any fault of theirs and sometimes because they have been doing their best. The hauntings in themselves constitute an upper layer of meaning; below that there is the ultimate mystery of the general condition of man, of which they are examples or symbols. Kipling had a profound sense of this strange and, to human judgment, unjust dispensation, as he had of the capacity of the human being for suffering and his loneliness in it. It is here that we find the likeness between these earlier tales and those of war injuries, which I consider later in this chapter.

If this is so, then any improbabilities that may appear in the medical parts of the tales, exceeding what might be expected as the result of the inevitable foreshortening of the form when its content is so complex, are only superficial flaws. They cannot split the heart of the tale. In these three stories, however, professional healers play a very small part. They appear only in 'In the Same Boat', and there they are concerned not with their patients' dreams, but with their addiction to a drug to which their misery has driven them. One of the specialists disbelieves in the dreams; the other has the imagination and boldness to attempt to break Conroy's self-centredness by putting his fellow-sufferer, Miss Henschil, in his charge on a night journey. Here, as in the other tales, it is love, of some kind, at some level, that is the true healer. The doctors, like 'I' in the other stories, place their patients in such a position that it can do its work. Their fellowship in misfortune, their efforts to help each other, have already saved and renewed their smothered souls, before Nurse Blaber, less sceptical and specialized than the doctors, is able to remove their last apprehensions. There is no need to comment on the lovers of 'The Dog Hervey'. In 'The House Surgeon' it is Miss Moultrie's distorted and despairing love for her sister that has haunted the house; when the despair is abolished, the unburdened love can do its work of renewal, and even the unhealthy, ageing body moves youthfully again.

There is not, then, in these three tales, anything that directly illustrates the new principles and techniques in psychiatry of the twentieth century. These may, however, have been in Kipling's mind. The interest in them provided a climate of thought in which traditional material, that had a deep symbolic meaning for him, could be related to the reality of daily life and explored for its human content. There is a great difference between the early supernatural tales, 'The Return of Imray, and 'The Lost Legion', on one hand, where the traditional material is accepted and the writer devotes himself to evoking an atmosphere that will engender faith, and 'The House Surgeon', 'In the Same Boat' and 'The Dog Hervey' on the other, which are moved by a positive moral force and by a far-reaching imagination, speculating on the unknown potentialities of human nature and the ways in which they may work. The likeness between the three later tales, however, does not permit us to assume that Kipling had a programme in writing them. The publication of them covers five years, and they are full of observations and interests and briefly seen sections of people's lives and occupations, as Kipling's later stories always are. He has told us in *Something of Myself* how a chance-caught remark in a local train at Cape Town fertilized a ten-year old memory of a woman's face and voice in New Zealand, so that the whole tale of 'Mrs Bathurst' slid smoothly into his mind. The tale naturally contained more than the logical product of the remark and the remembrance; the excitement had been passed through other layers of the memory and the imagination. It is only, then, if a writer tells us that we can be sure of the starting-point of a tale, though we can sometimes be sure of the memories it drew into its growth. It is plain—more than one critic has observed it—that in 'The House Surgeon' Kipling found the situation that would give meaning to the spirit of despondency which haunted the large, bright house at Torquay where he lived for a time, before it drove him away. The Moultrie sisters are developed from the three old maids who had inhabited it for thirty years, and to them he added, I believe, the unforgotten Evangelical woman of his childhood. I have sometimes wondered if the most striking scene of 'The Dog Hervey', the corridor behind the baize door, flanked with pitchpine doors of Gothic design, where the flagitious doctor kept his rewarding patients, is a 'metagrobolised' memory from his house-hunting days, 'when a "comfortable nursery" proved to be a dark padded cell at the end of a discreet passage!' The discovery, in its context of hopeful parental solicitude, is the sort of shock that is remembered, and shocks often generate the creative spirit. This is a guess, and guesses are of little validity in criticism, except to rest and refresh the intent 'ear' of the critic; but I am not unwilling to remind myself, in a study that is directed so much to the continuity and modification of Kipling's themes and subjects, that his tales often grew from some fortuitous, concrete datum. How strong, then, must the interest have been that shaped this multifarious material to the same purpose, setting the three tales the same burden to carry and the same hope of healing to aspire to.

Kipling's later tales hook into each other in all directions; if one is lifted up for inspection, several others come up attached to it; but the closest links are not always those that are at first apparent. Thus 'Unprofessional' has been related to 'A Doctor of Medicine' because both of them have to do with astrology, but the closer link is with 'Marklake Witches'. The two stories from *Rewards and Fairies* are companion pictures of medicine old and new, presented to the children, and no imaginative act of faith in astrology is required of them. Nicholas Culpeper's successful handling of the plague-stricken village is not, as he thinks, due to his reading of the stars, but to common-sense, devotion and a lucky chance. Puck takes his astrological expositions very lightly and puts down the victory to 'a high courage tempered with sound and stubborn conceit'; and the concluding verses, dismissing with amusement the world-picture of the introductory 'Astrologer's Song' as one of the 'enormous and manifold errors' of our fathers, praises their 'excellent heart', that wrought so well with such faulty tools. In 'Unprofessional', however, the influence of the stars is taken seriously, and the 'tides' they cause in human cells are traced and logged with the latest scientific devices. Like 'Marklake Witches' the tale deals with an advance in science, and with these two we may associate 'The Eye of Allah'. 'Marklake Witches' is simplest, as befits one of the tales that children were to read 'before people realized that they were meant for grown-ups'. René Laennec, French prisoner on parole, discusses his invention, the stethoscope, with the shrewd local wise-man, and meets the hostility of superstitious fear in the village folk and of conservative professional jealousy in Dr Break. It will not deter him, but his science will not save the high-spirited girl who tells the tale, in ignorance of its meaning and of her own disease, nor the outer ring of the momentarily seen sick—old Gaffer Macklin and young Copper—nor yet himself. This is a straightforward tale; 'The Eye of Allah' is complex. It tells of the possibility of a great scientific advance that looms for an hour and is declined, because it is untimely. Abbot Stephen destroys in the presence of Roger Bacon the microscope that John the artist has brought from the Moorish parts of Spain. But though the problem of scientific advance in a world not ready for it is central, the tale, like many of Kipling's, is doing several things at once. The scientist is contrasted not only with Abbot Stephen, the administrator, but with John of Burgos, the artist, 'to whom men were but matter for drawings'. John makes no protest against the breaking of the Eye of Allah; he has used it to get 'patterns' for the devils he has limned in his Great Luke, and has finished with it; his trade, he says, is with the outside shapes of things. Abbot Stephen, however, is a physician, like Roger of Salerno and Thomas the Infirmarian who, with Roger Bacon, plead against the destruction; he knows well what he does and why. The image of birth knits the themes together. John's Jewish mistress dies in childbed. He himself brings his stored conceptions triumphantly to birth. But when Abbot Stephen destroys the microscope under the hungry eyes of the men of science, a birth is aborted. 'The choice lies between two sins. To deny the world a Light which is under our hand, or to enlighten the world before her time.' When the little group of monks, ruler, artist, scientist and working physicians, walk on the leads to get foul water to put under the Eye of Allah, they see, in one of Kipling's marvellous compressed sentences of landscape, atmosphere, period and symbol

> three English counties laid out in evening sunshine around them; church upon church, monastery upon monastery, cell after cell, and the bulk of a vast cathedral moored on the edge of the banked shoals of sunset.

The moored cathedral is a ship of war, not yet wrecked on shoals in the blindness between one day and the next. The whole principle of order of their world lies in beauty and visible menace round them. It is not only that the audacious scientist would face the fire, but that in the struggle what order there is would be shaken and debased. The Eye of Allah would but bring 'more division and greater darkness in this dark age'. Western man is not yet ready to see with it. The claws of the *immedicabile cancer* that has gripped Anne of Norton are not yet to be blunted. The choir in the dark church sings '*Hora novissima, tempora pessima sunt*'. But Thomas, the doubting Infirmarian, who has feared lest his dream of the 'little animals of Varro' should be sin, has now seen them through the microscope, 'Life created and rejoicing—the work of the Creator', to be sanctified—though not yet—'to the service of His sick'.

The tales are further linked together by the verses attached to them. 'Untimely', the prelude to 'The Eye of Allah', leads directly to 'Unprofessional', as 'The Threshold', which follows the latter tale, points back to 'The Eye of Allah'. All the inventions of men, we hear in 'Untimely', have been discovered more than once. There is pity for the discoverer, who received 'oppression and scorn for his wages', and greater pity for the 'wise souls'

> *which foresaw the evil of loosing*
> *Knowledge or Art before time, and aborted*
> *Noble devices and deep-wrought healings*
> *Lest offence should arise.*

But, at last, 'Heaven delivers on earth the Hour that cannot be thwarted'. In 'Unprofessional' we share such an hour. All external obstructions are removed, and the three associated scientists—pathologist, surgeon, astronomer—backed by all that money can buy and the wit of man devise, held together by the bonds of a personal affection rising out of their war experience as well as by devotion to the job, explore 'the swab of culture which we call our world' and the 'influences' external to it, to such effect that Mrs Berners does not die of cancer, like Anne of Norton, but is healed. What is achieved is only 'some data and inferences which may serve as some sort of basis for some detail of someone else's work in the future'. Dawn has not yet broken, but the dawn-wind stirs strongly in the darkness, and the tale thrills with expectancy. 'What do you suppose is the good of Research?', asks Harries, and Loftie replies: 'God knows. . . . Only—only it looks—sometimes—as if He were going to tell.'

To get the emotion of such a story, the sense of the exacting and complex toil, of the endless recording of minute facts, the emergence of unexpected questions, the startling moments when the shadow of a colossal and distant truth is glimpsed—an intellectual passion, humanized in this case by being focused on to a particular patient, so that the measure of what pure knowledge means when applied to human pain can be kept in view—Kipling needed to draw on the detail of a specific line of inquiry. He could not achieve the effect by means of general terms, and it is not likely that he could, even with expert help, make use of any authentic research, past or present. The established achievements, such as Laennec's stethoscope, were too confined, and would hardly yield that trembling of the edges of revelation that he wished to suggest. The short story has no room for the normal pace of research, or for the prudent delays in the clinical application of its results. He was forced to make the project and the procedure 'unprofessional'. So he turned to the stars, whose influence on human lives was a commonplace of the India he knew, as he showed in *Kim* and much later in 'The Debt', and had been a commonplace in England, three hundred or so years before. 'We can't tell on what system this dam' dynamo of our universe is wound, but we know we're in the middle of every sort of wave as we call 'em. They used to be "influences".' We move through the tale from point to point of brilliantly illuminated detail, the logging and filming of minute stellar 'tides' in the cells of tissues, the timing of operations by planetary hours, the setting of the patient's bed on a compass bearing—an intricate fantasy, telling strongly in the laboratory setting of 'taps and sinks and glass shelves', typed papers and cages of white mice, until the astrology of 'A Doctor of Medicine' comes to look less like a historical curiosity than the clumsy and purblind beginning of a new science. The vision in 'The Astrologer's Song', of the predominance of the stars over all earthly things is restored on a vaster scale when Herries, 'drunk with the ferment of (his) own speculations', describes the ultimate heavens as 'all one generating station of one Power drawn from the Absolute, and of one essence and substance with all things'. This, 'The Threshold' tells us, was also the vision of 'resolute, unsatisfied Ionia', but the truth had been 'choked at birth'; and the imagination loops back to 'The Eye of Allah' and ties it up to the greatest historical example of the delayed dawn of knowledge. The advance comes at last through the spilt 'blood of the vanguards'.

The greatest obstruction that the friends have to meet is the suicidal impulse that draws the already convalescent Mrs Berners to the grave they have cheated of her. These spasms of insanity have been interpreted by Mr Edmund Wilson as the aftermath of the war, and it may be that they do indicate the contemporary situation of the human race, strung between the science that can save and a despairing trend to self-destruction. Kipling's later books are full of symbols and echoing implications that vibrate faintly in an enormous distance. These symbols, however, do not rise up from the unconscious mind to impose themselves upon the author's art. They are accepted and willed, and planted on the main path of a story; they do not subtly contradict what it asserts. Their first value is always that of a fact necessary to the working out of the tale. Thus Mrs Berners' suicidal impulse is primarily an example of the unforeseen, critical difficulties that may open on a team of scientists as the result of an apparently successful interference with the course of nature, requiring from them, on the spur of the moment, yet greater acts of imagination and devotion. In the same way cancer, in the several stories in which it appears, is there in each case because the tale requires the imposition of a long strain by a disease that can be slow, insidious, painful, secret and mortal. The victim must die hard, and with full consciousness of the act. This is the case with Bella Armine in 'A Madonna of the Trenches' and Grace Ashcroft in 'The Wish House', and with the Girl and Leo in 'The Children of the Zodiac'. Castorley alone remains in ignorance, as the history of Manallace's revenge requires. It has been often said that Kipling was obsessed with cancer. Perhaps; art is often made out of obsessions. Every age finds death dressed in some prevailing fashion, and cancer is specially a modern dread. It occurs a little more often in his work than tuberculosis, which I have not seen ascribed to an obsession or interpreted as a symbol. If, moreover, we accept cancer as a symbol for rejected and frustrated love, as Mr Edmund Wilson suggests, we must remember that the rejection and frustration are the material of victory. Except for 'Dayspring Mishandled', these are not tales of defeat.

In 'The Children of the Zodiac', the earliest tale in which cancer occurs, it is certainly symbolic, but certainly not of rejected love. The whole fable is an arrangement of symbols. It is a statement of the conditions of human life and of the spirit in which these can be supported, and the characters are drawn from the ancient Signs of the Zodiac. Half of these are the mysterious slayers of men from their heavenly Houses; the others (but Kipling counts the Twins as two and omits the Goat) wander on earth and, conforming in time to the modes of human life, are able, as half-gods, to strengthen and comfort men, though at the cost of sharing their experience. Given this scheme, it was obvious that the Archer and the Crab must be slayers, the lords of the quick and the slow doom. The procedure of the Crab is wholly appropriate; it touches the Girl on her woman's breast, and she goes on loving, and Leo, the singer, on the apple of his throat, and he sings his song to the end. But this gigantic Crab is much more than a specific disease; it is all the sorrow and evil of the world that tries to stifle the singer's voice and fastens on the heart of his wife. The arbitrary division of the Signs, not merely into the benevolent and the malevolent, but into beings of two different orders, confuses the allegory. By the end Leo is man confronting his fate. Yet since both the Houses—the agents of fate—and the Children, who show men how to endure it, are of heavenly origin, we perhaps have already the conception that is expressed in 'The Astrologer's Song':

> *Through abysses unproven,*
> *And gulfs beyond thought,*
> *Our portion is woven,*
> *Our burden is brought.*
> *Yet They that prepare it,*
> *Whose Nature we share,*
> *Make us who must bear it*
> *Well able to bear.*

'The Wish House' and 'A Madonna of the Trenches' (and 'The Gardener' may be counted with these, though it does not deal with cancer) are tales of love and death. Human love is opposed to the power that seems to defeat and nullify it. In the first two love triumphs; in the third it receives consolation, though without understanding it. In 'A Madonna of the Trenches', which is designed and painted very boldly, the lovers, Mrs Armine and Sergeant Godsoe, sure that they have all eternity ahead of them, can endure their several capitivities to disease and deprivation because 'an hour or two won't make any odds'. In 'The Wish House', Mrs Grace Ashcroft, with no clearer outlook on the issues of life and death than a yearning hope that 'the pain *do* count', forces her mortal disease to become the very medium of her love for Harry Mockler, and purchases his life with hers. The preluding poem, '"Late Came the God"', presents the wound of the poisoned knife, which is both her love and her disease, as the punishment for wrong and contempt, and the contempt, as the tale makes clear, has lain in Grace Ashcroft's cruelty and her unscrupulous taking of bodily love, before she found her master in Harry Mockler. She responds to punishment by making it the instrument of a sacrificial passion.

So she lived while her body corrupted upon her.
  And she called on the Night for a sign, and a Sign was allowed,
  And she builded an Altar and served by the light of her Vision—
    Alone, without hope of regard or reward, but uncowed,
  Resolute, selfless, divine.
    These things she did in Love's honour . . .
  What is a God beside Woman? Dust and derision!

It is plain that in these two tales and in 'The Gardener' death must confront love in palpable presence. So Helen Turrell's unacknowledged mother-love is set against the 'merciless sea of black crosses', the composed rows of the sacrifice of youth in the war-cemetery of Hagenzeele Third. But the love between man and woman, which is more immediately of the body than that of a mother for her grown son, must face the disintegration of the flesh by disease and death, the defiling and destruction of the earthly language of love. Grace Ashcroft is

bound face to face with death till death.

In her isolation she recognizes, foresees and invokes every pang. Her unexhausted physical passion and possessiveness, and the completeness of the offering they exact, cleanse her spirit by their very intensity. In the verses that follow 'The Wish House' love and corruption are again opposed in the figures of the leper and his woman under the loaded gallows, 'very merry, breaking bread'. She is 'whole and clean', but the corruption of his flesh does not hinder their delight in each other,

Since in perfect Love, saith Scripture, can be no excess at all.

Rahere, as he sees them, is relieved from the horror of darkness that has sunk his spirit.

In 'A Madonna of the Trenches' we hear little of Bella Armine's well-hidden 'trouble'. 'She'd 'ad a bit of a gatherin' in 'er breast, I believe. But she never talked of 'er body much to any one', is all her nephew knows of it. We see little of her. Sergeant John Godsoe holds the centre of the story, and his testimony is given amongst all the frozen dreadfulness of winter warfare in the trenches, where the landmarks are the four dead Warwicks and the two Zouave skeletons by the old sugar-boiler. This is one of the framed tales. It is drawn out of Strangwick, an ex-Runner of a South London Battalion, after he has collapsed at a Lodge of Instruction, by Brother Keede, Senior Warden and general practitioner, who had him under his hands on the Somme in 'Eighteen, when 'he went to bits'. Kipling had more than once approached a situation of high intensity through an imperfect and baffled narrator; here the lighting is thrown both ways and reflected back, more strongly than usual, on the teller of the tale. Strangwick, in seeing the meeting of his Aunt's spirit and John Godsoe, has had more than he can take. He has seen what has made nonsense of all his world and knocked the bottom out of all his presuppositions, and seen it expressed through persons whose age and humdrum closeness to his own life double the shock. 'There wasn't a single gor-dam thing left abidin' for me to take hold of, here or hereafter. If the dead *do* rise—and I saw 'em—why—why *anything* can 'appen.' He has masked his trouble as war-nerves, babbling hysterically about the creaking of the frozen 'stiffs' under the duck-boards, but this, says Keede, is the real thing at last. When the truth has been exacted from him, he sleeps quietly, and a step has been made towards his recovery. This, then, the first of Kipling's tales of neurosis in an ex-service man, is not really concerned with a war-injury at all, though the war setting throws all the values into strongest relief. We are helped to gauge the power and the range of the love streaming through Bella Armine and John Godsoe because the revelation wholly demolishes the defence-system of a cheerful young Runner, well-protected by youthful callousness and short views, and leaves him a nervous wreck. In the other cases the neurosis is at the centre of the story and is the direct product of the War.

It was natural that Kipling should be drawn to write of these obscure and tragic injuries. He had already explored the shadow-world, trodden in loneliness and fear by the mind that feels its sanity giving way under strain. He had also explored the mysterious borderlines of consciousness and haunted places and people. These hauntings are sometimes merely recorded, sometimes tentatively explained, but it is not until his later work that they are exorcized and the wounds of consciousness healed. With this change of interest, as I have already indicated, the tales take up a new element, that of detection. There enters them a character, often serving as narrator, who gropes for a clue and aims at a solution. He may be a professional healer or an amateur cast by chance for the part. The cases are often intricate, and there is more commentary and explanation than Kipling usually conceded. There is also in two of the pre-war tales, as has been seen, an irreducible element of the preternatural. With the appearance of the war cases, this preternatural element drops out. There was no need to look for strange and exceptional cases; too many were present in the accepted order of things. The thought that we are fearfully and wonderfully made had always been much in Kipling's mind. He had dealt in types, but he had been far from over-simplifying human nature. Now he shows himself more and more aware of the frailty of man's body and brain, his liability to manifold injury, his capacity for suffering and his fortitude in it. We have these treasures in earthen vessels.

We first meet the injured and shell-shocked men in the Lodge Faith and Works in ' "In the Interests of the Brethren" '. This tale was written during the War, and it is free from the notes of bitterness and apprehension that strike across those written in the subsequent peace. It is hopeful as to 'the possibilities of the Craft at this juncture', even if it sometimes crosses Brother Burges's mind 'that Grand Lodge may have thrown away its chance in the war almost as much as the Church has'. Men from hospitals and leave-trains, whose only practical creed since childhood has been Masonry ('The Fatherhood of God, an' the Brotherhood of Man; an' what more in Hell *do* you want?') find their way to the Lodge of Instruction, where their minds are helped by the fellowship and the ritual and their bodies succoured by the ham-sandwiches made from Brother Lemming's specially-fattened pig. 'All Ritual is fortifying,' says Brother Burges. 'Ritual's a natural necessity for mankind. The more things are upset, the more they fly to it.' So the casualty struck dumb with shock manages to articulate greetings from his Lodge in Wales, while in 'The Janeites', which begins in the same setting, Brother Humberstall, an enormous hairdresser with 'the eyes of a bewildered retriever', who was blown up twice but does not show it 'much more than Lazarus did', is found happily polishing the acacia-wood organ-panels. To all comes some solace and alleviation, even where the healing can be only partial. 'We had every day joy of the amendment of our sick,' wrote Bacon in *New Atlantis*, 'who thought themselves cast into some divine pool of healing; they mended so kindly and so well.' Such a pool of healing is the Lodge.

Here, however, we are dealing with the immediate and comparatively simple results of recent injury. In the four tales that recount in detail the healing of war-neuroses the diseased state is of long standing and in one case has taken years to show itself. These tales, which form a closely related group, were published between 1927 and 1930. Nothing certain can be made of their chronological order; the simpler and the more complex go hand in hand, and the distinction is reflected in the varying methods of narration. The plight of Martin Ballart, 'blasted, withered, dumb', brooding on 'one of those accursed Kodak pictures, of a young man in a trench, dancing languorously with a skeleton', is thoroughly understood by the priest of the village who tells the tale, but the essence of it is that his real self is suspended and inaccessible, and we do not enter that sealed mind. Indeed, we see little more than his shadow before 'the laugh of Faunus himself', his response to the involuntary ministrations of the group attached to the priest's umbrella, breaks the obsession. To the priest, though he is not ignorant of what he conveys by the term 'moral therapeuty', this is a miracle; and the design of the tale may remind us of some picture of a miraculous healing by an Italian artist of the Renascence, with its lost young man on a litter, the diamond-clear landscape behind him, and the cluster of ordinary people assisting at the divine intervention. The attention of all these figures is directed to the possessed in love or wonderment, but the painter's art has found richer material in the keen, experienced, humorous, devout priest, the atheist schoolmaster, with his thick black beard and his stomach, biting his nails with shame in the henhouse before he is caught in the backwash of the miracle, even in the 'yoke of gold and silver oxen with sheepskin wigs', ascending the hill before their driver and passing out of the picture.

John Marden, successful founder of an engineering firm, in 'The Woman in His Life', is to all intents and purposes as inarticulate as Martin Ballart when, after a bout of overwork, the 'forgotten and hardly held-back terrors' of his two years' experiences as a sapper beneath Messines ridge rise up to shatter him, and drink does him no good. The narrative here is forthright and in the third person, and we need no more comment than we get from his knowledgeable ex-batman who steers him back to sanity by means of the jet-black dwarf Aberdeen bitch, Dinah. For her sake, when she is caught in an old badger's earth, he once more crawls underground and defeats his fear. This, too, is a healing through love. Since John Marden's trouble is easily understood and accessible to treatment, much of this happy tale is given up to the skilled manoeuvres of that unexpected Æsculapius, Corporal Vincent Shingle, 'systematically a peculator, intermittently a drunkard, and emphatically a liar', and to the comically endearing behaviour of the pup Dinah.

The intricacies of 'Fairy-Kist' and 'The Tender Achilles' are reflected in the form. The tales are told conversationally, chiefly by Keede, the doctor of '"In the Interests of the Brethren"', but with interruptions, questions and supplements from his listeners. 'Fairy-Kist' is told among Masons, and the bond has helped the two 'detectives' to Wollin's confidence. For the elucidation of Wilkett's plight we need two medical men, Keede and the surgeon 'Scree', and liberal quotation from Sir James Belton, the Head of St Peggotty's Hospital. Both stories imply an interest in psychiatry, without attempting to reproduce its techniques. This is clear enough in 'Fairy-Kist'; the investigators are not analysts; Keede has a wide human and medical experience, but it is Lemming, the layman, who by chance—always an agency in Kipling's world—holds the key of the obsession. 'The Tender Achilles' is full of speculative elements that could not have been found in a tale of a generation before. Chance does not operate, for the tale follows step by step the process by which the nerve-shattered Wilkett is restored to his research work. Sir James Belton calls his treatment of his patient homeopathic; it is not analytic. Much of the comment on Wilkett's case is moral, while the title and other elements in 'Fairy-Kist' show that Kipling was brooding again on abnormal states and powers that, in a former age, were referred to magic and now, by a great advance in knowledge, are partly, but not wholly, exposed to the eye of science. Wollin's old housekeeper ('She was primitive Stone Age—bless her!' says Keede) looks on Keede and Lemming 'as a couple of magicians who's broken the spell on him', and the casual conversation of the friends about Lily the astrologer and the saying of the old woman at Barnet Horse Fair point in the same direction.

Both stories involve physical pain; it harrows Wollin and prepares his mind for the seeds of his obsession, and Wilkett's festering foot may be a safety valve for his mental trouble, is certainly a counter-irritant, as the 'Hymn to Physical Pain' confirms, and in the hands of Sir James Belton and his conscripted conspirators becomes a means of his cure. Wollin presents no temperamental difficulties. He is 'a not uncommon cross between a brave bully and an old maid', and more articulate than Ballart or Marden, full, indeed, 'of medical talkee-talkee'. Since he has resolutely worked out an odd and precarious adjustment of his life to his persecuting 'Voices', there is need of an external series of events to demolish this compromise and reduce him to desperation. This is provided by his involvement in the supposed murder of Ellen Marsh. His sense of the inexplicability of his actions, his conviction that, if he is brought to trial, he will be sent to Broadmoor, bring him to the point when he disappears for a month into his own cellar, with the means of death at hand, if the police arrive with a warrant. 'What a month! Think of it!', says Keede, indicating the central situation of this involved story. 'A cellar and a candle, a file of gardening papers, and a loaded revolver for company.' The picture is further emphasized by the earlier description of Wollin, 'a big, strong, darkish chap—middle-aged—wide as a bull between the eyes—no beauty, and evidently had been a very sick man'. He is the only one of these four cases to be described, and we carry this portrait in our memory when, the immediate danger over, he meets the amateur detectives once more ('He was burned out—all his wrinkles gashes, and his eyes readjustin' 'emselves after looking into Hell. One gets to know that kind of glare nowadays'), and again, when 'the pressures were off', and Keede says that he knows now how a redeemed soul looks. There is a pleasant tail-piece, too, not pictorial itself, but inciting the informed imagination to picture it, when, after the gruelling session during which his Voices have been accounted for and his trouble lifted from him, Keede sends him to bed 'full of his own beer, and growing a shade dictatorial'.

The complicated mechanics of this tale derive, rather as Meredith's do, from the necessity of accounting for the situations through which the theme is expressed. The appearance of the murder has to be evoked and dispersed, and that with a solidity of circumstance that belongs to the menacing rational world with which Wollin's nightmare world interlocks. Motives must be found—not very good ones, the reader may feel—for keeping the inquiry out of the hands of the police, and the shadow of Lemming's difficult wife hovers behind the rampaging young newspaper-men. The prints hanging in Wollin's study are needed to lure Lemming, a shy man, anxious to keep out of the business, to return to Mitcham. As is common with Kipling at this stage, these structural elements are developed with a Defoe-like attention to detail (Keede and Nicol, the village policeman, removing Ellen's body early on Sunday morning, commandeer a builder's handcart from some half-built shops and the shove-halfpenny board from the Oddfellows' Room at the 'Cup of Grapes'). But the comparison lies also with the Pre-Raphaelites of his early acquaintance, for, like them, he uses detail to signify his theme. Jemmy Tigner, Ellen's last young man, encounters the fate that Wollin dreads. The drastic proceedings of the genial ex-soldier Nicol introduce the War into the early part of the tale, before we are asked to consider its products. The prints that draw Lemming are portraits of great botanists, and this links up with Wollin's passion for plants and with Mrs Ewing's *Mary's Meadow*, which, read to him in hospital, shaped his obsessions. I have written in Chapter IV of the laying of a false trail at the beginning of the tale. The complexity of approach, here and in other tales of this period, has given rise to the supposition that Kipling's control of his form slackened towards the end of his writing life. This is not so; the tales never wander; but the density of the inwoven patterns sometimes baffles the eye. We have to peer as if through lattice-work to see Wollin as he sits in his cellar.

Compared to 'Fairy-Kist', 'The Tender Achilles' is almost stream-lined. From first to last we are with medical men, discussing the collapse and cure of their colleague and patient, Wilkett. A moral element enters into this case. It is Wilkett's 'bleedin' vanity' that makes him peculiarly liable to the strain of his work as surgeon—at which he is not very good—at a Casualty Clearance Station. But a further complication is his 'research temperament', ('That type of mind wants absolute results, one way or the other; *or* else absolute accuracy') which revolts at the conditions, the hit-or-miss decisions, the absence of any time to think. His vanity drives his sense of duty on to false ground, and his imagination, the first necessity in his research equipment, helps to overthrow him. 'You've got to acknowledge the facts of life and your own limitations,' says Scree. 'Ambitious men won't do that till they are broke.' But Wilkett, who regards himself as something special, can take no comfort from his participation in a common inadequacy.

> Then he wrung his hands and said, 'To whom much has been given, from the same much shall be required.' That annoyed me. I hate book-keeping with God! It's dam' insolence, anyhow. Who was he to know how much had been given to the other fellow?'

He keeps a list of the casualties he has 'murdered' by improper treatment, and when the wound, made in his foot by a splinter of metal, festers, he relates his injury to the self-inflicted instep-wounds he has treated in hospital, and, vanity still operative, 'said it was a judgment on him for shirking'. Back in England, he goes to pieces.

> He saw perspectives of heads—gunshot wounds—seen from above and a little behind, as they'd lie on the tables; with the pad over their mouths, but still they all accused him of murder. On off nights he had orderlies whispering to him to wake up and give some poor beggar a chance to live. Then they'd waggle his foot, and he'd wake up grateful for the pain and change the dressings.

Since, therefore, his mind is divided between an unhealthy humiliation and a still unchastened vanity that cannot accept failure as a natural incident, the lesson that 'In our Pro-fession we are none of us Jee-ho-vahs. Strange as it may seem, not an-y of us are Jee-ho-vahs' cannot be taught him simply and directly. He can accept it only by being himself the victim of a mistake in diagnosis and treatment, a mistake made not under the inhuman pressure of the CCS, but in spite of the full resources of St Peggotty's Hospital and its laboratories, and by finding the 'little affair' dismissed as regrettable but all in the year's work by its Head and his staff. This is the 'homeopathic treatment' at which Sir James Belton hints; but the discipline is supported by gentler methods. Wilkett is allured back to research by being placed once more in the atmosphere of a great teaching hospital; his surgeon and Sir James talk shop with him; finally his very vanity is thrown into the scale of recovery when Keede reminds his infuriated patient that he is now 'one bloomin' civil case in one bloomin' bed' (*sc.* in a hospital where he could be a power). By all manner of means Wilkett's brain is saved for research and his obsessions dispersed. He does not, it appears, understand what has happened to him, and the healing does not reach his moral nature. The heel of this Achilles is still vulnerable. Keede uses the present tense when he breaks off his narrative to ask Scree if Wilkett was '*always* as offensive as he is'. But the specialized instrument is repaired and put back to its proper work.

In 'The Enemies to Each Other', when the Mole reports that our exiled first Parents are rejoicing, in despite of the Curse, in the birth of Quabil, he is rebuked because he has wished to withdraw from them what alleviation is permitted. 'The Gardener' is a tale, not of healing, but of the alleviation that was permitted, or possible. This beautiful and highly concentrated tale keeps no secrets. The village knows that Lieut Michael Turrell is not Helen's nephew, but her son. Her anxious secrecy is useless, and its cost is high; she is a Magdalen whose burden is heavier because it is not avowed. When, after Michael's death, her companion on the pilgrimage to the war-cemeteries confesses her own unsanctioned love, in the need to be 'honest with some one', Helen's gesture of sympathy and avowal is useless to both of them. It is not from her counterpart that Mrs Scarsworth can get the purgation she wants; and, if Helen would now try to speak, there is no one to listen to her. Her past life is a tomb, sealed with the heavy stone of her silence; her present life is a black grave, like that she visits, 'not yet planted out'. Yet it is clear that such alleviation as was possible came to her, when, for the first time, she heard Michael Turrell called her son, though she supposed it was a mistake of the gardener. For one hour of one day of all her years, the stone was rolled away. The consolation that she could not ask came to her; and though she could not recognize it, yet it came. The parallel with the Fourth Gospel which signifies the identity of the gardener, and the point at which it ceases, are vital to the meaning of the tale. It is towards this that it moves. It is not a tale of chance consolation, but of 'infinite compassion' operating, to the limits of the possible, through what to the blindness of the sufferer still looks like chance.

The sobriety, the grave, compassionate irony of this tale are unbroken. This unity of tone arises from unity of interest. It is Helen we watch all the time, but with such a sparing regard as that which in life we turn on some acquaintance bearing a heavy grief. The setting, the briefly-seen people, the raw public clamour of motherhood in the Lancashire woman, are developed only as far as they bear on Helen. In Mrs Scarsworth she confronts her own image in homelier material and hears the confession she has never made. Professor Carrington tells us that this tale was begun on March 14, 1925, after Kipling had visited Rouen Cemetery, and finished nine evenings later at Lourdes. The precipitation seems to have been as immediate and smooth as that of 'Mrs Bathurst', and the product far simpler. Nothing seems to have been built in or adjusted. It is a classic and selfless tale.

There remain other expressions of the theme of healing of a quite different kind. These are the indulgences of the imagination, the oases, or mirages, of the wilderness. Like *Cymbeline* or *Winter's Tale*, they reveal a permitted play of the compassionate fancy, restoring, healing, renewing, 'making up' in terms of the imagination for the uncomforted miseries, the irretrievable mistakes, that lie outside the charmed circle. Sometimes Kipling draws the circle on common earth, enclosing common miseries, and, once it is drawn, not only are the miseries and the aching imagination that recorded them assuaged, but even the daily chattels within the circle are refined to an unmatched perfection. Thus he joyously elaborates the perfect equipment of a tobacconist's shop, a research laboratory, and a Masonic Lodge. Even in a tale that is not in the least concerned with healing, he will allow himself some unexpected salvage. In 'The Bull that Thought', Apis, the brilliant and brutal artist among bulls, comes alive out of a Spanish bull-ring, and Chisto, the inferior matador, 'a laborious, middle-aged professional who had never risen above a certain dull competence', retrieves and achieves for one miraculous hour 'the desire, the grace, and the beauty of his early dreams'. The French stock-breeder, who tells the tale, ascribes to Apis, the unique bull that thought, 'the detachment of the true artist who knows he is but the vessel of an emotion whence others, not he, must drink'. There is something less than such complete detachment in some of these tales of Kipling's old age, and the artist moistens his lip at the fountain of his own fantasy. Sometimes the charm detaches him from earth, and in a mood of mercy, veined with mischief, he designs, 'with brushes of comets' hair', the landscapes of Heaven and Hell, the impressive Department of Normal Civil Death, with the temporary extension of the war-sheds clustering round its knees, or the vast organization where the damned souls are 'reconditioned for re-issue'. Not all the products of this mood are his best work, but it is difficult to grudge them to an old artist who knows so well what he is doing. Nor does he ever carry us quite out of sound of the sea of human misery; indeed, it is a condition of the charm that it should not be forgotten. In the fantasy 'On the Gate' he produces, with relish, one after another, the stale and embarrassing data of the sentimentalist—the deserter before the firing-squad, the mottle-nosed major pushed into Heaven by his mother, the seraph whose sword is broken on a woman's gin-bottle—and keeps them all light and aerated by the wit that transfers the administrative organization of war to the 'reception' of Heaven, struggling with an unusually heavy entry. So delicate and gay is this tune played on the bones of death that, when we read that St Peter, busy at the Gate, 'caught up a thick block of Free Passes, nodded to a group in khaki at a passport table, initialled their Commanding Officer's personal pass as for 'Officer and Party', and left the numbers to be filled in by a quite competent-looking Quarter-Master-Sergeant', it is a moment before we envisage this incident from the earthward end—as we are meant to do. The mode of 'Uncovenanted Mercies', the companion-piece to 'On the Gate', does not allow of this sort of stroke. It is not a tale of the War, and the tendrils that hold it to contemporary life are not sensitive to such a tug. Yet the weight of human pain is conveyed, in a different fashion, when Gabriel, Azrael and Satan wait in the casualty-room in Hell during an endless interval, and submit themselves to the agony that creeps in from outside, 'dimming, first, the lustre of their pinions; bowing, next, their shoulders as the motes in the never-shifted sunbeam filtered through it and settled on them, masking, finally, the radiance of Robe, Sword, and very Halo, till only their eyes had light'. This is the myriad dust of suffering mortality which obscures these shining figments, and Azrael groans: 'How long? . . . How long?'

The material of this chapter is beginning to overlap that of the next. These fantasies, with their denial of ultimate loss and waste, are a permitted alleviation of the anguish of the imagination. They are also a design, pricked in points of light on the blackness of the abyss.

CHAPTER SEVEN

Man and the Abyss

If the title of this chapter sounds melodramatic, it is, at least, free from pretentiousness. It does not suggest that a developed metaphysic can be found in Kipling's books, though it is consonant with the existence of a philosophy of conduct. 'Abyss', moreover, has had many applications; there is an abyss of doubt and of ignorance, the abyss of Hell and the abyss of God's mercies. It is also a word that Kipling uses himself, in poetry and prose, and its melodramatic quality reflects the force of emotion with which he regards the unplumbed blackness in which the busy fates of men are suspended. This intimation of the unknown has a positive artistic force in some of his tales. The brilliantly lit scene at some point is seen to be bordered by darkness, or rather to be a small lighted enclave in it. From that moment the proportions of the story are altered. We see that an incalculable condition enters into human effort. The moment of recognition varies greatly in tone and effect. In the earliest tales it is slight enough, no more than a jerk of the thumb at the perversity of Fate, the residue of a propitiatory gesture, an acknowledgment of an irony more obscure than human ironies. It is very different in the later tales. There is nothing jaunty here. At the end of 'The Dog Hervey', when the lovers have been restored to each other, the tale ebbs quietly away in a conversation between the narrator and Mrs Godfrey, the older woman who had introduced him to Moira Sichliffe.

> 'Ella,' I said, 'I don't know anything rational or reasonable about any of it. It was all—all woman-work, and it scared me horribly.'
> 'Why?' she asked.
> That was six years ago. I have written this tale to let her know—wherever she is.

It is a surprising ending, a sudden and tangential sigh at the departure of one who, if we consider the story by orthodox canons of structure, is no more than a well-used piece of machinery, a commentator on Moira Sichliffe, an occasion for the journey to Madeira and the meeting with Shend. But to apply such standards at this stage of Kipling's work is stultifying; for the last few words give an extraordinary sense of actuality to the tale. More than the detail of Moira's ugly house or of Mrs Godfrey's illness, they establish the queer and alarming happenings in it as, nevertheless, a part of life on earth, taking place six years before in Sussex among a society of friendly people, all leading their own lives and cultivating their gardens, with the sun rising and setting over them. They do this because, for a fleeting moment, we have followed Mrs Godfrey who has passed out of the sun. It is a separation by a wider gulf of distance and ignorance than that which separated Shend and Moira; and the narrator, shaping his tale to satisfy her unanswered question, projects it across the gulf as Moira had projected her love in the 'strained half-soul of the dog'. But the tale ends on a dropping cadence, and it is a cold breath that blows in from the dark through the open window.

What usually turns the mind of the young writer to the abyss is death. Kipling insists on the closeness and familiarity of death in the Indian scene, both in his early tales and in the reminiscences of *Something of Myself*. When little Adam Strickland in 'The Son of his Father' is made much of by his father's Police, 'through all the conferences—one hand twisted into Imam Din's beard, and the other on his polished belt-buckle—there were two other people who came and went across the talk—Death and Sickness—persons greater than Imam Din, and stronger than the heel-roped horses'. They came and went, too, about the house on the Bombay Esplanade, near the Towers of Silence where the Parsees exposed their dead. The book that first struck the little boy in exile at 'Home' as 'a history of real people and real things'—Mrs Ewing's *Six to Sixteen*—begins in the house of an English officer in India, where his young daughter is doubly orphaned and the familiar setting of her life abolished with a suddenness that the reader must have recognized. The return to India and the profession of journalist brought a very young man face-to-face again with the continual presence, and now he was fully conscious of it and accustomed to consider it from every angle from the statistical to the personal. In Lahore, 'skulls and bones tumbled out of our mud garden walls', which, transferred to propagandist fiction, supplied one of 'The Enlightenments of Pagett, MP'. The early stories are full of death, by sickness, misadventure and violence, with some stress on the physical accompaniments in India, the buzzing of the flies in the Rest House in 'Thrown Away' and the water-logged burial-ground in Simla in 'At the Pit's Mouth'. Intermittently Nature 'audit(s) her account with a red pencil' and 'the torrent of cheap life' is directed in a formidable fall into the abyss, while the flat telegraphese, summoning men to fill the gaps, tells of the thinning of the white ranks. But always the hazards are near and the smallness of the British community forces every man and woman to deal with death as friend, nurse or executor.

In these conditions Kipling's vitality and curiosity, his strong physical sensitiveness, his life-long taste for marked contrast and ironical pattern produced a multitude of scenes and figures which provide a parallel to the mediaeval Dance of Death. Here is the Other Man, come back to Simla to visit the woman he loved, and sitting dead in the tonga, 'very square and firm, with one hand on the awning-stanchion and the wet pouring off his hat and moustache'; here is the nervous grin on the face of the Tertium Quid as his horse begins to slip backwards over the precipice; here is the bazaar-woman, dying on a clean mat with a nicely-wadded pillow, and her opium-pipe between her lips; and here is all that was left of little Muhammad Din, wrapped in a white cloth and carried in his father's arms to the Mussulman burying-ground. If we go beyond the first layer of the tales, the gallery is varied by the deaths of the soldiery in battle, camp and barracks. The man frenzied by heat or jealousy kills and is shot down; the troops perish in the rest-camp of cholera, 'like dumb sheep'; a private of the Tyrone has his head split, avenging his cousin in a Border fight, and 'wint down grinnin' by sections'. Some of the deaths are punitive or invited—Imray's servant and murderer treads deliberately on the poison-snake—but most of them are casual. The vitality of the young writer springs up to apprehend the brute truncation of vitality, the abrupt inversion of intention, the outrageous irony. His reaction combines shock, which he is determined to relay to his reader, with recognition of the common fate of man. There had been nothing at all like it in English literature for a very long while. At times there is a macabre oddity in his reports and inventions. 'The Pit they Digged' is a connoisseur's piece. Mumrath, a Bengal civilian is sick, and a beautiful brick-lined grave is prepared for him under a scheme of Government subvention. He recovers; and then begins the bandying to and fro of the unpaid account from department to department of the Provincial and finally the Supreme Government. At one stage the cost of his grave is deducted from his pay. Meanwhile a cobra lays her eggs in the unused grave. At last Mumrath gets the deduction recouped, drives out to the cemetery to chuckle over his hard-won victory beside the grave, and absently treads on a cobra's tail. The grave is filled and the account closed. Mostly, however, the deaths are not exceptional. They are part of a dispensation—much the sort of thing that happens. Often they are items in an enormous spilth of unfinished life. When Kipling came back to England again, he was contemptuous of the fuss the home-bred Englishman made over dying. What was it for a man to go in ripe years, with his family provided for and his friends round him? In India 'flesh and blood are very cheap'. He had considered the work of famine and cholera, the expensively bred young officer 'shot like a rabbit in a ride', the older man dying up-country, knowing that his friends will subscribe to send his wife home, and fearful lest the work that cost his life should crumble. The sheltered islander, Kipling thought, could not conceive that it is lawful to use up human life for anything. 'He believes that it has to be developed and made beautiful for the possessor'. So into the frame of 'The Courting of Dinah Shadd', the description of a bivouac during manoeuvres in India, he slipped a reminder that 'of all those jovial thieves who appropriated my commissariat and lay and laughed round that waterproof sheet, not one remains. They went to camps that were not of exercise and battles without umpires. Burmah, the Soudan, and the frontier—fever and fight—took them in their time'. A little later he devoted a section of 'The Song of the English' to 'The Song of the Dead'. The voortrekkers lie in the sun by their skeleton horses, and every ebb-tide drops our dead on the sand.

> *On the sand-drift—on the veldt-side—in the fern-scrub we lay,*
> *That our sons might follow after by the bones on the way.*

With the coming of middle-age the rattle of bones is less

insistent. This follows a natural curve of intellectual and imaginative change in men. Sussex, moreover, did not affront the eye with the swarming myriads of India; and Burma, the Sudan, even the Boer War were receding into the distance. Yet the shadow is never very far away, and Kipling had private griefs to feed his speculations. There is death in 'An Habitation Enforced', because there is death even in Arcadia, but there is no shock in the gentle departure of old Iggulden. 'They come down like ellum-branches in still weather', says the village nurse, and Sophie tells her husband: 'It's all quite natural for *them*', and feels even more closely bound to the old house that has seen so many comings and goings. With the War the pressure intensifies again. Here once more is the holocaust, the casual slaughter of the best with the worst. Now once more the multiplied embodiments of man's common fate are thrust at him and ride his imagination, and the imagination is the richer by age, experience and fatherhood. The bodies we loved are obscene and loll on the wire. Apart from the outcry of pain in 'The Children', however, there are few such images in the verse written during the War. In 'A Death-Bed', certainly, they are deliberately and dreadfully assembled, but in 'Epitaphs of the War' there are only two, and in 'A Recantation (To Lyde of the Music Halls)' only an archaic heroic type. In both these cases Kipling commits his work to the strict control of an ancient model—the epitaphs of the Greek Anthology and the Horatian Ode—and borrows composure from it. The 'Epitaphs' are not at all like a Dance of Death, though they record various ways—some ironical—in which life may be extinguished in war. They are strictly functional and commemorative. They suggest in turn a line cut on a headstone, or pencilled in a pocket-book, or scratched by the dead man's mates on a broken oar, upended in the sand. The dead confirm their natures, ('The Rebel', 'The Obedient', 'The Refined Man') or remember what they have left ('The Bridegroom', 'Pelicans in the Wilderness'). They record with acceptance or bewilderment what has befallen them ('Ex-Clerk', 'The Sleepy Sentinel'). Their fellows set down some token remembrance of them, ('A Grave near Cairo', 'Hindu Sepoy in France') and, from a greater distance, the parents recall the passing of their sons ('A Son', 'RAF (aged eighteen)'). It is when one starts to classify these tough shreds of verse that one sees how strong they are, and how much is strung on them. The tone and the verse vary; death is cited with defiance, with tenderness, and with stoical wit. The deaths commemorated are at once very near and seen in a long perspective of sacrifice. This perspective is also the effect of the classical locutions in 'A Recantation'.

Most of Kipling's war-tales were published several years after the War, the majority between 1924 and 1930, and in these the images of death are introduced sparingly, though with calculated force, and always in relation to some concept of value. The most pervasive of these values are the fellowship of common experience and the capacity of men under pressure for disciplined endurance. These were not new ideas; they had accompanied Kipling through his writing life; but they received confirmation of such a kind that the basic emotion transmitted by the tales is always wonder. The strongest images are found in 'The Tender Achilles', where the picture of the Casualty Clearing Station is needed to particularize the strain which Keede survived but which broke Wilkett, and in 'The Janeites', where they contrast every way with the exquisite art of Jane Austen, the strange but natural resource of the men whose duty it is to deal familiarly with carnage. They are needed, too, to suggest the full meaning of the quaint and innocently moving remark with which Humberstall, sound in body but always a little bewildered in mind, and now peaceably restored to his hair-dressing behind Ebury Street, ends his account of what was—though he could never describe it like that—the most deeply satisfying experience of his life:

> 'I read all her six books now for pleasure' tween times in the shop; an' it brings it all back—down to the smell of the glue-paint on the screens. You take it from me, Brethren, there's no one to touch Jane when you're in a tight place. Gawd bless 'er, whoever she was.'

But the abyss is more than death. It is, what it is to all of us, the whole mystery of the state of man; and since to Kipling man, and especially European man, and more especially the Englishman of the professional classes, is the creature who works, it is in connection with the work of man that the abyss opens its gulf on the rim or in the middle of his tales. 'The Bridge Builders' begins with a statement of legitimate ambition. 'The least that Findlayson, of the Public Works Department, expected was a CIE; he dreamed of a CSI.' This is the human scale. We are then shown pictorially what three years building a bridge over the Ganges mean in terms of labour, material and responsibility. The page is filled with construction-work and the activity and characteristic noises of the labour-gangs, framed between the 'huge stone-faced banks that flared away north and south for three miles on either side of the river'. A packed retrospective paragraph sums up the difficulties that have been surmounted by Findlayson and his assistant in their unsparing and complex toil; and now the bridge is near completion, 'lacking only a few weeks' work on the girders of the three middle piers'. The first note of menace is sounded by Peroo, the Lascar ex-serang and foreman of the overhead-men, who wonders what Mother Gunga will do, now she is bitted and bridled. In the brief interval before the telegram announces floods upstream, the two Englishmen talk lightly of Peroo's mixed religious observances and his denial of the efficacy of prayer. This, which at first reading is merely an entertaining touch of characterization, is the first suggestion of a widening of scale that is to reduce the enormous bridge and its swarming life to an atom, abolish the personalities whose driving force has effected the displacement of so vast a weight of material, and surround the infinitesimal by the immeasurable. But the abyss does not open at this point of the tale. Once again, with feverish tempo, we are plunged into weight, din, ordered and anxious acitivity as the gangs clear up the river-bed and do what they can in the few hours they can reckon on to strengthen the girders of the three middle piers. We are just a third of the way through the tale when 'a little wave hit the side of a pier with a crisp slap', and Peroo says that Mother Gunga is awake. There follows the description of the great flood, each phrase carrying its object and sound, and of Findlayson's agony of anxiety as his unfinished work is subjected to the fierce strain. By the mid-point of the tale he is adrift with Peroo in the stone-boat that he tried to save, on the wild river that comes more and more, as we listen to Peroo, to have purpose and life. Both men are drugged, for Findlayson, unable to eat, has swallowed the opium pellets that Peroo pressed on him, and in this state they are driven on a little island where the lightning shows them 'a clump of thorn, a clump of swaying creaking bamboos, and a grey gnarled peepul overshadowing a Hindoo shrine'. The tale moves into the trance of the drugged men. To this island come, in the shape of beasts driven there by the flood, the gods of India; and the Crocodile, who is Mother Gunga, complains to the Great Ones that the bridge has chained her; her power is spent and her waters are dropping, and still it stands. It is at this point, at what should be the triumph of Findlayson's labours, that they are reduced to nothing by progressive changes of scale. Indra chides the impatience of Mother Gunga: 'The deep sea was where she runs but yesterday, and tomorrow the sea shall cover her again as the Gods count that which men call time. Can any say that this their bridge endures till tomorrow?' Ganesh adds: 'It is but the shifting of a little dirt. . . . Let the dirt dig in the dirt ere it return to the dirt.' This chilling vision contracts again, from a geological to a historical scale, when Krishna, who lives with men, tells the other gods that, through the building of bridges and such works as the men from over the water do, the flame will die on their altars, and they will be as they were in the beginning, 'rag-Gods, pot Godlings of the tree, and the village-mark'. But, when they appeal to Indra, they get an answer that dissolves time and place and mass into insubstantiality. They and all things, even Heaven and Hell, are the dream of Brahm. This is the Riddle of the Gods. 'Be content. Brahm dreams still. The dreams come and go, and the nature of the dream changes, but still Brahm dreams.' With that the dawn comes, the divine presences withdraw, and the white man shakes off his trance as the solidity of his life and his responsibilities closes round him. The Lascar, however, still pursues the revelation. He too looked once into the abyss, when he clung to the ring of the ship's bow-anchor in a storm, tilted sideways on an enormous wave and looking down into the great deeps. In that moment, very near to death, he had asked himself if the gods whom he prayed to would abide at all. 'They are good for live men, but for the dead—.' The question is unfinished, for the white man's god, toil, claims them in the sunlight. The local Rajah's launch arrives to rescue them, and the last voice we hear is that of the young Rao Sahib, full of up-to-date inflections, regretting that he is 'due to attend at twelve forty-five in the state temple, where we sanctify some new idol. . . . They are dam-bore, these religious ceremonies, Finlinson, eh?' Brahm is dreaming and the dream is changing. We have seen beyond the toil and achievements of men; the great bridge to which Findlayson returns seems a mirage floating on vapour.

Findlayson, however, does return, shutting his mind easily to his vision, and rewarded, we may suppose, by the CIE or even the CSI. It is necessary to man's health in this world that he should be short-sighted. If he watches the great tides of the universe, he will lie, like poor Dowse in 'The Disturber of Traffic', with his eye to the planking, unable to speak. This is seeing unto madness, exposure to conceptions too vast for him, and it unfits him for his work in the world. Work is the great educator and consoler of man. 'The Four Angels', attached to 'With the Night Mail', presents Adam's sin in Eden as laziness, the refusal, even when the tutelary angels of the elements suggest it, to exploit his circumstances. Therefore the Angel of the Fire sets the flame of desire in his heart. The desire is for ever unattainable, but outside Eden-Wall it drives him to the mastery of the elements. It is thus through 'black disaster' that he fulfils his nature. This is the inverse of the argument in G. B. Shaw's *Back to Methuselah*, where it is the shortness of man's life that makes him irresponsible and careless. If he knew that he would live for a long term of centuries, he would be more diligent and careful. But Kipling, like Swift, did not define man as *animal rationale*, but only as *rationis capax*. Work as the source of strength and consolation is the theme of 'The Supports', published first in 1919 and afterwards attached to 'On the Gate'. The poet gives thanks for

> *the unregardful hours that grind us in our places*
> *With the burden on our backs, the weather in our faces.*
>
> *Not for any Miracle of easy Loaves and Fishes,*
> *But for doing, 'gainst our will, work against our wishes—*
> *Such as finding food to fill daily-emptied dishes.*

The artist, however, must at times support the distant vision, and it recurs intermittently through Kipling's work, but never again at the heart of a story. It is expressed in the epigraph, quoted from James Thomson, to 'A Conference of the Powers'; all the powers of man, creative and executive, are 'solid as ocean foam'. The lama in *Kim* takes this for granted. It is the burden of the verses that precede the Roman tales in *Puck of Pook's Hill*. The children are about to be told of Eternal Rome, with its roads, its colonies, and the long arm of its power. But before that they hear that

> *Cities and Thrones and Powers*
> *Stand in Time's eye,*
> *Almost as long as flowers,*
> *Which daily die,*

—a hyperbole so quiet in manner, touched with so humorous and gentle a melancholy, that it cannot alarm them. The next verse shifts ground to consider the daffodil, whose 'bold countenance' depends on her ignorance of the fate of last year's flowers. And Time has ordained that man shall be as bold and blind as the flower, so that in death he can take comfort in his works,

> *That in our very death,*
> *And burial sure,*
> *Shadow to shadow, well-persuaded, saith,*
> *'See how our works endure'.*

In the thin air of these distances the urgent appeal of 'A British-Roman Song' sounds remote and minute. Kipling here makes play with the same device as William Morris used in 'The Eve of Crecy', where the young French knight looks cheerfully forward to the morrow's battle, to win his lord's praise and his lady's love; the end of his hopes is in the title, and the end of Roman Britain in the date—A.D. 406. These verses are readily seen as a political act, a warning parable for the poet's contemporaries. They are certainly this, but they have a much wider significance. There is no exemption for any Empire from the universal process of coming into being and ceasing to be. Nevertheless the function of the workman is to work and spend himself, and this

> *Builds a bulkhead 'twixt Despair and the Edge of Nothing.*

It is not for his health that the window on the abyss should open too often or too long.

In the *Just So Stories* there is a curious expression of Kipling's sense of circumfluent mystery. It occurs in one of the pictures to the tale of 'The Crab that Played with the Sea'. This tale is about 'the Time of the Very Beginning ... when the Eldest Magician was getting Things ready', and telling the newly-created animals what they were to play at. The elephant is bidden to play at being an elephant, and does so to his own content and that of the Eldest Magician; and so with the rest of the animals. But the man is not included in this order, and when, towards the evening, he comes up with his little daughter on his shoulder, the Eldest Magician says: 'Ho, Son of Adam, this is the play of the Very Beginning; but you are too wise for this play', and the man agrees. The tale then passes on to the misdoings of the King Crab who would not wait for orders, but in the picture and in the commentary that faces it we can find out part of the 'play' of man and one of the orders he must obey. These pictures, which are developments of the text of the tales and full of the extra details that delight a child, also contain here and there Kipling's own self-delighting jokes. Such are the inscriptions on the bales of food that Suleiman-bin-Daoud has assembled to feed all the animals of the world, and that on the pouch of Old Man Kangaroo; but this picture is not all a joke. Behind the man as he stands talking to the Eldest Magician—a benign Buddha-like figure—are the intricate walls of a maze, and his foot is on the threshold of it. The commentary says: 'The thing that looks like bricks that the Man is standing in is the Big Miz-Maze. When the Man has done talking with the Eldest Magician he will walk in the Big Miz-Maze, because he has to.' The only critic to mention the Miz-Maze, so far as I know, is M. Robert Escarpit in his interesting and generous study *Rudyard Kipling: Servitudes et Grandeurs Impériales*, and I cannot altogether follow his interpretation. He concludes that the sole instruction of the Eldest Magician is that, since one exists, it is necessary to exist; it is no good asking questions, for there will be no answers; and he hears in the tale the suggestion that life is only a 'play', and that what is serious in it derives from the fact that we play it. This is too negative, and takes no account of parallel utterances, such as 'The Prayer of Miriam Cohen'. The man is set apart from the animals; he has outgrown their play. Like the Children of the Zodiac, who forgot that they were gods till the hour of death brought back the knowledge, he will forget that he has talked with the Eldest Magician. He will walk in the maze, and darkness and ignorance will be the conditions in which he does his work. The question is always how to get the maximum output out of human stuff, which works best blinkered. Kipling never attempts to define that element in man that is not animal, but he recurs to it in image and fable. Five years after the end of the War he addressed the Royal College of Surgeons on 'Surgeons and the Soul'. Man, he told them, still damp from the clay of the pit whence he was digged, claimed divinity. The gods conceded the claim but stole away his god-head and Brahm hid it in the man himself, so that he is 'an imperfectly denatured animal intermittently subject to the unpredictable reactions of an unlocated spiritual area'. But from this bafflement, as from the black disaster of Adam, came the impulse to search and the need to strive. 'Man, always a hunter, went up against the darkness that cloaked him and every act of his being, to find out what order of created being he might be.' This is an important point, and, because images and fables may be considered ambiguous indications of what Kipling thought, I will momentarily forsake my method and point to the direct biographical evidence in Rider Haggard's account of his old friend's conversation, printed in Lilias Rider Haggard's life of her father, *The Cloak that I Left*.

> I told him that I did believe that as a result of much spiritual labour there is born in one a knowledge of the nearness and consolation of God. He replied that occasionally this had happened to him also, but the difficulty was to 'hold' the mystic sense of the communion—that it passes. . . . Rudyard's explanation is that it is meant to be so; that God does not mean we should get too near lest we should become unfitted for our work in the world.

The darkness is felt for the space of a sentence in 'The Ship that Found Herself', when we hear the various parts of the untried ship talking together on her maiden voyage. 'Their conversation, of course, is not half as wise as our human talk, because they are all, though they do not know it, bound down one to the other in black darkness, where they cannot tell what is happening near them, nor what will overtake them next.' The irony hardly troubles the tone of the fable, which is, as it should be, ingeniously amusing and straightforwardly moral; yet it suggests another dimension to it. The surface statement of the tale is that machinery, however well tested its parts may be, needs to be run in, in working conditions—in this case, bad Atlantic weather—before it works as a whole. The different parts of the 'Dimbula' chatter, question and complain, until they discover their functions and adjust their relations with each other, and then their separate babble is replaced by the one voice of the new self-realizing ship. The statement can be referred from the artifact of men to men themselves in any form of association, since the success of this must depend on acceptance of function and co-operation of parts, and these can be established only in practice. All this is told with the utmost certainty, for this is the sphere of the Gods of the Copybook Headings, which are the unescapable conditions inherent in human nature, witnessed by history, ignored at our peril. But the Gods of the Copybook Headings have nothing to do with the abyss, except that submission to their discipline makes us more seaworthy under the assault of the storms that come out of it. They organize the limited and lighted ship, but below that is the ocean and around it the disturbed air —'circumstances', as the Steam calls them. Of these, Kipling says in his sardonic negatives, men are as ignorant as the parts of the ship, and like them 'bound down one to the other in black darkness, where they cannot tell what is happening near them, nor what will overtake them next'. More than once in his work the assertion, grave or ironic or even flighty, of ultimate ignorance is made before or during or after some display of certainty or dogmatism; it does not qualify the dogmatism in its own sphere, but reminds us of the ultimates about which the writer claims no knowledge. It is these ultimate powers that make the 'weather' which tests the ship, and by which she may one day be sunk, however well she has kept the law. But without the stress of 'weather' there is no supreme human achievement. He found a symbol for this conviction much later in life when, revisiting France after the war, he was allowed to go out on the roof of Chartres Cathedral and examine the reverse of those radiant windows. 'We found that every square millimetre of the glass had been microscopically etched by the years . . . and everywhere worked into a thousand varying planes to sift and glorify the light. . . . So we saw that it is not Man that makes perfection but the weather which his works must endure.' However much he may glorify the craftsman, Kipling's world is never a man-made one. External forces are the unknown partners in the work.

Nearly all the tales in *The Day's Work*, which we reach through the phantasmal arch of 'The Bridge Builders', belong to the well-lighted domain of the Gods of the Copybook Headings. It is a busy, limited world of personified machines and talking horses, of junior lieutenants, pearl-poachers, elderly naval engineers and Indian civilians seconded for famine work, all alike in that they give all they have to their work and receive from it the best they can enjoy, the assurance of their sufficiency for their charge. The abyss plays no part here or in the two farces towards the end of the collection, but an aspect of it looms faintly in 'The Brushwood Boy', before we close the book. This is a tale of the preternatural, of the abyss of strangeness within man himself. Findlayson's vision was forced on him. The reader can ascribe it to the opium he has taken, and see it as the uprush of that common knowledge of time and oblivion which all men have, and the active man does not take the risk of considering with any closeness. But the Brushwood Boy grows up with his dreams, though, since he is active and happy in all the aspects of his young life and firmly set on his duty, he keeps this strange extension of his consciousness in healthy subservience to his immediate living. The story, like 'The House Surgeon' and 'The Wish House', is just not rationalized. We are given hints about the material that was fantastically metamorphosed into Georgie's dream-country, and the dreams themselves are not unparalleled; but when the briefly-met little girl is not only swept into Georgie's dreams but infected by them, so that for years the two, unknown to each other and half a world apart, keep step in their dreaming, we have something that is outside our usual knowledge of human nature. Yet this sort of sympathy between two people can be conceived without bringing the transcendental into play; it can be considered in terms of the unexplored psychic potentialities of man; and the same kind of consideration will cover 'The Dog Hervey' and 'The Mark of the Beast'. But there are other tales in which powers are concerned which are either not human at all or are those of the human spirit altered by death.

I do not want to enter into any close examination of Kipling's early ghost-stories. It was natural that he should use this material when, as a young craftsman, he set his growing skill every kind of task. It seems that he sometimes started from local material, as in 'Haunted Subalterns', an account of poltergeist activity in Fort Lahore, in the main datum of the Simla tale, 'The Phantom 'Rickshaw', and in 'The Lost Legion'. Other tales, such as 'For One Night Only' and '"Sleipner", late "Thurinda"', read like bizarre inventions. There are a good many of these tales in the earlier layers of his work, and it is plain that this type of subject exercised a strong attraction on his imagination. Even in his 'Schoolboy

Lyrics' there are ghostly themes, and in *Something of Myself* he tells us that it was in 'The Phantom 'Rickshaw', written in his twentieth year, that he first felt the presence of his Daemon and made his 'first serious attempt to think into another man's skin'. This conscious advance must have resulted from the fervour with which he worked out his fantastic data. 'Some of it was weak,' he writes, 'much was bad and out of key', and this is true, but the badness is interesting. A complex mode of presentation seems to have suggested itself to him. Pansay, who is being drawn out of life by the ghost of the woman his cruelty killed, was to tell his appalling story in 'blood-and-thunder magazine diction'. An unliterary man, distracted by his incredible experiences and his incommunicable emotions, may have recourse to such diction. Kipling tried for an effect of emphasis, a way of heightening the horror. There was to be an inadequacy of language, corresponding to the inadequacy of Pansay's 'expressionless and commonplace' features that show no sign of his experiences. If, as the 'I' of the tale suggests, 'there was a crack in Pansay's head and a little bit of the Dark World came through and pressed him to death', the conception becomes more telling if the head in question is that of an ordinary, earth-bound, rather callous man, not at all predisposed for such an intrusion. The *clichés* duly appear—'Kitty in a regal rage'—and they are not like Kipling's own early errors; but the young writer had neither the tact nor the self-denying consistency to carry such a difficult mode to complete success. He managed better with a similar device in the contemporary 'Strange Ride of Morrowbie Jukes', where the horrible little burrows of the nightmare village of the living dead receive an added touch of ghastliness from being described to us in the practical, professional detail of an unimaginative Civil Engineer.

The haunting of Pansay is suspended between the credulity of the 'I' and the scepticism of Dr Heatherlegh who dismisses it as 'a Stomach *cum* Brain *cum* Eye illusion', due to overwork. Most of the other ghostly tales require the reader's belief, though the manifestations of 'My Own True Ghost Story' are explicitly rationalized, and 'The Sending of Dana Da' is a corrective jest. They vary in tone from the gravity of 'By Word of Mouth' to the shock-tactics of 'At the End of the Passage', and in technique from the brief sea-yarn, offered for what it is worth, in 'Of Those

Called' to the careful preparation of the reader in the longer 'Return of Imray' and 'The Lost Legion'. These last two tales and 'By Word of Mouth' might be called orthodox manifestations. It we accept the ghostly appearances, we have no difficulty in accounting for them. Mrs Dumoise, dead in a recent epidemic, appears to a servant to send her husband a message that she will meet him at Nuddea. Imray haunts his bungalow until his unburied body is found and his murderer detected. These are comprehensible motives in a psychic residuum. 'Of Those Called' implies some irregularity in the process of time. Three of the crew on a tramp hear repeatedly the voice and words they will hear in half-an-hour's time, when their ship will be run down in the fog by an ironclad. They alone hear them, and they alone are saved. But some of the shorter tales make their effect by a frightening irrationality. No explanation can be offered. 'There's no reason in it. It doesn't lead up to anything', says the red-haired subaltern in ' "Sleipner", late "Thurinda" '. In fact, the explanations glimmer and are lost, and the tale is all the more uncanny for that. If we say that the tough and solitary Jale, killed at a race-meeting, follows with indiscriminate, jealous violence, in the borrowed shape of the mare that killed him, her daughter Thurinda, whom he loves and has set his hopes on, we are driving the tale to a point of explicitness it never reaches. It is bizarre and unaccountable. The clatter of extra hoofs is heard alongside Thurinda and her new owner grimly renames her Sleipner after Odin's eight-legged steed; men who own or ride her are killed or maimed; a lathered stallion crosses her path. There are confusions and inconsistencies. The ghostly grey who pursues her, seen by a native jockey and by the fore-doomed Marish, has the markings of Thurinda's mother, Divorce, but when it passes Marish on the road he says: 'Look here! He's coming for the mare.' It is as if some disembodied violence of greed and resentment were approximating to an embodiment, informing and changing the nature of the dead beast that killed him, in accordance with his savage desire. As it stands, the tale is not only queer but illogical and confusing, and the assumptions that seem to lie behind the apparent confusions could hardly have been brought out more clearly without the bizarre lapsing into the ludicrous. It is evidence that the difficulty inherent in complexity of premise and severe compression is not confined to Kipling's later work. Even as it stands, however, I think it a better and more alarming suggestion of the darkness that lies

> *A stone's throw out on either hand*
> *From that well-ordered road we tread,*

than the stoked horrors of 'At the End of the Passage', which sometimes provoke a strong reaction in the reader. In that tale Hummil, the Civil Engineer, is caught and killed in the Dark Places of his dreams by demonic powers, and his agony is shown with pathos as well as terror. Also, in the loaded evocation of Indian hot weather in a railway bungalow on the plains, there is a readily perceptible streak of Kipling's determination to show the islanders in what conditions an Indian civilian may have to work. As a result, the two things get tangled in the reader's mind, and he finds himself protesting that demonic persecution is not the norm in India, even in hot weather. Mr Hilton Brown, indeed, is moved to assert that the four exiles 'had really very little to complain of'. There is a similar tangle of traces when Kipling drives the same two-in-hand in the slight but hyperbolical anecdote, 'The Last Relief', and the ghostly propaganda embarrasses. Spirits move more convincingly in a drier medium. There is no pathos in '"Sleipner", late "Thurinda"'. What mingles with alarm is irritation at Jale's 'ridiculous interference with a free gift', the intrusion of the passion and will of the dead into a life that can do so well without him; and when it has been agreed between the two men most concerned, with the fewest possible words, that that is what is happening, Thurinda's owner puts an end to the intolerable business by shooting her. It is a queer yarn, and not used to prove any point.

It will be noted that I have not assumed that what brought Hummil to the end of his passage were hallucinations. The tale could have been written like that, and it would have been a better, because a more single-minded tale; but I do not think it was so written. The invention, by which the dead man's retina preserves the image of the horrors that forced him out of life long enough to be recorded by a camera, is said to be without sufficient foundation for even a temporary suspension of disbelief; nevertheless, it was intended to substantiate the suggestion that seeps into the tale like foul smoke through the cracks of a building; and I take the occasion of what I consider a miscarried tale to maintain that the supernatural in Kipling's tales is never completely reducible to the illusory—though two or three cases of faked magic explicitly are. This is most evident in the least successful tales. Nothing explains the haunted theatre-box of 'For One Night Only'. Mostly, however, he deals in ambiguous appearances; yet, when we try to rationalize the story we come on some detail in it that will not fit the rationalization, and then our efforts to adjust or ignore it make us aware how strongly we are, in fact, directed not to do either. Dumoise in 'By Word of Mouth' might have heard of his impending transference to Nuddea as he passed through Simla, though he denies it, but then we have no reason for his servant's terror of the place. Or, to take an example from the later tales, where the point is more important than it can be in the early yarns, we are directly encouraged to ascribe the shapeless haunting of 'The House Surgeon' to a form of telepathy; but this will not cover 'the other thing', the helpless protest, the 'live grief beyond words' (as Kipling significantly says) which is felt after Miss Moultrie's ferocious, distant brooding is diverted from her old home. This can be no part of her projected mind. Among the diversity of Allah's creatures there are human beings with strange powers, consciously or unconsciously exercised; and outside the human race there is a darkness that can, at times, penetrate the rind of daily life.

Kipling's ghostly and demonic stories were written before he was twenty-seven. By then he had ceased to provide the two thousand word 'turnovers' that were so apt a frame for queer things; and, after the three full-length tales of horror in *Life's Handicap* and the classical 'Lost Legion' in *Many Inventions*, he discarded that type of work and found other means—dreams, allegories, symbols, charged ambiguities—to convey his sense of the darkness and the unknown existences outside life. It does not seem that his imagination ceased to throw up the perilous material, but he became much more wary in accepting it. In *Something of Myself* he tells how, during manoeuvres in 1913, in hazy, lowering weather, he

> conceived the whole pressure of our dead of the Boer War flickering and reforming as the horizon flickered in the heat; the galloping feet of a single horse, and a voice once well-known that passed chanting ribaldry along the flank of a crack

battalion.... The finale was to be manoeuvres abandoned and a hurried calling-off of all arms by badly frightened Commandants—the men themselves sweating with terror though they knew not why.

The notion, he says, obsessed him; he started on it at once, then rejected it on more advisement as 'absurd, unnecessary and hysterical', yet took it up again three or four times before, after the War, he finally threw the draft away. It would seem, then, that anything that passed such a censorship would carry a deeply-considered imprimatur. Actually there is not much that does pass. We cannot call '"They"' a ghost-story. It is not proposed for belief at the literal level. We can call it, perhaps, a serious fantasy, embodying an emotional truth and an acknowledged prohibition. It is true that we involuntarily think of the dead in terms of the personalities they wore on earth. It is hard to think of them any other way. The artist, to whom abstractions are little use, accepts this necessity and exploits it. '"They"' is related in its mode of imagination to 'On the Gate' and the gay and moving little poem 'Dinah in Heaven', where Dinah refuges under Peter's chair and waits for the master she has innocently helped to save. In much the same fashion the unreasonable, wounded mind may follow a dead child in its familiar shape into the unfamiliar world, and wonder what a young soul can do in such vastitudes. This habit of the human imagination provides a basis for the fantasy of the earth-seeking child spirits, drawn to the focus of the childless, blind, desiring woman with her innocent occult knowledge and to the perfect playground of the old house and garden she has made ready for them. But all this is a poetic hypothesis. It is a means for stating that the barrier between the living and the dead is not meant to be passed. Even if the road to Endor is as seductively lovely as the approach to the yew-studded lawn and the old house; even if one is brought there without intent, by the natural workings of one's own nature, and finds the barrier transparent; even if the dead is very young and much beloved, one must turn one's back on that road and return to the living world to which one belongs. This is the conviction that Kipling expresses in his own person in *Something of Myself*. I do not know if we are to deduce from the other figures in the tale—the butler and his wife and the village mother—that there may be exceptions to this ordinance. It is perhaps not a case for logical deductions within the fantasy. The tale needs subsidiary figures to move in its scenes, but it is entirely focused on the 'I', so unobtrusive at the beginning, so suddenly exposed to us in his grief and his renunciation when the moment of understanding comes at last, at the end of the tale.

These speculations do not trouble the children's stories. There is nothing supernatural in the jungle, and Mowgli laughs at Buldeo's superstitions. The characters that appear to Dan and Una are not ghosts; children understand the imaginative mode of Sir Richard Dalyngridge and Parnesius as well as they do that of talking animals and talking locomotives. The People of the Hills are spoken of, but all of them except Puck have left England long ago. There is no darkness here, though the children learn that gods have come and gone and that men have worshipped them in many ways. Three poems hover unalarmingly at the threshold of another world. A phantom breath blows delicately in 'The Way through the Woods' and the fairy maid takes the young man's heart in 'Brookland Road'. This last is a traditional theme, and so is Lord Leicester's ghost, scratching on the door of Queen Bess's room in 'The Looking-Glass'. The traditional supernatural of English songs and ballads survived in Kipling's work the fading of the alarming panorama that India spread before him. It can be used with unquestionable seriousness. The spirit of the newly-dead walks in 'A Madonna of the Trenches' and a woman strikes a bargain with an evil thing in 'The Wish House'; and surely the speaker in 'Gethsemane' is the man whose cup has not passed from him, who has drunk the gas and is looking back on life, like the spirit that comes to Margaret's bedside in the ballad, or the first speaker in A. E. Housman's 'Is my team ploughing?'

The supernatural, then, remained part of Kipling's total world, though it is very sparingly touched in his latest work. He himself specifically disclaimed in *Something of Myself* any disposition for the 'psychic'. Only once did he pass beyond 'the bounds of ordinance', in an unimportant prophetic dream, fulfilled to the letter some six weeks later. The power of dreaming, which De Quincey calls one of the inlets of the dark sublime into our minds, was certainly his. He built only one story on dreams, 'The Brushwood Boy', but the evidence of his dream-life is scattered through his books in simile and reminiscence; and so, I think, is that of his acquaintance with the Horror of Great Darkness, which he ascribes to Rahere, 'moods and tenses of black depression and despair', of which he warned the boys at Wellington, when he addressed them. Such experiences, waking and sleeping, are a source of morbid and terrifying imagery and nightmare sensations. I cannot be sure that the 'blind face that cries and can't wipe its eyes', which appears with horrific facetiousness in 'La Nuit Blanche' in *Departmental Ditties* and as pure horror in 'At the End of the Passage', rose in Kipling's own dreams, but he himself has told us in 'Brazilian Sketches' that once in a child's dream he wandered into a Fifth Quarter of the world and 'found everything different from all previous knowledge', and the memory of that dream must have provided the groundwork for George Cottar's wanderings into

> a sixth quarter of the globe, beyond the most remote imaginings of man, [where] he hurried desperately, and the islands slipped and slid under his feet, the straits yawned and widened, till he found himself utterly lost in the world's fourth dimension with no hope of return. Yet only a little distance away he could see the old world with the rivers and mountain-chains marked according to the Sandhurst rules of map-making.

Whether his dreams ceased as he grew older or he declined to use what they offered, their track grows much fainter and is only to be suspected occasionally in an image. In his last tale, 'Proofs of Holy Writ', the Oxford scholar, Miles Smith, hears in Macbeth's speech 'Tomorrow and tomorrow and tomorrow...' 'a parable, as it might be, of his reverend self, going down darkling to his tomb 'twixt cliffs of ice and iron'. This is dream-scenery.

What survives, strictly controlled, in the last phase of Kipling's work, of so strong a bent for dark and strange imaginings, is worth close consideration. There is a moment in 'A Friend of the Family', before Bevin begins to tell his tale of Hickmot the Australian, when it seems as if the reminiscences of the ex-servicemen at the Lodge will open on pure supernatural horror, but it is 'choked off': that tale is not to be told. The three tales that are told are 'The Gardener', 'A Madonna of the Trenches' and 'The Wish House'. They were all published close together in 1924, half-a-dozen years after the end of the war, and together they define the extent to which Kipling was now prepared to let the supernatural enter his work. They have all been rationalized by readers, and it is nearly possible to do it successfully. None of them can be so bedevilled by rationalization as Henry James's 'Turn of the Screw' has been; but, like all stories that include a supernatural element, exposure to this process impoverishes them. Indeed, if it is assumed that Strangwick's vision of the dead woman in the trenches is a hallucination, it is difficult to see what coherent story is left at all. But there are plenty of suggestions that make such an assumption difficult. Strangwick, when he tells his tale, is certainly a nervous case, but it is made quite clear that his nerves were in a perfectly good state before he saw the spirit of Bella Armine, that he did not know of his aunt's death and had no idea that she was dying. Nor is there any reason to suggest that the conviction that he has seen her is a retrospective delusion, one of the manifestations of 'shell-shock', for the movement of the dialogue is all the other way. Keede, probing through what he sees to be a protective obsession with the frozen dead, presses to elicit what really happened on the day when Godsoe was due for leave, and comes, not as he expects to do on murder, but on a revelation of love surviving death. But this is a revelation that Strangwick, as he is drawn, would never expect to have, and did not want. His are the agonies of the reluctant convert, struggling against what is making nonsense of life as he supposed it to be, and imposing new and unwished standards on him. Read like this, the whole tale is closely integrated; rationalized, it is pointless. How idle would be the intricacies of the approach, if they led simply to a painful record of a collapse and a delusion. I have sometimes thought that the charges of failing craftsmanship brought against the later tales must in part arise from the inability of readers to 'take' the supernatural in Kipling. The climax, in the light of which the organization is clarified, is not there for them, because they cannot admit it. There is a sort of dialectic of faith and scepticism in 'A Madonna of the Trenches'. There had been a similar one at the end of *Kim*, but there the balance tilts perceptibly towards Kim's practical interpretation of the circumstances of the lama's trance. In this tale, the uncompromising challenge of the enclosed narrative is set at a distance; we see it through a lattice of criss-cross suggestions—shell-shock, hallucination, the angels of Mons, the very title of the story, Keede's acceptance of second sight and his remark: '*That's* the real thing at last.' The stories of the war require this modesty of method, since they handle real and recent wounds, and the healer dare not claim too much.

There is no such intricacy of organization in 'The Gardener'. In any case, Helen receives her one hour of comfort through what seems to her chance. What the medium of that comfort is depends upon the interpretation of 'infinite compassion' in the last lines of the story, where the meaning hangs in a hair-fine poise. We can take it as a usual hyperbole, running off the pen of a writer who had dealt much in hyperboles, but who had nevertheless been writing this tale with grave and exact restraint; or we can accept that it means what it says. The tale ends in a hush, weighted with ironies and unspoken questions. The vision is circumscribed by Helen's unbelief. The light is so folded in cloud that we ask if it is there at all. There is a humility, a wistful desire to see rather than an assured sight, that is very moving. This is perhaps Kipling's 'Karshish'.

'The Wish House' is a different case, because, with a very large allowance for coincidence, it can be rationalized; that allowance, however, is a heavy price to pay, and it is not Kipling's habit to exact it from us. Grace Ashcroft's headache stops 'quick as bein' kicked', after the little girl has spoken through the letter-box of the empty house and taken the pain on herself, and Mrs Ashcroft admits that the incident lay at the back of her mind. If this is coincidence, then it provides the soil for her delusion later, when she herself goes to the Wish House to take Harry Mockler's trouble on her. The manifestations there—the chair pushed back in the basement-kitchen, the feet on the stairs, the breathing behind the shut door—are all such as a superstitious and agitated woman might imagine. The injury to her leg next morning and Harry's recovery during the hopping-season are then coincidental, and so is the accident that befalls him when her running sore is nearly healed, and the good news about him as soon as she has caused it to break out again. In the years that followed, Mrs Ashcroft tells her friend, she 'took an' worked [her] pains on an' off', and learnt to know 'by the feel of it' when Harry was in need. This we could dismiss as a delusion; but she is a practical woman who puts her impressions to the test. 'Then I'd send another five shillin's to Bess, or somethin' fer the chillern, to find out if, mebbe, 'e'd took any hurt through my neglects. 'Twas *so!* Year in, year out, I worked it dat way, Liz, an' 'e got 'is good from me 'thout knowin'—for years and years.' At this the rationalizer can only say that Mrs Ashcroft's obsession must have obscured the plain sense of her sister's letters, or perhaps that she is lying to her old friend at their last meeting, or that Kipling is a very clumsy craftsman. And while we are reversing all these fingerposts, what is happening to Grace Ashcroft? There is still a good deal of her left, since her sublime and unrewarded devotion remains even if the occasion on which she exercises it is illusory. She is still, in some measure, the unsanctioned Alcestis, who goes down into Hell to save her lover. But not in the whole measure, since she has become a psychopathic case, and much of the reader's attention is diverted to making reservations he was never meant to make, and draining Mrs Ashcroft's words of their full meaning. He is, in fact, standing against the current of the tale instead of going with it, and his foothold is shifty. Mrs Ashcroft does not speak like a hysterical subject; indeed, she has never spoken before. She was cautious and slow to believe that her bargain was an effective one. 'I won't lay two an' two together *yit*', she says after the third coincidence. Her friend believes her implicitly.

It is better to see in this tale the power of love opposed to the powers of death and hell, and to listen to what the writer says. I do not know where he got his appalling Token from—in the tale Mrs Ashcroft says that the charwoman's little girl heard of it from gipsy children—but by its means he makes the pit of darkness open in a London by-street in a hot Edwardian summer. Town is empty, and a middle-aged cook from Sussex bargains with the evil thing at a little terrace-house, with the paint off the door and a strip of walled garden in front. This evocation of the darkness 'a stone's throw out' from the familiar, in an England whose social changes are precisely marked in the tale, is much finer and subtler than even the admirable 'Lost Legion', where weather, place, time and tension are all conducive to the effect required. Here the evocation is passed to us through Mrs Ashcroft's shrewd and resolute mind, in an account that confines itself strictly to what happened and wastes no word on her own reactions beyond saying that afterwards she was 'fair flogged out'.

In what I have written I have, I know, taken the key-conception, the abyss, in different senses. This is inevitable, since we are not dealing with a metaphysician or a psychic researcher, but an artist. Darkness is the implied background to his shaped work, or an element in the design of it, or a sliding speck on the rim of his vision. 'A mote it is to trouble the mind's eye.' There is, however, another artistic use for the abyss. It is the vast black cloth presented to the mental vision, inviting the artist to project his own designs upon it, to trace his own beliefs and hopes and hatreds in masterful shapes. 'The 'brushes of comets' hair' splash over the myriad-league canvas, suspended between star and star, as Dick Heldar painted his sea-devils and sea-angels in strife for the naked, choking human soul in the empty lower-deck of the ship. This process may tell us nothing about the abyss but it tells us a good deal about the artist and the pressure of his consciousness of the abyss on him. This projection Kipling called the work of Romance, and in the verses 'To the True Romance', which serve as a prelude to *Many Inventions*, he declares:

> *Oh 'twas certes at Thy decrees*
> *We fashioned Heaven and Hell—*
>
> . . . .
>
> *A veil to draw 'twixt God His Law*
> *And Man's infirmity,*
> *A shadow kind to dumb and blind*
> *The shambles where we die.*

The glittering spume of rhyme and assonance obscures the argument, if argument there is. There is certainly a conviction that this Romance, this 'handmaid of the Gods', conveys some truth. Kipling speaks at times of religions and mythologies as if they were such designs, drawn on the dark by the craving mind of man. What he himself inscribed there was, in 'Tomlinson', a justice that requires positive action from the soul, preferring the sinner to the parasitic intelligence; in 'On the Gate' a conception of transcending mercy; and in 'Uncovenanted Mercies' a speculation as to how waste human material might be 'reconditioned for re-issue', and what the true nature of spiritual 'output' is. In such work the writer ascribes to the abyss the qualities that he cannot bear it to be without. By such work, also, he temporarily hides the abyss and comforts his imagination. He may hope, perhaps, that the conception has travelled both ways, and that his mind has reflected a truth before he casts it back on the dark. This kind of writing is extremely exposed to criticism, and the critic, who undertakes to assess it, is extremely exposed to his own preconceptions and the peculiarities of his own tastes and beliefs. It can be called anything from space fiction to a parable—a term that Kipling sometimes applied to his tales, but not to these. The writer can be envisaged as grasping a celestial megaphone to proclaim his personal creed, or as performing an act of hope and faith, in order that hope and faith may grow. There is, to my ear, something of the megaphone in 'Tomlinson', but the tales sound like tentative acts of hope.

The celestial fable is an established literary form. It has been turned to their own purposes by sophisticated poets, dressed in the appearances of human society, and sometimes tied closely to particular historical events. To find an example, we need go no further than to Byron's 'Vision of Judgment', which may have counted for something in 'On the Gate', as 'Tomlinson', with its horror of exposure in the void, may ultimately draw from the lyke-wake dirge, 'This ae Night'. At any rate, to read Byron and Kipling together is to give both inventions keener definition. Both men had been exposed in early youth to the Calvinist emphasis on damnation. Kipling says that he had never heard of Hell before he was introduced to it 'in all its terrors' at Southsea, at six years old. Traces of that initiation are seen as late as 'With the Night Mail' and 'The House Surgeon', and the ultimate result was a complete rejection of the concept. Byron, for his part, was left with a recurrent obsession with the emotion of sinfulness, and the temperamental habits of defiance and disrespect as defences against it. In the 'Vision', however, a happier mood is dominant. The witty burlesque of a conventional conception of Heaven is shot through, once and again, by a perception of its beauties, and the controlled fluctuations of the tone vary from momentary sublimity to farce. 'On the Gate' begins as a reversal of Byron's conceptions. Byron's St Peter is not at all busy, for as men get worse, fewer candidates for entry come to the Heavenly Gate. The only busy official is the recording angel, who has been provided with a handsome board of six angels and twelve saints, and even these are not sufficient, for

> *at the crowning carnage, Waterloo,*
> *They threw their pens down in divine disgust—*
> *The page was so besmear'd with blood and dust.*

Here perhaps is the starting-point of Kipling's 'Tale of '16'; but his angelic guard is overworked, and St Peter's effort is not to exclude but to admit. This is not a vision of judgment but of mercy. Like Byron, Kipling borrows his comparisons from clay ('Being clay myself') and leads us from the dark Aberdeen granite Normal Civil Death Offices, where 'Death as men have made him —in their own image' is in control, and the clerks, who receive the autophonic reels of last dying speeches, try to knock them into conventional shape, to the Domestic Induced Casualty Shed, with its couriers and its telephone-indicators, and back to the crowded Gate and the vast convoy stretching far across the plain outside, beset by 'busy, discreet emissaries from the Lower Establishment'. There is a brilliant gaiety of fantasy and satiric invention, and a great, even excessive, tenderness of sentiment. Judas Iscariot telling stories to children gives way, somewhat to our relief, to Judas peddling his shame aloud with Oriental effusiveness to the distracted troops. 'This way, please. Many mansions, gentlemen! Go-ood billets! Don't you notice these low people, Sar.' The fantasy is no more detached from earth than Byron's. The dying voice of Lattimer comes on the autophonic reel with complete reality and a precise connotation of place and time. 'You go back to your Somme doin's, and I'll put it through with Aunt Maria. It'll amuse her and it won't hinder you.' The delusions of created man cannot obstruct celestial mercy, and the advanced atheist enters Heaven unconsciously, arguing with John Bunyan. 'St Christopher,' St Peter says happily, 'will pass anything that looks wet and muddy.' Death as men have imagined him— the King of Terrors—is distinguished from Azrael, the Archangel, whose function, as we are told in the companion tale, is to dismiss to the Mercy, though very certainly not without terror. Against those so dismissed, the gates of Hell shall not, or shall not long prevail. The self-pitying, confusedly-resentful deserter is, after the enactment of a military procedure familiar to him, marched off there; he will have a bad time, but they will not keep him a day longer than his sentence. This may be called the Wesleyan as distinct from the Calvinistic Hell.

> *But I surely shall feel*
> *E'er I fall into hell,*
> *That the arms of Thy love are beneath.*

So Charles Wesley wrote in his Penitential Hymns, remembering Psalm 139: 'If I go down to hell thou art there also.' The 'ruling' that covers the deserter's case, however, consists of the words of the Woman of Tekoah, to which Kipling had referred, some fifteen years before, in 'The Rabbi's Song':

> For we must needs die, and are as water spilt on the ground, which cannot be gathered up again; neither doth God respect any person: yet doth he devise means, that his banished be not expelled from him.

It is not Kipling's business in this story of '16 to consider the problem of the wicked will, as it appeared, for instance, to the Jacobean imagination. He does not ever consider it. There is plenty of cruelty, meanness and callousness in his world, and plenty of passionate or enforced violence. They are the result of various sorts of pressure working on human material. Human material is faulty. 'Oh, Lord! What *do* You expect for the money?' says Sir James Belton, after observing the condition of Wilkett, the moral and nervous war casualty in 'The Tender Achilles'. It is what we say of goods of inferior stuff and workmanship that break down under hard use. In 'The Legend of Mirth' the human race, who receive the zealous ministrations of the Archangels, are described as 'gross, indifferent, facile dust'. They have, however, other potentialities. Azrael says in 'Uncovenanted Mercies': 'I've seen wonderful work done—with my sword practically at people's throats—even when I've had to haggle a bit'; and he adds later: 'A hard lot. They frighten me sometimes.' In 1916 all kinds of weakness and hardness were elicited from human material at home and abroad. The pressures were very heavy. There might be said to be almost enough 'Hell' on earth to suspend the notion of retribution, always strong in Kipling and recurrent later. What further payment should be exacted from those who were muddy and wet and did not desert? We have often heard of the malice of the civilian in the first Great War. There were also moments of helpless love for all the ordinary, normally rather unlovable people in a bus or on a platform. 'On the Gate' is the imaginative satisfaction for such moods; and the satire, the fancy, the deliberate gay use of sentimental but natural *clichés* show that we are never for a moment supposed to forget that that is what it is. The amusingly contemporary décor, the romantic beauty of the angelic militia (for which Byron offers a hint), the dove-coloured patch on the pinions of the volunteer Imp, the fluttering of the papers on the desks 'beneath the draught of his furious vans', as he launches himself earthward on his mission, these are not merely self-indulgences, but also directives. This is a fable. There is no harm in calling it a fairy-tale, if we remember how deeply the roots of fairy-tales run into the needs and hopes of human beings.

Man is a creature of time, and there can be no absolute value in his productions. It is not only that what served the hour must appear to lose validity when the hour is past. It is that the oppressive hour may harrow up a truth that we can hardly recall or recognize when it is over. We do not commonly love the crowd on a platform or our fellow-passengers on a bus. There are passages, as every teacher knows who has had to take them, that reveal new meaning in times of war. Henry V's remark that it is 'good for men to love their present pains Upon example', Bunyan's *Holy War*, the second part of Dryden's *Annus Mirabilis* —these are hardly 'there' in peace-time; and I have been aware in what I have written of an undergraduate with whom my relations are sometimes close and sometimes very remote, who used every night on the homeward journey to see the hospital-train at Charing Cross, and the London flower-women climbing on the steps of the ambulances, as they slowed down to turn into the Strand, to throw in their bunches of flowers. This memory might be a drawback, if my aim were strictly literary assessment. For what I have to do, I do not think that it is.

The Hell of 'Uncovenanted Mercies' is not a tender jest, like the Heaven of 'On the Gate'. It is a realization of human suffering in terms of sick hope and repeated disappointment; and since it has been equipped in the most modern fashion with a large railway-station, a hotel, a casualty-room, and platforms where people meet train after train that does not bring the face they expect, there are moments when the reader ceases to feel it as a fantasy at all. This intensity of effect is given off by only a few passages, and they are interspersed with satire on the temperament and departmental methods of the Archangel of the English and with evocations of space-travel through the depths and heights of creation, terrifying and joyful. The shifts of tone are more abrupt than in 'On the Gate' and the rough-and-tumble end suggests that Kipling found some difficulty in getting his tale out of Hell. In the case of the unnamed shabby man, subjected to the test for Breaking Strain in one of Satan's shops, he is, if we like to take it so, going back to, or going beyond, the case of McIntosh Jellaludin in 'To be Filed for Reference', the last of the *Plain Tales* of his youth, as Shakespeare in his Romances went back to, and beyond, the sins, errors and losses of his tragedies. The very title is echoed. When Satan asks what has happened to the two hand-picked souls, from whose carefully-arranged cultured felicity the Archangel of the English had hoped for 'the happiest influences on their respective entourages', Azrael replies: 'Both filed.' The file is re-opened. After the Archangel of the English has cut his losses, Hell—that is, the reconditioning power—thinks there is still a little more work to be got out of the man.

> 'So we made him do it—rather as Job did—on an annuity bought by his friends, in what they call a Rowton lodging-house, with an incurable disease on him. In *our* humble judgment, his last five years' realization-output was worth all his constructive efforts.'
>
> 'Does—did he know it?' Gabriel asked.
>
> 'Hardly. He was down and out, as the English say.'

What is indicated here is the generation of a positive spiritual force in despair and degradation; and the requirement of the test for Breaking Strain is that the subject shall resist the offer of oblivion and persist in self-acceptance, with the painful consciousness of all he has lost and discarded. He is then, in the language of the Infernal industry, reconditioned for re-issue. This is a heavy burden for a fantasy to carry, and its gait, in consequence, is lop-sided. The mercies that are outside the Covenant—and very far outside the sphere of the Gods of the Copybook Headings, who know nothing of them—derive from the belief, natural to an artist if he believes at all, that nothing can break the bond between creature and creator, that God is God not only of those who acknowledge him but of those who do not, and for these mercies it is difficult to find satisfactory images.

Setting aside these inventions, we may well ask what it is that, beyond parable, fantasy or supernatural story, Kipling repeatedly says of the abyss. The answer can be given only in the most general terms. It is simply that the abyss is not empty; that it is the abode of power or Powers; that out of it come influences that affect the life of man. No man was less of a materialist. No writer has been less able, or less willing, to ascribe shape or nature to that which filled him with awe. But it is perfectly clear that through all his writing life 'the darkness stayed at his shoulder-blade'. The Gods of the Copybook Headings are explicable in terms of history and psychology; the darkness is not. Sometimes there is an ambiguity in his references to the gods. Modern machinery, he cries exuberantly, is 'everything on earth except the Gods'. Which gods? I do not know; any would serve at this point; but for the purpose of the critical understanding of Kipling it is important not to confound the two conceptions. The Gods of the Copybook Headings are generalizations from human behaviour, rhetorically worked up into pronouncers of the law that is their essence; but the ultimate Powers are not worked up at all. They are not, outside the acknowledged fantasies, shadows of desire. Perhaps it is in order that they should not become such that they remain so formless—so without form that one cannot choose between the singular and the plural pronouns in speaking of them, or between power and Powers. In an early poem, 'Evarra and his Gods', Kipling had imagined man, the craftsman of gods, shaping his divinity in accordance with his circumstances. In four incarnations he shapes four different gods, to cast them out of Paradise with laughter when at last he comes there. In 'The Bridge Builders' Krishna tells his brother gods that they forget whence they came, implying that it is men that give them shape and nature. None the less, a mind so addicted to patterns and ritual, to correspondences and analogies as Kipling's was must express itself as Evarra did, the difference being that what Evarra claimed as a fact he knows to be a symbol or hypothesis. As an artist he draws on the symbols and language of more than one faith. He had met many of them in the Masonic Lodge at Lahore which first gave a very young man, exposed to strong and various experiences, what he says he needed. Atheism, moreover, as that young man wrote in 'The Conversion of Aurelian McCoggin' (a brilliant young civilian, a little man, over-engined for his beam, whose grandfathers on both sides had been Wesleyan preachers) makes men too responsible and leaves too much to their honour. The appeal of Islam to his imagination is evident in the very early 'City of Dreadful Night'. 'My life had lain among Muslims,' he wrote in *Something of Myself*, 'and a man leans one way or other according to his first service.' When, after over twenty years' absence from the East, he came to Cairo, as he tells us in 'Egypt of the Magicians', he found its spirit waiting for him.

> Then we came upon a deserted mosque of pitted brick colonnades round a vast courtyard open to the pale sky. It was utterly empty except for its own proper spirit, and that caught one by the throat as one entered. Christian churches may compromise with images and side-chapels where the unworthy and abashed can traffic with accessible saints. Islam has but one pulpit and one stark affirmation—living or dying one only—and where men have repeated that in red-hot belief through centuries, the air still shakes to it.

Nevertheless, he also speaks through the Hindu pantheon in 'The Bridge Builders'; and the whole complex of ideas concerning law, retribution and sacrifice wakes the echoes of Old Testament language. It is on this ground that the boundary runs between the highest territory of the Gods of the Copybook Headings and the mystery of the ultimate powers, and it would be a difficult task to chart it. Later in his life, when the compassion that is apparent at all stages in his work, though not in all he wrote, strengthened into a conception of absolving love and mercy, he turned sometimes to the language and figures of the Christian faith. He does this very seldom, and always at a remove. The ballads of 'Cold Iron', 'Eddi's Service' and 'Our Lady of the Sackcloth' have the reserve of their traditional form, and 'A Nativity' is shaped as a dramatic lyric. In the tales we see the Apostles from the standpoint of an urbane Roman administrator or through the memories of an impressed but uncomprehending Scythian and a proud, rationalist Sidonian. They are men shaken and supported by the Spirit, as were the holy men of which, in *Kim*, we are told that India is full. The prefect takes a civilized interest in their doctrine, but we do not hear it preached. Indeed, there is very little of the formulation of any religion in Kipling's work. If we look for doctrine, we find only the most universal utterances —there is no god but God; all is Spirit; suffer the little children.... In *Rewards and Fairies* St Wilfrid, Archbishop and missionary, converts the South Saxons, but it is his own 'conversion' that the title of the tale records, and this 'conversion' is a move towards the inclusiveness of 'Jobson's Amen'. Altar-gates, as Dan explains anxiously, 'are just *the* one pair of gates which no man can shut'. On the islet where he is shipwrecked St Wilfrid not only learns—which delights all children—to value the faithfulness of Padda, the tame seal, but in the simplicity of his exhaustion to deal with Meon, Padda's pagan master, with the equal respect owed by one soul to another. 'One should deal kindly with all the creatures of God,' he concludes, 'and gently with their masters. But one learns late.' In the preceding ballad the fellowship of all created things before their Creator is acknowledged when Eddi preaches in his empty chapel on Christmas Eve to an old marsh donkey and a weary bullock that shelter there.

> *'How do I know what is greatest,*
> *How do I know what is least?*
> *That is My Father's business',*
> *Said Eddi, Wilfrid's priest.*

Even in the four or five thousand year-old tomb of the ancient Egyptian Minister of Agriculture Kipling, only temporarily checked by the brute-headed gods, surmised a fellowship. Man's needs have been the same in all ages; he has asked the same questions of the abyss; what answer he has thought to hear has come in the language of his time and place. Yet, especially as one grows older, the language of one's own people has most meaning and readiest access. There is a curious touch in the Appendix to 'With the Night Mail', which takes the shape of a number of the Gazette of the Aerial Board of Control. It occurs in a review of the life of Xavier Lavalle, discoverer of the Laws of the Cyclone, and Kipling is enjoying himself 'rendering' a certain type of formal French prose. The reviewer turns from the scientific achievement to the 'ground-life' of his subject:

> I would specially refer such as doubt the sustaining influence of ancestral faith upon character and will to the eleventh and nineteenth chapters, in which are contained the opening and consummation of the Tellurionical Records extending over nine years.... 'Pray for me', he says upon the eve of each of his excursions, and returning, with an equal simplicity, he renders thanks 'after supper in the little room where he kept his barometers'.

To the last Lavalle was a Catholic of the old school, accepting —he who had looked into the very heart of the lightnings— the dogmas of papal infallibility, of absolution, of confession— of relics great and small. Marvellous—enviable contradiction.

But to Kipling, speaking with his own voice in one of his last poems, the 'Hymn of Breaking Strain', the power whom he addresses is still a

> *veiled and secret Power*
> *Whose paths we seek in vain,*

working through apparent injustice, afflicting man, alone in Creation, with the 'twin-damnation—to fail and know we fail', yet manifested when overthrow and pain lead to new growth, and we

> *In spite of being broken,*
> *Because of being broken*
> *May rise and build anew,*
> *Stand up and build anew.*

Two speculative ideas accompanied Kipling through his work as symbols or examples—it is difficult to tell which—of inflowing mystery. These are the influence of the stars on men and the rebirth of the soul through a succession of lives. Both must owe a great deal to his Indian experience, but both were fully represented in his own literature and in the intellectual ferment of the time of his youth. The most interesting conception of stellar influence is in 'Unprofessional', and the most striking use of rebirth is in '"The Finest Story in the World"', though here it seems to have presented itself, as I hope to show, chiefly as the solution of a technical problem. None the less, it was a speculation that attracted him. In 'With the Night Mail' it has become the orthodoxy of the future, disposing for ever of the horror of damnation. Moreover it is one of the hypotheses by which he seeks to explain inspiration. The 'I' in ' "The Finest Story in the World"' believes that in tracing the former lives of Charlie, the bank-clerk, he has 'discovered the entire principles upon which the half-memory falsely called imagination is based'. The 'I' at this point is a good deal above himself, and has to be reduced by Grish Chunder's: 'These things are not allowed, you know. As I said, the door is shut.' Man is not meant to live in a state of plenary illumination. There are also other theories or images of inspiration, reflecting more clearly than that of metempsychosis Kipling's conviction that it comes from outside. This we must accept as his literal belief, not to be disposed of by talk about the Unconscious. Dick Heldar says explicitly: 'Good work has nothing to do with —doesn't belong to—the person who does it. It's put into him or her from outside.' The impulse is 'given'; the artist's response is faithfulness and craftsmanship. Kipling's own Daemon remains ambiguous; and his namesake, the Demon of Irresponsibility, is a very familiar imp, without any connection with the abyss. The ingenious parallels of '"Wireless"' cannot be pressed logically home; they run out in mystery, as they are meant to do. It is the fault of this story, inherent, I think, in its material, that it rouses too fretful an inquisitiveness and dowses it with too heavy a shock of awe; but in its main bearing, it is consonant with all that Kipling says on this theme. The most conclusive statement, however, is outside his works, and is to be found in Rider Haggard's account of a visit to him in 1918, to which I have already referred. The grieving father found no consolation in his fame.

> He thrust the idea away with a gesture of disgust. 'What is it worth?—What is it all worth?' he answered. Moreover he went on to show anything any of us did well was no credit to us; that it came from somewhere else, that we were, in fact, only telephone wires. As for example he instanced some of our successes—'You did not write *She*, you know,' he said, 'something wrote it through you.'

As Blake said: 'I dare not pretend to be other than a secretary; the authors are in Eternity.'

We are, then, surrounded by Powers; but we are in the dark, and the dark means dread, bewilderment and separation. If we are under orders, we do not know them. In 'Uncovenanted Mercies' we are told of Orders for Life, 'that sentence, written on the frontal sutures of the skull of every three-year-old child, which is supposed, by the less progressive Departments, to foreshadow his or her destiny'; but the Archangel of the English, who is very progressive, dismisses them as 'no more than Oriental flourishes', counteracted nowadays by training and environment. The tale confirms their validity, but the directions given to each soul are known only to its guardian angel and the higher powers. 'You know, 's well's me,' says Mrs Ashcroft to her friend, 'that na'un happens to ye till it *as* 'appened. Your mind don't warn ye before'and of the road ye've took, till you're at the far eend of it. We've only a backwent view of our proceedin's.' Kipling's convictions about the nature of man always assume this ultimate ignorance. The trumpet-calls of his moral imperatives, the crack of his whips in his noonday, cannot be understood unless they are heard echoing down these unfathomable precipices of night. In the half-lighted world we know, it is better to be a drilled man, but the trained movements are only provisional, not perfect.

There are two convictions which emerge strongly in Kipling's work, both deeply-rooted. The first is that man is a creature that can do his best work only under pressure. He is radically imperfect, originally sinful. But he has potentialities of great work in him. Therefore the early tales are full of courses of training and of the ordeals that test it and the capacities of the material. Tests of all kinds continue through his later work, and they are often cruelly difficult. They are tests for breaking strain, like Wilkett's agony at the CCS, sprung, it may be, without preparation and not to be passed simply by adherence to a code. In 'Uncovenanted Mercies' the assertion of the slightly pot-bellied Archangel of the English that it is happiness ('impeccable surroundings, wealth, culture, health, felicity') that gets the best out of people is met by the polite scepticism of Gabriel, Azrael and Satan. Hardship and storm are the proper conditions in which man can exercise himself in the virtues which are the natural but not spontaneous fruits of his spirit. This conviction accounts for the calm acceptance with which in 'The Storm-Cone' (1932) Kipling confronted the mustering of yet deadlier weather over England.

The other conviction is that the adult human being is in service. He wears some yoke or harness, whether it be the obligations of a profession or a position, the demands of his genius or those made by society on the Sons of Martha. Some carry a lonely load, but most men are harnessed in a team, or interact like pieces of machinery. I do not think that this insistence on the yoke that a man, to be completely a man, must carry conflicts at all with Kipling's insistence on independence and self-ownership. The Brushwood Boy fulfils each of his duties to his regiment and lives a wholly remote and independent life as well; and in some way every man has to make the adjustment. Kipling has no use at all for the irresponsible; and complete freedom—freedom from the rut, the yoke, the time-table, from the giving and receiving of orders, from the accepted values and the usual expressions—is too great a burden and too great a solitude for most men.

It is not claimed that there is anything unusual about the point of view illustrated in this chapter. It could be considered as a natural result of a Methodist heredity, a wide view of the world, and the intellectual climate at the end of the nineteenth century. One of the 'Epitaphs of the War' is that of the man who received no sign but none the less served the Gods. My object has been to show how deeply this common point of view was apprehended and how important it is in the perspective of Kipling's art. It is entirely fitting that *Something of Myself*, published after his death, should come to its end with such an effect of perspective. He is describing his work-table:

> Left and right on the table were two big globes, on one of which a great airman had once outlined in white paint those air-routes to the East and Australia which were well in use before my death.

The sudden, light, glancing blow is delivered in a subordinate clause, and its meaning is underlined by the cessation of the book. The desk, with its crowded equipment, and the writing hand are suddenly seen far away, receding from us, a small illuminated point in a sea of shadow. In his earlier work, as we have seen, the shutters of the house of life had clapped to and fro with casual violence; but in his later work it is, at moments, as if the very walls of the house had grown transparent.

CHAPTER EIGHT

Change and Persistence

The limitations within which I have designed this book tell more adversely against this chapter than against any of the others. It may well be felt that to discuss change and persistence in Kipling, while ignoring the political and social incitements to either, is to leave out too much. I have considered omitting the following pages on the ground that the changes and persistence in his art, which come within my scope, have already been exemplified in various places, both as to his themes and his technique. Yet there remain a good many things that I should like to say on the subject, so I have let them stand. What follows must be regarded rather as a sampling than an investigation of this field.

Kipling had both a very acquisitive and a very tenacious mind. With the acquisitiveness went in his early years a large measure of precocity. It is natural, then, that the books with which he filled his enormous literary appetite as a boy and a young man should still feed the roots of his later works, and that the literature of the Eighties and Nineties should count for something in the tales and verses of the mature Kipling. Some of these debts he has acknowledged in *Something of Myself* and elsewhere—the childhood reading that cropped up in the *Jungle Books*; Browning's 'Men and Women', which shaped his monologues in verse and prose and provided him with the figure of Fra Lippo Lippi, who seems to have accompanied him through life. Fra Lippo too rejoiced at the diversity of God's creatures and, moreover, said with irritation to the watch that apprehended him

You need not clap your torches to my face,

a remark that Kipling annexed for one of the chapters of *Something of Myself*. Browning's strongest influence, however, was necessarily early. Some of the short tales of Kipling's twenties are

Browningesque in their acceptance of the centrality of love in a man's life, and others in their presentation of special cases in love. 'In Error', 'On the Strength of a Likeness' and 'Wressley of the Foreign Office' are subjects that Browning might have used, and 'Bitters Neat' is a negative illustration of

> *Oh, the little more, and how much it is!*
> *And the little less, and what worlds away!*

I do not think, moreover, that we can set any limit to the effect of Browning's example in charging a poem with completely appropriate, substantiating, absorbing detail. The two poems which, besides 'Fra Lippo Lippi', are mentioned by name in *Something of Myself* are 'The Bishop Orders his Tomb' and 'Love among the Ruins'. They were cardinal discoveries. This line of enquiry could be followed much further, but I am chiefly interested in the tenacious survival of an appropriation, not its immediate effect. I shall therefore say nothing of his discipleship to Bret Harte, obvious and recognized by contemporary reviewers, and shall do no more here than mention *The Wrong Box*, though he declared in *Something of Myself* that he would even then back himself 'to take seventy-five per cent marks in a written or *viva-voce* examination' on it. Swinburne, one of his many masters in metre, reappears, as the stars of our morning have the habit of doing, in his evening skies. When, against all his expectations, his inauguration as Lord Rector of the University of St Andrews broke up, as he says, the frost at his heart and changed and renewed his spirit, it was in the style and verse of Swinburne that he greeted the city and her young men:

> *And the roar of the wind shall refashion*
> *And the wind-driven torches recall*
> *The passing of Time and the passion*
> *Of Youth over all.*

Later still, John Godsoe quotes 'Les Noyades' in 'A Madonna of the Trenches', and in 'Uncovenanted Mercies' Azrael, who has experience of men, utters four resonant and tragic lines from the second chorus of 'Atalanta in Calydon'; and since McIntosh Jellaludin of 'To be Filed for Reference', who, as I have suggested, seems to have something to do with this story, had once recited the whole of that play in the native quarters of the Serai, 'beating time to the swing of the verse with a bedstead leg', we may indeed say here that the morning and the evening star are the same.

But some of the leaves he turned have disintegrated in the compost. There is no substantial evidence to support my impression that Anstey's *Vice Versa* lay somewhere behind 'The Tie', that the singing House of Commons in 'The Village that Voted the Earth was Flat' is somehow connected with the singing House of Lords in *Iolanthe* (there are allusions to Gilbert and Sullivan in 'Dayspring Mishandled' and 'Uncovenanted Mercies', and there were crowded London revivals of the operas after the War) or, most tenuous of all, that Joaquin Miller's 'Ship of the Desert'—Miller was Kipling's latest 'infection' when he wrote the prize poem in 1882—counts for something in the arid scene and the destructive love of 'Mrs Bathurst'. There are many little excavations in *Something of Myself*, shafts run down to the levels where his work, like that of the King in 'The Palace', is bedded upon the structures of his predecessors. Sometimes he tells us about them, as when he indicates a boyish reading of Manon Lescaut as one of the origins of *The Light that Failed*, but often he leaves it to his reader's perception. He does the same with the incidents and encounters he records. It is often a far cry from the first impression to the re-emergence. The critic can point with assurance to the origin of Pennsylvania Penn of *Captains Courageous* in the thirty-sixth chapter of *From Sea to Sea*, and with less certainty to the Japanese artist in the eighteenth chapter, who did his best work when he was drunk, as one of the notions fused into the last third of *The Light that Failed*, but he must be wary when he sets out to trace the contribution of General Booth, Kipling's fellow-traveller in 1891 and his fellow-Doctor at Oxford seventeen years later, to the Apostle Paul of the two stories published more than twenty years after that. Yet Kipling makes the connection himself, and surely the stamp is there, though other impressions have been superimposed on it. A reference to Kipling's works will often suggest a reason for the seemingly haphazard selection of material in the second half of his autobiographical sketch. It is not possible, however, unless the author helps us, to trace the vitality that is drawn from the deepest layers of all. William Morris, mounted on a rocking-horse in the Burne-Jones nursery, cleared his imagination of the magnificence of the saga of *Burnt Njál* to the two young children there. Since not only was the occasion unforgotten but the saga could be recognized long afterwards, 'when I was old enough to know a maker's pains', the impressions must have gone deep. De Quincey tells us how two lines from Phaedrus on the statue of Æsop, raised by the Athenians, gave him his first jubilant sense of the moral sublime, and elaborates the incident according to his custom. Kipling never elaborates such hints. All that we can say is that *Burnt Njál*, with its stoicism and humour and violence, even when less than half understood, is strengthening food for a young imagination.

The debt, moral in the first place, to Walter Besant's *All in a Garden Fair* was acknowledged personally to the older novelist. The young Kipling, oppressed with overwork and loneliness in the Indian heat, read of another young man, poor and obscure, who made his way by writing and saw the door to the future open. In *Something of Myself* he touches also on the literary debt. The young man of the book 'came to realize the possibilities of common things seen' and found themes in the crowded life of the East End. Here, though the change in pace from Besant's easy amble is complete, is the end of the clue that led to Dick Heldar's vision of the city of London as the artist's 'loot' and to 'The Record of Badalia Herodsfoot'. It may be, too, that we have here a directive that turned the young writer—he was not yet twenty-one—from strange rides and phantom 'rickshaws to such 'common things seen' as 'In the Pride of His Youth', 'A Bank Fraud', 'Gemini' and 'Jews in Shushan'. But this is to enter very far into the realm of conjecture. It is not a conjectural link, however, that suggests itself between C. G. Leland's *Hans Breitmann* ballads and 'The Incarnation of Krishna Mulvaney', for Kipling used lines from 'Hans Breitmann's Ride to Church' as an epigraph. The tale has displeased many, and with some reason. In intention, however, it is an attempt to annexe for Mulvaney part of the territory of Leland's cynical, hard-living, battered exile of '48, who quarters his troop in a church, swills whisky in the aisle with grim indecency, and listens with genuine emotion to a fellow-exile playing on the organ the melodies of the fatherland. Investigators of Kipling's relations with the literature of his youth may well follow up both these contacts. They will find much that is prophetic of Kipling's practice in Besant's lecture to the Royal Institution on *The Art of Fiction* in 1884, and, as Professor Carrington has done, a passage of what is now called Kipling mannerism in *All in a Garden Fair*.

In his *Autobiography* they will find a reference to his 'Titania's Farewell', which appeared in *Once a Week* in 1869 and treated, he says—for I have not been able to find it—'the last night of the fairies in this island', some forty years before '"Dymchurch Flit"'. (But the departure by boat seems to derive from 'The Elfin-Grove' in *Grimms' Tales*.) They will find in a letter of C. G. Leland's in 1893 a rejection of 'the Horrors of Namby-Pambyism and feeble Despair' even more violent than the utterances of Kipling on this subject, a year or two before, since the old adventurer explicitly prefers 'all the Horrors of War'—which he had seen—as 'less disgusting'; and in the early pages of his *Memoirs* (1893) they will come on a fragrant evocation of the Philadelphia of his boyhood and, through the memories of the oldest inhabitants, of fifty years before that, which seems to me a very likely starting-point for 'Brother Square-Toes', nearly twenty years later.

To abide by the book, however, which means by what Kipling himself explicitly indicates or lets fall, the work of Besant and Leland was a stimulus consciously received and soon worked off. I now have to propose another author, whose work provoked in Kipling, if I am right, both an immediate and a deferred reaction. This was Edwin Lester Arnold, whose *Wonderful Adventures of Phra the Phoenician* was serialized in the *Illustrated London News* from July to December 1890. In this lively, picturesque, cheerful romance, written with homely vigour and, in the early scenes at least, almost free from tushery, Arnold, who like Kipling had close links with the East, uses a fantasticated metempsychosis as a structural device to connect a series of historical scenes, from the arrival of a Phoenician trader in pre-Roman Britain to an explosion in the laboratory of an Elizabethan alchemist. The book was widely read at the time and is readable now, though the supply of everything in it is too ample, and conviction leaks away. Kipling's '"The Finest Story in the World"', treading close on its heels in July 1891, reads like a craftsman's reaction to the entertaining, vivid, sprawling thing. The notion is seized, the manifestations trimmed, condensed, intensified. *Phra the Phoenician* is not mentioned; the book that the 'I' lends to Charlie, in order to find out if the boy has any suspicion of the origin of his 'dreams', is Mortimer Collins's *Transmigration*. 'What rot it all is', says Charlie frankly, and he is right. It was neither a new nor a successful book, and there was nothing in it for either Kipling or Charlie except the bare introduction of the concept of reincarnation, and that is not used, as Arnold and Kipling use it, as a principle of continuity between historical periods or as a means of injecting an eye-witness's immediacy into them. Kipling's problem is to achieve imaginative conviction in the presentation of the remote past, and he transfers this problem to the 'I' of his tale. The device of reincarnation appeals on more than one ground, and Kipling improves on Arnold by presenting his reborn hero as a weedy London bank-clerk, in whose intermittent but brilliantly immediate memories the 'I' sees his material for a unique and masterly work, a landmark in the history of the human mind. But it will not do. The disconnected memories—intense moments of experience, loaded with physical sensation—look, when they are sorted and recorded, like the draft of any other book-built historical novel. In the tale, the 'I' cannot achieve his object, but, by the tale, Kipling does achieve his; for what the 'I' finally records is the baffling relationship with Charlie. In a moment and for a moment, as the coals shift in the grate or a cow bellows on a barge below London Bridge, Charlie's former lives come through in incomparably vivid single jets. We see the sunlight sliding between oar and oarhole on the lower deck, where the galley-slaves row, and we hear the laugh of a 'much shrewder' Charlie as he remembers how the bellowing cattle on Thorfin Karlsefne's ship scared the Skraelings. The difficulty of sustaining conviction is met by refusing to attempt to sustain it. The reader is magnificently handled. As we strain to distinguish and piece together the scattered hints of Charlie's former lives, we share the anxiety of 'I' for a full vision, take in our stride the postulate of reincarnation and, in effect, get a much stronger imaginative impression of the past from disjointed fragments than we could have done from a complete picture. The fragments glow with conviction because we are infected with excitement at a revelation so imminent and so completely unrealizable. The very fact that the attention of 'I' is divided—he is even more eager to produce evidence of the multiple lives of men and thus abolish the fear of death than he is to write the supreme historical novel—leaves them to pulse with unobstructed light. By complicating the frame of his story Kipling has completely disencumbered the moments.

Ten years later Arnold published *Lepidus the Centurion*. The device here is the prolonged trance of the hero who, when his grave is broken into, wakes to take his part in contemporary life for a time, revisiting the countryside he knew some fifteen or sixteen hundred years before. I do not think that one can read this book without recalling the Parnesius stories of *Puck of Pook's Hill*. Here is the same easy, gentlemanly Roman, quite at home in an English country-house, though liable to take the dinner-gong for the alarm of a barbarian raid, as Parnesius mistakes Una's catapult for a British sling. Here is the casually vivid evocation of sights and sounds in a Roman homestead, and the pleasing interplay of familiar and unfamiliar.

> 'Where are they, comrade?—Where are the brass-clad legionaries; and the naked British children; and the tall dogs quarrelling over yesterday's refuse; and the white oxen munching their hay by the stone-wheeled carts in the courtyard; and the hucksters in their sheds bartering Gaulish stuffs for new-plucked boar fangs, or wolf-skins?'

It is on method and style, the cheerful, casual tone and the precise, scattered detail, that the case must rest, but there are other grains of evidence. In both of Arnold's books there is local continuity of scene, and this becomes central in the *Puck* tales. Then, too, Kipling tells us that the first tale he wrote in the *Puck* series—he rejected it afterwards—envisaged the departure of the legions from Britain from the ship of a Saxon raider. Phra the Phoenician also, in his second incarnation saw this departure. His third leads him to the battle of Hastings, where Kipling's Norman knight fought. These last grains, it must be admitted, weigh very light. The withdrawal of Rome and the Norman invasion lie in the fairway for any author who builds a series of historical tales about a house and a hillside in Sussex.

In *Something of Myself* Kipling says more about *Puck of Pook's Hill* and *Rewards and Fairies* than about any other of his books. He tells us of the immediate human and local stimuli—his cousin's suggestion, his children's performance of scenes from *A Midsummer Night's Dream*, the peacock-hued slag of the Elizabethan mule-tracks crossing his land, the Roman horse-bit in his well, the Neolithic axe-head in his pond. Professor Carrington offers us E. E. Nesbit's *The Phoenix and the Carpet*, and we accept this admirable children's book gladly as a precipitant. Kipling's

Daemon, however, whose presence was continuously felt during the writing of these tales, had a powerful metabolism, working sometimes with great rapidity and sometimes as slowly as the mills of God, sometimes in the full light of the intellect and sometimes in darkness and obscurity. A writer can remember, without knowing what it is he remembers; and he can (like Charlie) remember without knowing that he is remembering at all. I do not know if Kipling remembered Arnold when the 'Puck' tales came flooding into his mind. It does not matter. Nothing that I have suggested impugns his originality. I did not, in fact, undertake any special search for sources or models when I was planning this book, but in following up Kipling's own allusions to writers of his youth I came on certain possibilities that seemed to shout from the page that they were facts. I cannot claim this status for most of them, for the Daemon in assimilating his nourishment has destroyed much of the evidence; but I must not be so false to whatever minor imp is assigned to scholars as not to record my conviction that these are the crumbs of the Daemon's meal.

This sort of persistence is one of imaginative impression. In the case of an adult artist the impression is probably fused, while it is being received, with the conviction that the thing could be done better, the problem of presentation could be more satisfactorily solved; and it is therefore the fused, not the simple, impression that generates in time the new work. There are many other kinds of persistence in his books. In his autobiographical sketch, *Something of Myself*, he conformed to the standards of his youth, though the pattern of autobiography and the expectations of readers had changed around him. It has been called evasive. It says nothing directly of the trouble in Vermont, nothing of his relations with his wife, nothing of the deaths of his elder daughter and his son. But it is entirely in harmony with the autobiographical utterances of many Victorian gentlemen who were authors. The plan of these works was, I believe, laid down by Thomas Hood, when he was discussing with his friend Wright the book which became *Literary Reminiscences*. 'Although declining to give a life,' he wrote, 'I thought it not out of character to give the circumstances that prepared, educated, and made me a literary man.' So far a gentleman could go. This was the ground later occupied by Trollope, Walter Besant and, one might add, the American C. G. Leland, who believed himself to be exemplifying an unconventional degree of outspokenness. The intimacy of the earlier pages, of the remembered stresses and chances of childhood and youth, gives place, once the writer has emerged into public knowledge, to a much more restricted communication. The perspective alters. It is now with his public self that the autobiographer deals and the doors of his private rooms are shut. We may hear of the material openly offered by fortune to the writer, of the development of his literary methods and the changes in the literary world during his career. But we must go to Trollope's private letters to learn how he loved his wife and his sons—and even to understand the full strength of his passion for his work, on which subject Kipling is not unduly reticent. By the side of these books, indeed, his will appear normal. His reticence is not more marked than theirs; it is less marked than that of Tennyson, who carried a similar distaste for personal publicity to the point of wishing, in his old age, as Mrs Ewing reports, that he had never published *In Memoriam*. What is remarkable about *Something of Myself* is the survival of this accepted form, unaltered by contemporary pressures, some fifty years beyond its time. In his seventieth year Kipling was writing the kind of personal statement that was approved in his twentieth, and it was 'not out of character' for him to do so. Fifty years before it would have been thought a modest and informative memorial (even De Quincey, if we discount the exotic nature of his material and of his imagination, had not given much more; nor, when we have allowed for protective and playful mystifications, denser to his own age than to ours, had Lamb). To this generation, eager for psychological evidence, often more interested in what is suppressed than in what has been selected for expression, *Something of Myself* appears defiant and uncommunicative enough.

The persistence of certain dominant themes through the work of an author is not unusual, They are the patterns of moral experiences that impinge on his mind in his youth and are confirmed in his maturity; it is in expressing them that he learns his art, and unless they and the art that explores them cease to develop, their persistence is no ground for saying that the author's experience has fossilized. I have tried to show in the chapter on Revenge that one of Kipling's dominant themes does indeed develop and reaches its most subtle, tragic and profound expression in his last collection of tales; and in the chapter on Healing I have traced the emergence of a theme which, barely touched in his earlier work, becomes dominant in his later phases. Other themes could be followed up in the same way. Professor C. S. Lewis has pointed out that Kipling was the first writer of fiction in England to deal with that large and often passionate area of experience that includes the relation of a man to his work and to the men whose work interacts with his. This line runs right through from the sketch of the young Gallio in 'The Judgment of Dungara' to Castorley in 'Dayspring Mishandled' and Wilkett in 'The Tender Achilles'. The bond between ex-servicemen, never central but often in support in the later tales, is from one point of view a specialized aspect of this theme.

The themes of the ordeal and the tribal sacrifice have very ancient roots in primitive life. Kipling showed himself well aware of this in some of the speeches to schools and service groups reprinted in *A Book of Words*. Stories of sacrifice, he said, are to be found in all mythologies, and many describe at length how the selected man prepared himself for the oblation. The most primitive expression of this theme is 'The Knife and the Naked Chalk', but it is one aspect of 'At the End of the Passage'. This is not the sacrifice of the meek. There is a passage in the early journalism of *From Sea to Sea* where he remembers in Japan the gods of the Northern imagination, fit recipients, he says, of the sacrifice of the rebellious human spirit. But in the final story on this theme, it is neither god nor tribe that receives the sacrifice of Grace Ashcroft's life, through long-drawn preparations to the accomplished payment, but merely the unwitting man she loves; and she alone exacts it. Though sacrifice in the full sense is seldom the acknowledged subject of his tales, one may say that his characters commonly prefer something else to their personal interest, whether it be the stability of a bridge, the peace of a district or the honour of the Armies in Hind, and this makes the demand for sacrifice at some level always a latent possibility. One must always risk one's life, or one's soul, or one's peace, or some little thing, as Maximus says—though his risks were incurred for his own ambition.

There is something the same shift in accent from the tribal ethos to the condition of the individual spirit in Kipling's handling of the theme of the ordeal. This is one of the most pervasive of all his themes. The test of fitness, the test of manhood, is a qualifying examination. It is always moral, though the morals need not be universally accepted. It can be imposed as a violent jest by the entered members of a group, as it was on Mr Wontner in 'The Honours of War', or by authority, as in 'Regulus', or by chance operating within an established and public framework, as in 'His Private Honour'. These tests are the equivalent of primitive ordeals. The young man who has passed them enters into full membership of his group and receives his full share of responsibility in it. The last tale to turn on such a testing is 'The Honours of War', published in 1911. After 1914, we may say, the tests were too universally and stringently applied and too tragically made good for the theme to retain its special colouring. Or, more likely, the moral discoveries, to which the later tales move, are the more complex ones of the older man and woman, with a lifetime's habit behind them. Here we pass into that intensification of the theme that Professor Bonamy Dobrée has pointed out, the test for breaking strain. This ordeal does not propose a standard to be reached; it is a full test of what human material can bear. It is not a wholly new theme. It is faintly discernible at the end of 'Mrs Bathurst'; but now, in the war tales, the tales of war injuries and in 'Uncovenanted Mercies' we are called to consider the dire pressures, the unappeasable obscure exactions that break, or stop just short of breaking, a man or woman. There are no rules in this game. Nothing suffices but the utmost, and that not always.

There is little room here to examine Kipling's conception of the love between man and woman. It is easy to underestimate the part it plays in his work, since, after his early tales, he seldom builds a story round it. Moreover in presenting the wife and helpmate his touch is not always happy. Dinah Shadd has to be seen through Mulvaney's emotional eloquence. Agnes Strickland and Lady Jim bear those period marks that do so much more harm to the figure of the domestic woman than to that of her rebellious sister. William bids fair to be a staunch service-wife, as good as gold, identified with her husband's interests and talking his language. Janet McPhee, already stout and middle-aged, was 'wholesome and antiseptic' to love, we are told, and so, no doubt, McPhee had found her. Most of these wives are middle-aged and they play bit parts and make brief appearances, but they are not therefore a negligible body. Mrs M'Leod of 'The House Surgeon', a fat Greek woman 'with a heavily powdered face, against which her black long-lashed eyes showed like currants in dough', is sensitive and courageous, motherly and wifely. Mrs Burges, who sees her husband off to his Lodge, has borne with him the loss of their only son, and they are still together. This is the sanity of the affections, the established reliance, the fruit of domesticated love, as much of comradeship in life as life allows. That it is not a static condition but subject to the strains of human nature, that a fundamental hostility may co-exist between man and woman with a fundamental love and need, is what Kipling said in 'The Enemies to Each Other'. It was an aspect that he had not touched before; it comes late in his work, and is given the Oriental stateliness and playfulness of a fable.

Love the destroyer is much in evidence in the early tales. The violence and irrationality of it is typified by the action of the charm in 'The Bisara of Pooree'. This is a knowing little tale, unsympathetically told. It speaks of the quite unsuitable and 'really blind attachment' of the displeasing Pack, who makes himself a 'nuisance' and is 'nearly mad' and ready to go beyond all reason and to steal the charm. When he does so the girl, whom he had merely embarrassed up till then, falls into the same blind folly. Wressley of the Foreign Office, too, is made and unmade by an irrational passion for a silly little girl who cannot understand him, for whom he first writes and then destroys his brilliant work on the Central Indian States. The ashes of Athira and Sukhet Singh in 'Through the Fire' are the remains of such a conflagration. It drives men and women out of their true—or their acquired—natures. In 'Beyond the Pale' Trejago's 'madness' deprives him of all common caution, and poor, bullied Mrs Schreiderling in 'The Other Man' is seen 'kneeling in the wet road by the back seat of the newly-arrived tonga, screaming hideously.' There is a strong note of violence and abandonment in these drastic scenes and anecdotes, however curtly they are told. The narrator, for all his knowledgeableness, is sometimes appalled. It is in this region of grotesque and tragic illusion and grotesque and tragic reality that we find what is permanent in Kipling, not in his precocious and cleverish dealings with Simla flirtations and Mrs Hauksbee. The components of 'Mrs Bathurst' are already assembled. The kind of woman that Mrs Bathurst is—the vessel of a power whose effects can go counter to her willed character and her natural kindness—is already noted in Mrs Vansuythen in 'A Wayside

Comedy', and in Mrs Delville in 'A Second-Rate Woman', where dowdiness and unhappy languor cannot nullify the attraction. 'Mrs Bathurst' is the culmination of the theme of destruction. After that he does not touch it again until he shows how love, starved, misplaced and entirely unacknowledged, betrayed Mary Postgate. Last of all, in 'The Wish House' and 'Uncovenanted Mercies', of which I have already said enough, we follow out, first in time and then in eternity, the fierce alchemy by which the deadly elements of this energy are transmuted into agents of purification.

The friendship between men is never central in Kipling's tales, unless it may be held to be so in 'The Man who would be King' —but that is a tale that changes its prevailing colour, like an opal, whenever it is read. It is the assumption in all the tales of Mulvaney, Learoyd and Ortheris, and is occasionally asserted with emphasis. In *The Light that Failed* it is emotionally handled. It is never so strongly lighted again, but it recurs constantly. *Captains Courageous* has the odd partnership of Uncle Silas and little Penn. The bond between Sir Richard and Brother Hugh, like that between Parnesius and Pertinax, is more than a convenience of the story-teller. 'Beauty Spots' has its pair of young ex-servicemen, and there are close personal relationships between the scientists of 'Unprofessional' and the Masons in 'Fairy-Kist'; but these are older men, and their stable relations are not demonstrative. The parental or quasi-parental bond, often stained with the colour of loss or potential loss, recurs in the tales from 'The Story of Muhammad Din' and 'Without Benefit of Clergy', through *Kim* and the Taffimai tales to 'The Gardener', 'The Manner of Men' and 'Beauty Spots'. Qabil has lost his son at sea and softens to the audacious young Balearic captain. The tobacconist Burges has now no heir to his money or the historic treasures of his trade that he has collected. 'Beauty Spots' touches delicately Mr Gravell's poignant pleasure in the companionship of the son who has been restored to him, and his concern for his health (he has been gassed), and doubles the effect by the natural reversal of function by which Jemmy unobtrusively but firmly safeguards his father. None the less, since 'each of the Seven Ages of Man is separated from all the others by sound-and-X-ray-proof bulkheads', these relationships, and all other forms of love, never abolish, though they assuage, the essential loneliness of the human spirit.

The last of these persistent themes that I shall mention is vanity. This is not pride nor egoism. It springs from the uncontrollable pleasure and exultation in the functioning of one's own power and brilliance. 'Und I work miracles—und dey come off too' as old Muller says in 'In the Rukh'; and the satisfaction is not very different when the 'miracle' is a successful bluff. It is hardly possible for the young genius to avoid this encrustation on the surface of his humility, and if he is tender-conscienced he may wonder uneasily how deep the crust really is. Kipling chastens this type of vanity steadily, all the way from 'The Conversion of Aurelian McGoggin' to 'The Tender Achilles'. Landmarks on this path are the 'I' of '"Brugglesmith"', Suleiman-bin-Daoud, Hal o' the Draft, the four archangels of 'The Legend of Mirth', St Paul of 'The Church that was in Antioch', and poor Wilkett. The most insidious subtlety of vanity is not the simple showing-off of Suleiman-bin-Daoud, when he gratuitously undertakes to feed all the animals in the world, but the zeal 'that with superfluous burdens loads the day', springing not from the demands of the job or the crudities of emulation, but from the vain man's conception of the standard of performance that is appropriate to him. Aurelian McGoggin always went beyond his instructions, and Wilkett could not be content to make mistakes like other men.

These themes and others are expressed through different subjects and in different settings. Occasionally Kipling repeats what is essentially the same story, but the difference in handling obstructs recognition. I have indicated the likeness and the differences between 'The Man who Was' and 'The Tree of Justice'. It could be done between 'By Word of Mouth' and 'A Madonna of the Trenches' and between the groups of the consumptive girl and her two lovers in 'On Greenhow Hill' and in 'Marklake Witches'. In setting his tales his art moved with his life, allowing for the natural interval of delay during which the impressions he had received were worked off. The deep impression of India takes nearly a dozen years to embody itself, but there is nothing after *Kim* except, divided from it and from each other by long intervals, 'In the Presence' and 'The Debt', both of them anecdotes about English Emperors of India, recounted by Indians to each other, and illustrating a standard of honour and a spontaneous courtesy that all races recognize. There is no harking back to the American or the South African scene, once contact with it had ceased, though Americans are introduced against an English background, On the other hand, as I have shown, the war is not left behind. Kipling lived in full view of its results, and only one of his later tales omits it (excepting, naturally, the historical tales) and that is 'The Wish House'. In his rural settings he is at once deeply aware of, and reassured by, the traditional elements in his scene, and quick to record changes. I have heard the two hedgers in 'Friendly Brook' called anachronisms, and certainly the strict local containment of these old Wealden oaks is now a thing of the past; but the tale was published in 1914, and Jabez and Jesse (they bear the Scriptural names of their generation) might be the grandsons of the men who fought at Waterloo, as their own grandsons may have fought with the Royal Sussex, in whose ranks Lord Moran found the last examples of Wellington's 'yokel' soldiery. Kipling tells us that some of these old rural craftsmen worked for him, when he first settled at Burwash. Captain Mankeltow of 'The Captive', however, later Lord Marshalton, reflects a changing society, since, by the time of 'The Edge of the Evening', he is glad to let his Georgian mansion and park to Laughton O. Zigler because of the death-duties on his inheritance; and, less than twenty years later, in 'Beauty Spots', the touring charabancs and picnic litter of democracy are making all rural solitude precarious. Scientific and mechanical advance is immediately reflected in his tales. The motor-car replaces the horse in them as the railway does the stage-coach in Dickens's novels. The early wireless in the tale of that name and the early cinematograph in 'Mrs Bathurst' are turned to his artistic purposes; and the early stages of the conquest of the air stimulate him to a long-term political forecast, which has not yet been matched against the event, and to the creation of one of his most detailed imagined worlds. Even his Infernos are up-to-date in their fantastic equipment. The approach to the Limbo of Lost Endeavour in 'The Last of the Stories' is like that to a big railway junction. The incoming souls stop at the distance-signal for line-clear, and whistle. The Hades of 'The Benefactors', twenty years later, is a vast engine-room, with tier on tier of platforms and gratings, and the stokers of Nos 47—53 Auxiliary Furnaces standing easy in the morning watch over their bowls of raw cocoa. Fifteen years later still the Satan of 'Uncovenanted Mercies' commands a super-cinema, a talkie before its time, among the resources of his modernized Hell.

These changes, however, do not affect the inmost nature of man or invalidate the truths of the Gods of the Copybook Headings, under whose authority he stands. Speaking to the Royal Geographical Society in 1914 on 'Some Aspects of Travel', Kipling first stressed the difference that air-travel would make to the whole outlook of the traveller—'The old mechanism is scrapped; the moods and emotions that went with it follow'—and then concluded: 'Only the spirit of man carries on, unaltered and unappeasable'. At St Andrews, nine years later, with an unfamiliar world taking doubtful shape around him, he reaffirmed to the young men who listened to him: 'Nothing in life changes. The utmost any generation can do is to rebaptize each spiritual and emotional rebirth in its own tongue'. This is the point of view of Satan in 'Uncovenanted Mercies'. In face of the sanguine and progressive Archangel of the English, whose solicitude for his people, now refined by social welfare, leads him to suggest that Azrael should modify the cruder features of his 'despatch-work', he insists that nothing is new, and especially not the sins of men. Human language is speciously inventive. In the sixteenth century English souls had come down to Hell 'positively Caxtonized' with words, but, after a little boiling and peeling, their novel transgressions were all found to be reducible to the old Imperfect Octave. We do not therefore find any 'new men' in Kipling's stories. The well-behaved subalterns who disquieted Stalky turned out to be much the same as he had been himself. It is not the absence of the historical sense that makes Valens and Baeticus and Parnesius so like Bobby and Moorshed and Tallantire. New crafts and conditions produce new skills; new languages are born; he notices a special look in the eyes of airmen; but man does not change.

Any summary description of Kipling's characters is likely to fall far short of their variety. The Kipling man, as he is supposed to be, is not Baxter, the gentle and slightly devious lawyer, nor Wollin, nor Shend, nor Sulinor, the big, dish-faced Dacian with his dread of the beasts of the arena, nor Manallace, nor Wilkett. None of these even represents what Kipling from first to last so delights to contemplate, the complete fitness, natural and acquired, of a man for his work. They are none of them, except perhaps Wilkett, the best of their kind; and Wilkett's excellence is strictly limited to his professional function and precariously supported by an undeveloped moral nature. It is more possible to classify the characters of the first half of his writing life. First there are the ordinary people, the creatures and sometimes the sport of circumstance, who appear in large numbers in the Anglo-Indian scenes and give substance and reality to the English ones. A reviewer in the *Home and Colonial Mail* wrote of the earliest tales: 'His knowledge of Anglo-Indian human nature, which is ordinary human nature under great provocation, is profound—we were going to say awful.' Profundity is not easily shown in summaries and anecdotes of two thousand words in length, but an episode or a gesture can be charged with an illustrative significance which will lay bare a way of life. The behaviour of ordinary people is exposed to the provocation of circumstance. In the longer tales Kipling labours this point somewhat, but it is real, and sometimes alarming. It is ordinary people who make and inhabit the little Hell at Kashima, since 'all laws weaken in a small and hidden community where there is no public opinion' and the judgment of God is 'almost as distant as Narkarra'—a hundred and forty-three miles away. Secondly there are the fully-developed types, the triumphs of decorum, standing up superbly in their shafts or shifting their loads with the last ounce of heart in them. *Kim* is full of them; the Stricklands, father and son, belong to this *élite*, and Hurree Babu, and Corbyn, and Findlayson, and Lord Lundie, and Disko Troop, the best skipper on the Banks, who thought like a cod when he was following the shoals. These are the masters of circumstance, unless the tribe requires a sacrifice or fortune is in an ironical mood. Lastly there are the 'humours', the eccentrics in the English tradition, equipped with speech and mannerisms that cry out to be acted, larger than life but based on truth. It is not always possible to draw the line between the second and the third classes, since the completely specialized man easily becomes grotesque. Mulvaney's private sorrows keep him on the hither side of eccentricity; the fantasy of the parrots in 'A Naval Mutiny' propels Winter Vergil into it; Emmanuel Pyecroft with his remarkable vocabulary and his unflinching professionalism varies from tale to tale. In the later tales the divisions merge. L. Maxwell M'Leod, the Jewish fur-dealer of 'The House Surgeon', knows where all the rarer furs come from and go to, and has the finest collection of narwhal tusks in the world. He is therefore the best of his kind;

but he is also provided with small oddities of manner which make his a character-part, and, as the tale shows, he is in addition affectionate, sensitive and tenacious. This is a substantial figure enough for a secondary character in a thirty-page tale.

'The House Surgeon' will do, as well as any other story, to illustrate Kipling's remarkable power of conveying the personal presence of his characters. At this stage of his work he no longer makes much use of the introductory description. If it occurs, it is short. Zigler in 'The Edge of the Evening' describes Lord Lundie as 'like a frame-food and soap advertisement', and the eminent Judge of Appeal rises before our informed eyes. Nor are the most convincing speeches—those that seem actually to vibrate on the air—any more the climactic ones. It had been a finely-managed and traditional moment when, in the early 'On Greenhow Hill', old Jesse Roantree, standing in his house-door, discharged his grief as a father and his disapproval of the man his dying daughter had chosen through his musician's disgust; 'Thou'lt never be good for naught i' th' world, and as long as thou lives thou'll never play the big fiddle', and then shut the door softly between Learoyd and his love. But in the later tales Kipling works by scattered, and sometimes tangential, observations. In 'The House Surgeon' M'Leod is suddenly substantially there, on the second page, by means of an intonation and a casual quaintness of gesture:

> 'A man and his family ought to be happy after so much expense, ain't it?' He looked at me through the bottom of his glass.

Baxter is formally introduced as a 'large, greyish, throaty-voiced man'. He is meant to appear ambiguous. Presently the narrator, harbouring 'well-developed theories' of misappropriation of moneys, and worse, against him, wishes that he were not 'so gentle, and good-tempered, and innocent-eyed'. Four pages on, he says definitely; 'You're a good man . . . A very good man'; and in some way I do not understand, this effect is visually confirmed a dozen lines later when Baxter appears 'in an ulster over orange and white pyjamas, which I should never have suspected from his character'. Something boyish is suggested in the middle-aged lawyer, something that matches the innocence; and this is more comprehensibly underlined when he wakes up from his sleep in the hall of the redeemed house:

'I've had a heavenly little nap', he said, rubbing his eyes with the backs of his hands like a child.

His cousin's bitter obsession and cruel, condemning love have never touched him. We feel as if we should know him in the street—or on the links—and recognize his voice, not from any remarkable mannerism but from the habitual confirmative endings of his remarks: 'Never was', 'Never would', 'Always did', 'Elizabeth doesn't matter. Brain of a hen. Always had.'

One type of character appears all through Kipling's work. This is the resourceful young officer, military or naval, carrying heavy responsibilities with a cheerful countenance, formidable in jest or earnest. He met these young men in India and South Africa, at Portsmouth and Simonstown, in peace and war. The Infant, back from the Burmese War; Judson, that 'ship's husband' and mandolinist, quelling a revolution; Stalky, besieged in a Border fort; Moorshed, tyrannically elaborating his gaudy jests on sea or land; the officers of the destroyer in 'A Sea Dog'—these are the same young men, functioning according to the circumstances in which they find themselves. They are brothers of the young veterans of 'The Trade', of whom he wrote with strong emotion in *Sea Warfare*. He called them children, and they cannot have liked it, if they read him. But this spontaneous, unchastened emphasis of admiration and protest at the intimacy of youth with the business of death was not new in 1916. It can be found in the Boer War journalism in 'With Number Three' and earlier in 'The Drums of the Fore and Aft'. Distanced and depersonalized, the address 'child' is appropriately placed in the mouth of old Allen in 'A Burgher of the Free State', when he confronts the gun of a very young, very tough loyalist among the roses of his garden.

Kipling, then, took shape early and held it tenaciously; but the contract with his Daemon forbade him to follow up a success, and the willed changes of the craftsman's experimental drive interacted with the natural changes of years and experience. There are no facile repetitions in his work. Even the young officers, of whom I have just spoken, function according to their circumstances, and the circumstances differ widely between 'Judson and the Empire' and 'A Sea Dog'. In the latter tale, moreover, it is not the Skipper or even his dog that is the object of Kipling's curiosity, but rather the mixed crew and 'Cywil', the

Crystal Palace-trained RNVR man, with his plans for 'mowally delousing' them. The Daemon apparently regarded the two *Jungle Books* as one work, since the tales were written consecutively, but had to be placated over *Rewards and Fairies* by the invention of a 'plinth', by which the architecture of the second group of *Puck* stories was varied from that of the first. The return to the scenes and characters of *Stalky & Co.* deserves examination. The original tales were written in Kipling's early thirties. Some ten years later he wrote 'Regulus', in which we hear King, a magnificent teacher though rather too acid, take a class through the Fifth Ode of Horace's Third Book; and it is a fair guess that Kipling was stimulated to this *amende honourable* by his own change of mind toward Horace, which he records in *Something of Myself*. The remaining three tales, 'The United Idolaters', 'The Propagation of Knowledge' and 'The Satisfaction of a Gentleman, were written in his early sixties, nearly a generation after Stalky first showed his qualities. *Stalky & Co.*, Kipling says, is a parable. The obvious interpretation—there may be others—is educational; a wise negligence, particularly of the emotional side of a boy's life but also of his minor outbreaks and adventures, combined, when these get out of measure, with a sufficiently heavy discipline that makes no pretence to be perfect justice, is the best preparation for a resourceful, well-adjusted maturity, since it is not false to the general conditions of life. The terms of the parable are somewhat hyperbolical, though not more so than those of many school tales of the period. Boys and masters are a little over life-size, and the unusual features of the school they inhabit add to the legendary colouring. But beneath the hyperbole there is enough of the recognizable and real. Anyone who has known schoolmasters knows the sort of men who, in the sight of their charges, at once unkindly keen and necessarily limited, were King and Prout and Hartopp. An element of fantasy enters into such episodes as the ruining of King's books and the grand manifestation of the dead cat under the dormitory floor, the fantasy of the adolescent who, as the tales duly show, is not yet a match for, though he is a nuisance to, the adults whose job it is to instruct and control him. With the later tales, however, the question of dimensions hardly comes in. The characters are life-size. The tales, especially the three last, suggest a long retrospect, the memory of an ageing man revisiting the scenes of boyhood with that spontaneous amusement and enjoyment that comes when the elderly go back in company over their common youth. The 'unforgotten innocent enormities' are seen for what they really were, and masters and boys restored to their true stature. The boys that swarm through the pages act and speak with complete credibility. Vernon, looking like an earnest elderly horse, who will never be higher than the top of the second class, because his virture is costive; Study Five preparing for the English examination; the fags who are lifted up in waste-paper baskets as heave-offerings, till the bottoms fall away—the whole lively, grubby, noisy community is there, with the masters irritated, supercilious, mutually intolerant, yet possessed by that unreasonable 'caring' of the teacher for the pupil as the recipient of his ministrations, and occasionally by his need of reassurance that all his effort has not been wasted, that 'something sticks', as King says, 'even among the barbarians'. This is done to the life. The 'level beams' of eventide do indeed show more truth than the midday sun had done, a truth of exact and humorous recognition. Writing these tales was an act of pleasure that had no need of a didactic intention to complicate it. 'Regulus' stands a little apart, for it can still be classed as a parable, but it would be difficult to find such a meaning in 'The United Idolaters' or 'The Propagation of Knowledge'. 'The Satisfaction of a Gentleman' is less successful as a tale, but relevant to this discussion, because in it every man is out of his humour—the infallible Head, confessing to an adult Pussy how he was once badgered by an irate Governor into giving an unjust licking; the wily and audacious boys, not a day older than their years, involved in a comically unheroic 'duel' in the sand-pits; even Foxy, whose twinkling eyes suggest that this time he is not baffled but silently in the know. For full measure, Pussy's report on the Head's confession leads an older Stalky up the garden path, so that his: 'Knew it all the time', is baseless swagger. Stalky, however, had already played second fiddle in 'The United Idolaters'. The effect is not so much one of deflation as of the recovery of the real scene. The tales are not a recession to his earlier vein, nor a breach of compact with the Daemon.

At Westward Ho! the Head often told his boys that there was not much justice in the world, and Kipling often repeats the lesson and sometimes illustrates it. But the moral nature of man is outside the sphere of fortune, and carries its own scourges.

This is the conviction that controls '"Love-o'-Women"', and it is enforced by Mulvaney with a plainness that is worlds away from the suspended judgment of 'Mary Postgate'. Nevertheless, we ought not to assume that this reserve was a lesson of age. Obscured as it sometimes is by passion or prejudice, it was learnt early, and is found in the epigraph of 'To be Filed for Reference' at the end of Kipling's first book, *Plain Tales from the Hills*. All three are tragic tales; and in what follows I use the word tragic without exact definition to indicate the tale that turns out badly. There is not a high proportion of tragic tales in Kipling's work, and most of these, if we estimate by titles, belong to his earlier books. But we cannot estimate by titles. The intense scrutiny of 'Mary Postgate' outweighs, as an imaginative effort, any number of the salted and bitter little chips of calamity that bestrewed the Indian scene. These, however, have a cumulative importance; the young man's world included from the beginning the acids of failure, the hopeless harvest of misunderstanding, the pathos and the terror of death, and the savage ironies of circumstance. These subjects were dealt with in many modes and tones, some of which, as is common with artists, failed to survive into his later work. Singly, they have a simplicity of effect that does not appear in the longer tales. The impression of 'Beyond the Pale' is one of shock and hopelessness, of coming up against an impassable blank wall. Trejago does not even know where the door of the house is, where he found little Bisesa. He limps back into the beaten paths and gets on with his work. It is characteristic of Kipling that he writes the last paragraph of this tale. His narratives seldom come to a tragic stop. The burden is carried on; the bitter food is digested. Trejago pays his calls regularly, and, but for a slight limp, 'there is nothing peculiar about him'. It seems to me that this is the way in which Kipling's sense of the tragic in life naturally developed. It is not isolated in the conception of a tragic hero, but diffused through a crowded scene. It is given an episodic expression. Even the sharply-focused tragic fragments of his earliest books never really stand alone; we are always aware of all the other tales, told and untold, and of the multifarious existence of which these episodes are a small and momentary part. Terrible things happen to men, and those who survive carry their experiences hidden in them. This effect is very strong and real.

There are, however, scattered through Kipling's works, few in number but prominent in their nature, certain tales where the focus is close and the tragic pitch high. '"Love-o'-Women"' is one of these. The limelight is full on here, and nothing is held back. Guilt, remorse, punishment, the final mingling of despair and atonement are given us with maximum intensity. The dying gentleman-ranker quotes *Antony and Cleopatra*, and Mulvaney serves as a sort of Enobarbus, comprehending and condemning. The writer goes all out to rouse emotion, and the power and the crudity, the real and the doubtfully real, the understatement and the overstatement strike us all together. It is heavy, close hitting; and it is by way of a great many strong emotions that we reach the tragic loading of the verandah. 'At the End of the Passage' is similar in its method. Here there is no distancing at all. Life is counted in days, and we are shut round by thick heat.

The last of these tales of close focus—the greatest and most terrible—is 'Mary Postgate'. We are forced to look at everything till the very end. Reflection, if it comes at all, comes later, after we have survived the shock. It is not concurrent with the reading of the tale. This is the last tragic catastrophe that Kipling shows us at so close a range—so close that the heat of the furnace and Mary's coarse clamour make us recoil. Thereafter, as before, the tragedies are elements in a larger scene; they are bits of flotsam that we see moving on the dark and crowded waters of life. They are subsidiary to the main business of the tale, but they are indisputably there, and their existence gives a deeper perspective to it. The casualty lists are, as it were, interfoliated with the stories, and we catch names as we turn the page. Findlayson in his agony of suspense over his bridge, 'remembered the half-pitying things that he himself had said when Lockhart's big water-works burst and broke down in brick heaps and sludge and Lockhart's spirit broke in him and he died'. Jimmy Tigner is destroyed by the same fortuitous series of events by which Wollin is redeemed. Mr Gravell has got his son back, only a little damaged, but Mr Burges has lost his. Where in these later tales a tragic subject is central, it is part of a large tract of time and national experience, and it is handled in so meditative a mode—or perhaps I should say a mode requiring such a contribution of thought from the reader—that we find ourselves asking if we can call these stories tragedies at all. Grace Ashcroft's masterful sacrifice of herself for her unknowing and departed lover is self-fulfilment and self-purgation. Sergeant Godsoe's suicide is quite a different matter from the despair of 'Click' Vickery. The barrier between him and Bella Armine has been removed; he can go through, and he does so with a preparation and composure that the Sikh Regimental Chaplain of 'In the Presence' would have approved. These people follow out the processes natural to their beings, love and suffer and seem to 'answer the end of [their] being created'—whatever that end may be. We watch them through years and have pride in their endurance. Perhaps the only thing that remained completely tragic—immedicable—to Kipling in his old age was the prolonged mistake, the error that becomes a tyranny, a vampire or a prison. He made such mistakes the subjects of 'The Gardener' and 'Dayspring Mishandled'. There is no high state of excitement in these tales. They are told with mature irony and unspoken compassion. At the end Manallace and Helen are shut into their several limbos. In middle life, in the cheerfully serious verses of 'A Pilgrim's Way', Kipling had insisted that

> *Heaven and Hell which in our hearts we have*
> *Show nothing irredeemable on either side the grave.*

As a young artist, loyally open to all that was 'given', he had not needed this fortifying chant. As an old one, he was content to separate what he saw from what he hoped, and to present his hopes with a fantasy that acknowledges the insufficiency of the human imagination before ultimate mystery.

To trace change and persistence in Kipling's style would take much more space than I have left at my disposal. He was richly and variously gifted, and he disused none of his gifts. Some, for a time, he abused. His zest for the English vocabulary and for words that 'should tell, carry, weigh, taste and, if need were, smell' did not decline, and he never cared to write a neutral-coloured prose. What I shall call, by extension, the taste-buds of his nature were active and widely responsive. Everything came to him fully-flavoured and sharply defined. He often aimed at maximum impact; but his equipment was genuine and original, and he might have said, modifying Dickens: 'It is a pleasure to work with taste-buds like mine.' From the beginning, however, he could damp down his style for dramatic purposes, as we can hear in the exhausted, repetitive, indifferent sentences of 'The Gate of the Hundred Sorrows', written before he was nineteen. The sentences that tell of the end of the child Muhammad Din are like pebbles dropped into a little pool; the rings spread and are stopped by the margin, and the small disturbance is over. It is in a passage like this that we can discern the potentiality of the styles of 'The Miracle of Purun Bhagat' and of 'The Gardener'. The principle of selection in these quieter pages is not moderation; economy is an object, certainly, and dramatic consistency, but what these considerations license comes with the old strength of response. Helen Turrell, on her pilgrimage to her son's grave, gets information from 'a Central Authority who lived in a board and tar-paper shed on the skirts of a razed city full of whirling lime-dust and blown papers'. The chastening principle is reverence for human experience, especially human grief, and the older Kipling goes softly before it.

The examples that are usually selected to prove the homogeneity of Kipling's style through all his work are emphatic and often mannered. They are taken from his *opus alexandrinum* ('smoking mists that changed from solid pearl to writhing opal') or from his weighted satiric lines, stabbing with every word ('the trained sweetness and unction in the otherwise hardish, ignorant eyes') or from his spinning sentences, hung on participles or a sequence of verbs, and conveying simultaneous complex activity. ('Then everybody shouted and tried to haul up his anchor to get among the school, and fouled his neighbour's line and said what was in his heart, and dipped furiously with his dip-net, and shrieked cautions and advice to his companions, while the deep fizzed like freshly-opened soda-water, and cod, men and whales together flung in upon the luckless bait.') They illustrate the strong physical sensitiveness that is so marked an expression of his vitality ('that terrible first night at school when the establishment has been newly whitewashed, and a soft smell of escaping gas mingles with the odour of trunks and wet overcoats'), or even the challenging sit-up-and-listen tactics of his youth ('Four men, each entitled to "life, liberty, and the pursuit of happiness", sat at a table playing whist') or the esoteric (and doubtful) erudition with which, as he admits with amusement, he sometimes brought off his bluffs. It cannot be denied that all these strands, even the last flagrant one, are twisted into his yarn to the end, though some become thin and intermittent, so that their recurrence finds us unprepared. We are unprepared to read in 'The Tender Achilles' that 'the tiny muscle that twitches when we feel certain sorts of shame showed itself beneath Scree's lower eyelid', and we are vexed and incredulous. What muscle? How extravagant a generalization from an individual idiosyncrasy, and how disturbing a break in a tale that has been describing pain and strain with such grim force, and moving round such unanswerable questions. This habit and others of the same kind are facets of his writing personality that continue to come into play in certain moods and certain tales, while they are wholly absent from others. There are none of them in the passage in 'An Habitation Enforced' where Sophy finds old Iggulden dead in his chair by the fire, 'a thistle-spud between his knees', or in that in 'The Gardener' where Helen feels herself 'being manufactured into a bereaved next of kin', or in the beginning of 'The Miracle of Saint Jubanus'; but these are not the pages that are usually quoted. The statement that the characteristic flavour of his prose is so strong that every sentence exudes it is like the statement that used to be made about speeches in Shakespeare, that every one could be assigned, by ear, to the proper speaker. Neither statement is literally true; both convey an important truth hyperbolically. The following brief passage comes from 'Letters to the Family'. When we know who wrote it, we see that it is characteristic, and yet I must doubt whether any uninformed reader, on meeting it, would identify it:

> We sat around on the farm machinery, and, in the hush that a shut-up house imposes, we seemed to hear the lavish earth getting ready for new harvests. There was no true wind, but a push, as it were, of the whole crystal atmosphere.

What all Kipling's prose shows, from beginning to end, is conciseness and that 'natural momentum in the syntax' which W. B. Yeats in 1926 ascribed, with reluctant justice, to his verse. It is a quality that stylistic critics say too little about. One measure of it is the ground that a sentence can cover with a fluid and easy movement. It can often be said of Kipling's sentences, as it has been said of the stanzas of Burns, that the end is out of sight of the beginning; but this quality is more convincingly illustrated by a moderate than an exceptional sentence. I quote from one on the second page of '"My Son's Wife"'. Midmore has had to leave London in winter for the 'dank country' to attend the burial of his aunt:

There he faced the bracing ritual of the British funeral, and was wept at across the raw grave by an elderly, coffin-shaped female with a long nose, who called him 'Master Frankie'; and there he was congratulated behind an echoing top-hat by a man he mistook for a mute, who turned out to be his aunt's lawyer.

Yeats suggested that Kipling was able to achieve natural momentum in the syntax because he kept to the surface. Certainly these fifty-seven words cover a good deal of surface. The funeral is enacted, and two new characters are introduced, in appearance and attitude, and their relation to Midmore is indicated. Further, the scoffing, slightly inhumane note of the description tells us that we are seeing the scene through Midmore's eyes. We have had a sample of his tone already, and it is to be confirmed immediately after by the 'bright account of the funeral' he sent to his mother. Moreover, we have been told that Fate has chosen to play with Midmore. The sentence, couched in his language, necessarily displays him in his fastidious hostility and irritation. But he is also part of the scene, as he stands on the brink of unexpected experiences. What is called satirically the bracing ritual of the British funeral is really bracing—much more so than his mother's nebulous pseudo-mysticism, of which we have heard; and, since Midmore faced it, he may well face other bracing experiences. The whole tale has been moved a long, smooth step forward, and the free gesture of the sentence is such that it is only as we read on that we see how much it carried in its pace, and learn that the long nose of the anonymous female was not a mere decoration.

What more I have to say about the development of Kipling's style and handling can all be classed under the head of relevance. It is not to be supposed that, with his strong sense of form, his love of pattern and his severe journalistic training, he could have erred much or grossly in this matter. It is not easy anywhere in his tales to find passages that are specifically irrelevant. The intrusion of the Member for Lower Tooting into 'Without Benefit of Clergy' is beyond defence, and so is the narrator's dream of a territorial army in India in 'His Private Honour'. There is also in the longer tales of his earlier collections a certain amount of what may be called tangential material, especially in the frames. It belongs to the life that he describes, but not always particularly to the story he has to tell. The description of the guard on a hot night in 'With the Main Guard', for instance, has little to do with the fight at Silver's Theatre, but accounts for Mulvaney's toast, echoed by Ortheris at the end of the tale and so strange in our ears: 'Bloody war! North, South, East, an' West.' But the subject of the soldier tales is really an area of life, of which some of the conditions are set in full relief by an episode; and some of the tales of the Great War are of this kind, though they are more intricately designed. The dense associated detail is necessary, since we cannot understand the episode without a continuous sense of the life. When, however, the tangential material is not dramatized, but given us by the author from outside the scene, the structure is loosened too far. This is the fault of 'The Drums of the Fore and Aft'. It is the longest but one of his Indian stories ('The Man who would be King', which is a little longer, is fuller of material and more highly wrought) and it is more than a third longer than the average length of his middle and later tales, excluding the double tales. Kipling has, in fact, given himself too much room. It was much admired in its own generation, when the courageous novelty of the treatment was more striking than it can be now. It presents the valiant action of two drummer-boys, who were partly drunk at the time and coarse little scamps at all times, set in an account of the breaking of an unblooded regiment in an Afghan fight, and accompanied by an attempt to show war from the professional point of view. Parts of it are excitedly overwritten. Aggressively understating images and euphemisms lead to the crowning exasperation of alliteration when the Lancers make their attack 'with a wicked whistling of wind in the pennons', and the author calls it 'a dainty charge, deftly delivered'. The merit of the tale is that it tries honestly to convey what Border marching and fighting really were to the men, the officers and the Brigadier in charge of operations. The material is built out by a sort of logical agglutination, which is quite different from relevant development. The regiment will break, and so Kipling lays before us, in his own person, the conditions that may predispose a regiment to do so. The regiment comes back and fights, and he compares the mental attitude and technique of a Gurkha, a Highland and a Midland regiment, and adds the Bengal Lancers, with a note on the recovery of the lance. At the end a correspondent arrives, and the mismanagement and failure are suppressed in the concoction of a satisfactory communiqué. The tale is a composite; and the *Barrack-Room Ballad* 'That Day' is a much better, as it is a much shorter, treatment of a rout.

There is no other tale that presents such a target as 'The Drums of the Fore and Aft', though there are some where the skilful infixing of extra material, however entertaining, may leave a doubt. 'Steam Tactics' is composite, and makes no pretence to be anything else. In 'A Matter of Fact' the powerfully imaginative vision of the sea-beasts has both a preparation and a sequel. They are journalists who are appalled by it, and some space is expended on establishing their toughness and their experience. After the event, the question arises as to what they are to do with their scoop, but, even before the 'awful orderliness' of the English scene shuts round them, two of them have accepted that they can do nothing with it, except in fiction. So far, so good; but Kipling lets himself be carried on to exhibit the third journalist, the American Keller, determined to work 'the biggest thing ever vouchsafed to paper', resolving to bypass his own newspapers because 'everything goes in the States, from a trouser-button to a double-eagle' and he wants to 'see the Britishers sit up', but finally cowed by the sight of *The Times*, Winchester Cathedral and Westminster Abbey, the age and unmoved solidity of the Old World. This is miching mallecho, and done with cheap materials. Kipling might well wish, as a craftsman, to set his wild wonder against the non-conductive sobriety of the civilized world, and need an extreme type of journalist to make his point; he did not need to show Keller at a disadvantage with British phlegm.

There would be no purpose in underlining the structural weakness of early or minor works of an author, whose original equipment is so strong that even in them he can carry his readers with him, except to make the point that in his later tales these weaknesses do not occur at all. The discipline of the last two collections, especially, is very strict; the average length of the tales is shorter, and the material dense and closely-packed. In what have been called the enigmatic tales, as I have tried to show, every stroke is relevant. On the other hand, the natural hold of the born storyteller has been imperilled by—or perhaps consciously bartered for—investigating subtlety and depth of meaning. It does not seem to have been lost. 'The Bull that Thought' is full of narrative force, and so is 'The Church that was in Antioch' and 'A Sea Dog'. The satisfactory integration of a genuinely complex tale as distinct from a composite one—one which presses towards its crisis by an obscure path or in which the chief event is a focus of diverse interests—depends upon either the structural necessity of the parts or upon the light they shed on the central idea. 'Dayspring Mishandled' is an example of the first type, and 'The Eye of Allah' of the second. There is nothing very like the first type in Kipling's earlier work. His tales not infrequently advance to the confirmation of a moral truth, but here the path is underground. 'The Eye of Allah', however, may be regarded as developing from the composite tale. The Moorish microscope is a strong enough focus to hold in place the description of the Abbey—the embodiment of a principle of order which its survival would wreck—and the artist's nature of John Otho, essentially different from that of the scientists, but with its own generic ruthlessness, using their instrument for his particular investigations, and ready to let it go, when it has supplied his need. ' "The Finest Story in the World" ' is the first of Kipling's tales to be integrated in this manner round an idea, but the splendid flashes of his natural equipment in it are such that the reader does not very much mind whether it is integrated or not. Whatever he started from—and I have assigned the primacy to the problems of historical fiction—transmigration brought with it a number of speculations, and these—the nature of the imagination, the origin of the imperfect artist, the lifting of the fear of death to which the western world clings, the ordinance of the shut door—are all focused on the narrator and on Charlie, the unique instrument that breaks in his hand. Even when the narrator dances among the 'dumb gods of Egypt' (whose testimony is no longer heard) in the British Museum, his overweening exuberance is absurd, but not out of step.

For a tale of this kind to be fully successful, some warmth must be imparted in it, either the glow of the furious imagination or an informed sympathy with the destinies of men. There are few connoisseurs of structure among the readers of fiction. To most a passage will appear to belong to, or not to belong to a tale; and it is warmth that fuses it into its place, to be accepted until it is understood. It may be the absence of warmth that makes 'The

Prophet and the Country' an awkward tale to approach. It is the only one in the last two books that might be called composite, excepting the farce 'Aunt Ellen', which is so by definition, one damn thing after another. It is not quite without detached pity, but the atmosphere is chilly. Kipling has several subjects in hand, but we are not immediately convinced that they belong to each other.

So far as we have evidence, his imagination was generally set going by a specific and often concrete detail, a name, a phrase, a place, an anecdote. 'I move easiest from a given point', he writes. It is possible, therefore, that 'The Prophet and the Country' started with a face above a yellow raincoat, a caravan, a phrase ('the Ne-mee-sis of Presumption') the behaviour at Monte Carlo of American tourists under Prohibition, or the wonderful language and procedures of the American Movie industry. But once the given point is activated, it draws conceptions old and new to itself. What was drawn to it, in this case, was disquietude about America, serious enough in spite of its satirical and extravagant trimmings, as Tarworth, the prophet of the tale, is serious. Kipling did not write directly about Isolationism but about Prohibition, seen as an expression of the same state of mind, the dangerous will to an artificially 'virg'nized civ'lization' in a world that is not virgin—'the Zeenith of Presumption'. Such a criticism to make its full effect, must be put in the mouth of a 'one-hundred-per-cent American'—and best in that of a prophet whose vision is mixed with a streak of madness. From this consideration the thin strand of grotesque pathos in the tale derives. It is on his return from his wife's burial that Mr Tarworth receives his 'Revelation *qua* Prohibition', and acts on it with all the energy and resource that have made him a successful business man. Twice in the tale, near the beginning and at the end, 'I' speaks of the fracture of the magneto make-and-break, 'that tiny two-inch spring of finest steel, failure of which immobilizes any car', and it is an obvious symbol of the psychic injury the American has received. The inevitable consequences under the 'Collective Outlook of Democracy' follow; the prophet is disbelieved and persecuted. He bears his testimony in exile, beside the English road on which 'I' has already been stopped that day by the 'witch-doctoring' of a motor-licence control. It is not only in the States that the 'Herd Impulse' and 'the counterbalancing necessity for Individual Self-expression' are at odds.

This potentially serious material is treated for most of the tale as a comic extravaganza. Tarworth is an eccentric, and the amazing scenario of his projected anti-Prohibition film is in Kipling's old style of cumulative, concrete, hyperbolic detail. In his attempt to convey his disquietude in the insinuating vehicle of farce, he goes through the long-disused ritual of the night, the Demon, and the wind that heralds the dawn. But the Demon is inactive, and what the dawn-wind preludes is the passage of a hearse, evoking a queer, cracked note of pathos from that distressed patriot, bereaved husband and possessed seer, Mr Tarworth. There is a moment in the caravan when 'I' has no desire to laugh; and though the last words of the tale carry the image of the broken spring, the upshot of the whole seems to be: 'This is not altogether fool, my lord.'

I am less certain of my interpretation of this tale than of any other in Kipling's last collections. The others have unfolded themselves smoothly over the years, offering me another and then another aspect, so that it seemed I had only to accept what lay before me. But I have had to worry at 'The Prophet and the Country' and be ingenious; and I can readily believe that I may be quite wrong about it. It leaves the impression of something difficult, hammered into shape. The extravaganza of the film scenario, however, expands itself with the accustomed fertility of spontaneous comic invention into a vast bubble, gleaming with portentous and preposterous hues. It is unlike his former extravaganzas only in the fact that it is not an arabesque—an ornamental adjunct to the tale—'a small and curious flourishing', as Cotgrave defines it—but supports the whole structure.

The arabesque, says R. L. Stevenson, is the first fancy of the artist. This is widely true, and the fact often surprises the non-writer, who does not conceive that the desire to express precedes the possession of—let alone by—a subject. Images, parallels, parodies, sequences of exuberant, detailed invention, fireworks of every kind, these are not so much the exercises in which a writer develops his strength as the natural expression of the fact that he is a writer. They are found in the early work of many poets, and the richer the natural equipment, the more plentiful they are likely to be. They will be disciplined in mature art by the necessities of the style and type of subject on which the writer concentrates; but one whose temperament is originally exuberant and whose fancy remains fertile will never wholly lose the delight in playing with the tools of his trade. Shakespeare did not; nor did Dickens. Except in the highest and most serious art, it is a sour and Puritanical critic and one of weak digestive powers who demands that every image shall show its worker's pass. Austerity is not among the cardinal virtues, though prudence and temperance are. What we may fairly ask is whether the play hinders the work, whether the distraction is a refreshment or a misdirection. Arabesques of both kinds appear freely in Kipling's work. The elaboration of the state of the three old guns, which are the only fire-arms of the infantry of the Gilbertian little Himalayan kingdom in 'Namgay Doola', is relevant to the description of that kingdom and amusing even to those who have never handled a gun, whereas the detailed account of how Spurstow in 'At the End of the Passage' put Hummil's guns out of action disturbs us with its inappropriate relish for technical procedures. Kipling's images, especially those which reinforce sense impressions, come with great spontaneity, but in the earlier work they are sometimes commended to the writer himself by an ingeniousness that should have made them suspect. In 'The City of Dreadful Night' silence closes on the Muezzin's cry 'as the ram on the head of a cotton-bale', and, though this certainly conveys a stifling suggestion, its chief effect is to direct attention to the young journalist's recent experiences. The comparison in *The Light that Failed* of the lanes opened in the Mahdi's forces by the camel-guns to 'the quick-closing vistas in a Kentish hop-garden, seen when a train races by at full speed', confuses the desert scene with Kentish agriculture, and the lightning that, in 'The Return of Imray', 'spattered the sky as a thrown egg spatters a barn-door' has an odd double effect; one sees the lightning, but pauses to wonder when Kipling was present at such an occurrence. Yet if we were to call this imagery 'Jacobean', instead of simply 'showy', we should be aware, even in its excess, of its likeness to the imagery which those leaping, forcible, all-experiencing minds fetched from too far off, or too near at hand, to please Doctor Johnson. It has not their intellectual quality, but it has their appetite. But there are also images, even in the earliest tales, of unquestioned appropriateness. The drunken mirth dies out of Duncan Parrenness 'as I have seen the waters of our great rivers die away in one night', and India stretches its foreign landscape round the shaken young Writer; the Ganges under Findlayson's bridge 'lifted herself bodily, as a snake when she drinks at midsummer', an effect of living menace. There are images that are not only descriptive but appropriate to the speaker also. When Ortheris remarks in 'His Private Honour' that Mulvaney 'whistles like a bloomin' bullfinch up there in 'orspital', and that Learoyd lying down to shoot 'looks like a sea-lion at Brighton Aquarium', it is the Cockney who speaks, whose ambition is to keep a taxidermist's shop 'in the 'Ammersmith 'Igh'; and when Simple Simon says that Drake 'drew our spirits up in our bodies same as a chimney-towel draws a fire' and that in one of his risky manoeuvres 'we clawed off them sands like a drunk man rubbin' along a tavern bench', we have the speech of a homely burgess of Rye. This is the fully dramatic use of imagery, which not only illumines the object described but confirms our sense of the speaker.

What Kipling the craftsman had to learn was to avoid checking his reader's progress, which included discriminating between tales in which he could operate in the overt strength and variety of his stored and venturesome fancy, and those from which he must in part withdraw. Images in the wider sense, pictures called up in the reader's mind, mark all his stories, which rise in the memory first as scenes and then as a sequence of voices; but images in the sense of similes become much fewer as they become more significant. There are none in 'The Gardener' until we come to Helen's sight of Hagenzeele Third, 'a waist-high wilderness as of weeds stricken dead'. But he never put his senses on a lowering diet, and the metaphorical quality of his style, though not always salient, is constant. The self-pleasing arabesque, however, is relegated in his later tales to those pages where the reader shall be at leisure to enjoy it. The farces are hospitable to these side-shows, and rightly so. 'Aunt Ellen', the last of its kind, easily accommodates a witty set-piece, something in the tradition of Petruchio's horse, on the state of 'a canoe-ended natural wood sporting-machine' after ditching.

> Her left fore-wheel inclined, on its stub-axle, towards (technically speaking) the Plane of the Ecliptic; her radiator sweated like Samson at Gaza; her steering-gear played like all Wordsworth's own daffodils; her swivelling headlight glared fixedly

at the ground beneath it like a Trappist monk under penance; but her cranking-handle was beyond comparison, because it was not there.

The pot has not yet gone off the boil. Over the page, the car has 'the look and gait of a dachshund', while in overtaking 'her infirmities made her deadlier than Boadicea's chariots'. Nor does it matter, on this night of nights, how long we dally by the roadside in contemplation of her. The arabesques in 'Aunt Ellen' have an unexpectedness that can be found in Dickens, together with a literary allusiveness which was outside his range.

The adjustment of means to ends included the control of the 'I'; indeed, that is indistinguishable from the control of image and arabesque, for, where these disturb or exceed, the effect is always that of a personal irruption of the author. What must now be briefly considered, however, is the 'I' as a character in the tales. The 'I' is a dramatic character. He is often in what we know was Kipling's situation; he presents, at times, certain recognizable aspects of his character; at other times, perhaps, the figure which he wished to cut, and occasionally a slightly parodied or belittled version of him. He is not therefore to be carelessly identified with Kipling. He is the link between the characters and the reader; he is not an autobiographer, and, with very few exceptions, the tale is not about him. It is therefore a mark of insufficient control when the writer's excitement overflows and the 'I' intrudes too far into the story and disturbs the focus of our attention. There is a little too much of 'I' in 'The Man who would be King', and there is a good deal too much of him in 'His Private Honour'. 'I' has plenty of legitimate business in this tale; he has to be the anxious friend both of Ortheris and of the young officer who struck him, and he is the witness of the offence. But it is quite unlikely that he would have followed up the Colonel's rebuke by administering more of the same medicine to Ouliss. The focus jerks. We are turned from Ouliss's plight to attend to the narrator's inflamed feelings ('If Ortheris had slipped in a cartridge and cleared the account at once I should have rejoiced') and to consider him as the mouthpiece of the Law and the understudy of Destiny. This is the worst case, and there is nothing at all like it in the later tales, where 'I' occupies his place with reserve and offers no distractions. In 'The Miracle of Saint Jubanus' he is so far depersonalized that he is 'the visitor' throughout. I have noted, too, that whereas the 'I', as at first conceived, is knowledgeable, and sometimes exuberantly so, the 'I' of the last books sometimes betrays an incidental ignorance. In 'Fairy-Kist', for instance, he knows nothing about gardening or about Goya. It is a light touch, but seems to fit him more firmly into the circle he describes, and to prevent the least taint of showmanship. These are the extremes; the intermediate variants are to be found in such tales as 'The Captive', 'Garm—a Hostage' and 'The House Surgeon'.

Once or twice in this study I have used the epithet 'Elizabethan' of Kipling's work. This was not done without consideration. The historical accidents of his life, the geographical accidents of his youth, his dedication to the short story, a form to which no major English prose artist before him had so largely committed his genius, have unduly obscured the truth that we have in him a traditional writer with a traditional and recurrent cast of English temperament. I have no wish to play down the importance of the Empire to him, as a physical and political fact and a moral agent, for some half of his writing life; after that it was replaced by a preoccupation more familiar to us and to the Elizabethans, England fighting for existence. In any comprehensive view of his work it will always be necessary to consider his political position and its repercussion upon his reputation, then and later; but it has been my effort, by following up selected aspects of his writing, to establish its nature as far as possible—it is not completely possible—in detachment from politics.

Kipling felt that fascination for extreme things that marks our greatest drama. It can have been no surprise to his readers to learn from Professor Carrington's book that all his life he delighted in the Elizabethan dramatists. Man in a state of strong excitement, stretched beyond his normal stature on the rack of anguish, passion, or his own will, was as much his theme as theirs, though in him the will is directed rather to service than to self-assertion. In Kipling, too, as in his elder brothers, the moral and the sensational go hand in hand. Strain, the oppression and horror of melancholy, throw up for him, as for them, eccentricities of behaviour which he observes with curiosity, and open on tracts of mental experience, of which he seeks to convey the strangeness. Meanwhile his lively comic sense rejoices in 'humours', men shaped by professional conditions, local persistences, a decisive and unfettered personality, or special experience of any kind. These humours he embeds, where space allows, in the substantial detail of their lives, and puts into their mouths a speech of quintessential flavour and, at its best, superbly natural cadence. Like the Elizabethans, he had an original and unembarrassed love of eloquence. Words had for him history and personality, and in sequences their sounds could acquire a symbolic fitness. He believed that some subjects could not be properly handled without eloquence; and, when he dispensed with it, his reserves have the 'bursting' quality of theirs, and imply the head of passion that is dammed back. His danger, and theirs, was excess, the premature outbreak of the imagination into extravagant emphasis and unsupported hyperbole. But the excess was always vital, even when, occasionally, it was also absurd.

Pattern and intricacy of all kinds delighted him, and he loved to play with his tools and his material. As his work deepened, the intricacies sank into its grain, and he produced that figured art, which perhaps appeals particularly to the English literary mind, where the full meaning has to be developed from image, symbol and hint, and the reader must also be an investigator. He provided texts for the minute verbal inquisitions, that are now one of the dominant fashions in literary criticism, before those fashions were widely established. It is no very far-fetched analogy to compare the passage from his earlier to his later works with that from Elizabethan to Jacobean literature. In both cases the exuberance was reduced, and deliberate eloquence confined in its operation, though never wholly disused; a range of quieter, strictly contemporary tones was explored, without loss of flavour; and complexity and conciseness united to prefer the 'pregnant' style before the explicit and rhetorical.

I have chosen to develop the Elizabethan parallel, because in that I have now the support of Kipling's known preference, and because it is the most comprehensive. But I could also have matched him, in many respects, with Dickens. Kipling's great popularity seems to me far more likely to be due to his satisfaction of a traditional taste in his public than to his 'Imperialist' mission (the inverted commas are his, in *Something of Myself*) and this would also account for its survival, as the popularity of Dickens survived, through a period of critical disapproval.

There are certainly things to be disapproved of in Kipling's writings; and, since we have it under his hand (though on Dick Heldar's tongue) and marked by his characteristic lavish overstatement, that four-fifths of everyone's work must necessarily be bad, we may safely assume that he disapproved of some of them himself. There is enough left. A writer must accept his own nature and his own development, or he might as well throw away his pen. The worst faults, as the strongest evidences of original genius, are in the first half of his work. His later tales deserve more impartial study than they have received. If Kipling 'limps' in them, as Mr Edmund Wilson avers, it is because he has travelled a long way. 'Shrunken' I cannot accept; to me his stature is increased. The virtues of poets are much more important than their faults, as is confirmed by the survival of that very faulty but vital poet, Byron. 'After all,' as this one writes, 'mankind is but made of earth and water; and our hearts, like muddy streams, cleanse themselves as they go forward.'

List

of the books, tales, essays and verses by Kipling alluded to in this study, with the date of their first appearance and the volume of his works in which they can most readily be found. Pieces uncollected in his life-time are referred to the volume of the *Sussex* edition of his works in which they appear, except where they have been added to *The Complete Stalky & Co* or *Collected Dog Stories*. Some of them are also to be found in the American *Outward Bound* edition or in the *One-Volume Kipling* (New York 1928, reissued as *Selected Prose and Poetry of Rudyard Kipling*, 1937).

Abaft the Funnel	1909	*Sussex ed., vol. xxix*
(contents 1888, 1889, 1890)		
Actions and Reactions	1909	
Among the Railway Folk	1888	*From Sea to Sea*
Arrest of Lieutenant Golighty, The	1886	*Plain Tales from the Hills*
As Easy as ABC	1912	*A Diversity of Creatures*
Astrologer's Song, An	1910	*Rewards and Fairies*
At his Execution	1932	*Limits and Renewals*
At Howli Thana	1888	*In Black and White*
At the End of the Passage	1890	*Life's Handicap*
At the Pit's Mouth	1888	*Under the Deodars*
Aunt Ellen	1932	*Limits and Renewals*
Baa Baa, Black Sheep	1888	*Wee Willie Winkie*
Ballad of East and West, The	1890	*Barrack-Room Ballads*
Bank Fraud, A	1887	*Plain Tales from the Hills*
Barrack-Room Ballads	1892	
Battle of Rupert Square, The	1889	*Sussex ed., vol. xxix*
Beauty Spots	1931	*Limits and Renewals*
Below the Mill Dam	1902	*Traffics and Discoveries*
Benefactors, The	1912	*Sussex ed., vol. xxx*
Beyond the Pale	1888	*Plain Tales from the Hills*
Bisara of Pooree, The	1887	*Plain Tales from the Hills*

LIST OF TALES AND POEMS

Bitters Neat	1887	*Sussex ed., vol. I* and *Plain Tales, Outward Bound ed.*
Bonds of Discipline, The	1903	*Traffics and Discoveries*
Book of Words, A	1928	
	(contents 1906–27)	
Brazilian sketches	1927	*Sussex ed., vol. xxiv*
'Bread upon the Waters'	1896	*The Day's Work*
Bridge Builders, The	1893	*The Day's Work*
British-Roman Song, A	1906	*Puck of Pook's Hill*
Brookland Road	1910	*Rewards and Fairies*
Brother Square-Toes	1910	*Rewards and Fairies*
'Brugglesmith'	1891	*Many Inventions*
Brushwood Boy, The	1895	*The Day's Work*
Bull that Thought, The	1924	*Debits and Credits*
Burden, The	1926	*Debits and Credits*
Burgher of the Free State, A	1900	*Sussex ed., vol. xxx*
Butterfly that Stamped, The	1902	*Just So Stories*
By Word of Mouth	1887	*Plain Tales from the Hills*
'Captains Courageous'	1896–7	
Captive, The	1902	*Traffics and Discoveries*
Carol, A	1900	*Rewards and Fairies*
Cat that Walked by Himself, The	1902	*Just So Stories*
Centaurs, The	1926	*Debits and Credits*
Centurion of the Thirtieth, A	1906	*Puck of Pook's Hill*
Charm, A	1910	*Rewards and Fairies*
Children, The	1917	*A Diversity of Creatures*
Children of the Zodiac, The	1891	*Many Inventions*
Church that was in Antioch, The	1929	*Limits and Renewals*
'Cities and Thrones and Powers'	1906	*Puck of Pook's Hill*
'City of Dreadful Night, The'	1885	*Life's Handicap*
City of Dreadful Night and Other Places, The	1891 (contents 1888–1890)	*From Sea to Sea*
Cold Iron (poem)	1910	*Rewards and Fairies*
Cold Iron (tale)	1909	*Rewards and Fairies*
Comforters, The	1917	*A Diversity of Creatures*
Conference of the Powers, A	1890	*Many Inventions*
Conversion of Aurelian McGoggin, The	1887	*Plain Tales from the Hills*

Conversion of Saint Wilfrid, The	1910	*Rewards and Fairies*
Courting of Dinah Shadd, The	1890	*Life's Handicap*
Crab that Played with the Sea, The	1902	*Just So Stories*
Day's Work, The	1898	
Dayspring Mishandled	1928	*Limits and Renewals*
Deal in Cotton, A	1907	*Actions and Reactions*
Death-Bed, A	1919	*The Years Between*
Debits and Credits	1926	
Debt, The	1930	*Limits and Renewals*
Departmental Ditties	1886	
Devil and the Deep Sea, The	1895	*The Day's Work*
Dinah in Heaven	1932	*Limits and Renewals*
Disturber of Traffic, The	1891	*Many Inventions*
Diversity of Creatures, A	1917	
Doctor of Medicine, A	1909	*Rewards and Fairies*
Dog Hervey, The	1914	*A Diversity of Creatures*
Dray Wara Yow Dee	1888	*In Black and White*
Dream of Duncan Parrenness, The	1884	*Life's Handicap*
Drums of the Fore and Aft, The	1888	*Wee Willie Winkie*
'Dymchurch Flit'	1906	*Puck of Pook's Hill*
Eddi's Service	1910	*Puck of Pook's Hill*
Edge of the Evening, The	1913	*A Diversity of Creatures*
Egypt of the Magicians	1914	*Letters of Travel*
Elephant's Child, The	1900	*Just So Stories*
Enemies to Each Other, The	1924	*Debits and Credits*
Enlightenments of Pagett, MP, The	1890	Sussex ed., vol v, and *In Black and White*, Outward Bound ed.
Epitaphs of the War	1919	*The Years Between*
Evarra and his Gods	1890	*Barrack-Room Ballads*
Expert, The	1932	*Limits and Renewals*
Eye of Allah, The	1926	*Debits and Credits*
Fairy-Kist	1927	*Limits and Renewal*
'Finest Story in the World, The'	1891	*Many Inventions*
Five Nations, The	1903	

LIST OF TALES AND POEMS

For One Night Only	1890	*Sussex ed., vol. xxxi and One-Volume Kipling*
Four Angels, The	1909	*Actions and Reactions*
Friend of the Family, A	1924	*Debits and Credits*
Friendly Brook	1914	*A Diversity of Creatures*
Friend's Friend, A	1887	*Plain Tales from the Hills*
From Lyden's 'Irenius'	1904	*Traffics and Discoveries*
From Sea to Sea	1899	
	(contents 1887–90)	
From Tideway to Tideway	1892–5	*Letters of Travel*
Gardener, The	1926	*Debits and Credits*
Garm—a Hostage	1899	*Actions and Reactions*
Gate of the Hundred Sorrows, The	1884	*Plain Tales from the Hills*
Gemini	1888	*In Black and White*
Gertrude's Prayer	1932	*Limits and Renewals*
Gethsemane	1919	*The Years Between*
Gow's Watch	1904 / 1926	*Verse, Definitive ed.*
Habitation Enforced, An	1905	*Actions and Reactions*
Hal-o'-the-Draft	1906	*Puck of Pook's Hill*
Half-Ballade of Waterval	1903	*The Five Nations*
Haunted Subalterns	1887	*Sussex ed., vol. i and Plain Tales, Outward Bound ed.*
His Gift	1923	*Land and Sea Tales*
His Private Honour	1891	*Many Inventions*
His Wedded Wife	1887	*Plain Tales from the Hills*
Honours of War, The	1911	*A Diversity of Creatures*
Horse Marines, The	1910	*A Diversity of Creatures*
House Surgeon, The	1909	*Actions and Reactions*
How Fear Came	1894	*The Second Jungle Book*
How the First Letter was Written	1901	*Just So Stories*
Hymn of Breaking Strain	1935	*Verse, Definitive ed.*
Hymn to Physical Pain	1932	*Limits and Renewals*
If—	1910	*Rewards and Fairies*
In Black and White	1888	

In Error	1887	*Plain Tales from the Hills*
In Flood Time	1888	*In Black and White*
'In the Interests of the Brethren'	1918	*Debits and Credits*
In the Presence	1912	*A Diversity of Creatures*
In the Pride of his Youth	1887	*Plain Tales from the Hills*
In the Rukh	1893	*Many Inventions*
In the Same Boat	1911	*A Diversity of Creatures*
Incarnation of Krishna Mulvaney, The	1889	*Life's Handicap*
Janeites, The	1924	*Debits and Credits*
Jews in Shushan	1887	*Life's Handicap*
Jobson's Amen	1917	*A Diversity of Creatures*
Judgment of Dungara, The	1888	*In Black and White*
Judson and the Empire	1893	*Many Inventions*
Jungle Book, The	1894	
Just So Stories	1902	
Kaa's Hunting	1894	*The Jungle Book*
Kaspar's Song from 'Varda'	1904	*Traffics and Discoveries*
Kim	1900–1	
King's Ankus, The	1895	*The Second Jungle Book*
Knife and the Naked Chalk, The	1909	*Rewards and Fairies*
Knights of the Joyous Venture, The	1906	*Puck of Pook's Hill*
La Nuit Blanche	1887	*Departmental Ditties*
Lamentable Comedy of Willow Wood, The	1890	*Sussex ed., vol. xxx and One-Volume Kipling*
Land and Sea Tales for Scouts and Guides	1923	
Last of the Stories, The	1888	*Abaft the Funnel*
Last Relief, The	1891	*Sussex ed., vol. xxx*
'Late Came the God'	1926	*Debits and Credits*
Leaves from a Winter Note-Book	1900	*Letters of Travel*
Legend of Mirth, The	1917	*A Diversity of Creatures*

LIST OF TALES AND POEMS

Legs of Sister Ursula, The	1893	*Sussex ed., vol. xxx and One-Volume Kipling*
Letters of Marque	1887–8	*From Sea to Sea*
Letters of Travel	1920	
	(contents 1892–1914)	
Letters to the Family	1908	*Letters of Travel*
Life's Handicap	1891	
Light that Failed, The	1890	
Limitations of Pambé Serang, The	1889	*Life's Handicap*
Limits and Renewals	1932	
Little Foxes	1909	*Actions and Reactions*
Little Tobrah	1888	*Life's Handicap*
Looking-Glass, The	1910	*Rewards and Fairies*
Lost Legion, The	1892	*Many Inventions*
'Love-o'-Women'	1893	*Many Inventions*
Madonna of the Trenches, A	1924	*Debits and Credits*
Maltese Cat, The	1895	*The Day's Work*
Man who Was, The	1890	*Life's Handicap*
Man who would be King, The	1888	*The Phantom 'Rickshaw*
Manner of Men, The	1930	*Limits and Renewals*
Many Inventions	1893	
Mark of the Beast, The	1890	*Life's Handicap*
Marklake Witches	1910	*Rewards and Fairies*
Marrèd Drives of Windsor, The	1908	*Verse, Definitive ed.*
Mary Postgate	1915	*A Diversity of Creatures*
Matter of Fact, A	1892	*Many Inventions*
Miracle of Purun Bhagat, The	1894	*The Second Jungle Book*
Miracle of Saint Jubanus, The	1930	*Limits and Renewals*
Moral Reformers, The	1899	*Stalky & Co*
Mother Hive, The	1908	*Actions and Reactions*
Mother's Son, The	1932	*Limits and Renewals*
Mowgli's Brothers	1894	*The Jungle Book*
Mrs Bathurst	1904	*Traffics and Discoveries*
Muse among the Motors, The	1900–1930	*Verse, Definitive ed.*
Mutiny of the Mavericks, The	1891	*Life's Handicap*
My First Book	1892	*Sussex ed., vol. xxx*

My Lord the Elephant	1893	*Many Inventions*
My Own True Ghost Story	1888	*The Phantom 'Rickshaw*
'My Son's Wife'	1917 (written 1913)	*A Diversity of Creatures*
My Sunday at Home	1895	*The Day's Work*
Naboth	1886	*Life's Handicap*
Namgay Doola	1891	*Life's Handicap*
Nativity, A	1916	*The Years Between*
Naulahka, The	1892	
Naval Mutiny, A	1931	*Limits and Renewals*
Necessitarian, The	1904	*Traffics and Discoveries*
New Knighthood, The	1909	*Actions and Reactions*
Of Those Called	1895	*Abaft the Funnel*
Old Men at Pevensey	1906	*Puck of Pook's Hill*
On Greenhow Hill	1890	*Life's Handicap*
On the Gate	1926	*Debits and Credits*
On the Great Wall	1906	*Puck of Pook's Hill*
On the Strength of a Likeness	1887	*Plain Tales from the Hills*
Only a Subaltern	1888	*Under the Deodars*
.007	1897	*The Day's Work*
Other Man, The	1886	*Plain Tales from the Hills*
Our Lady of the Sackcloth	1935	*Verse, Definitive ed.*
Palace, The	1903	*The Five Nations*
Penalty, The	1932	*Limits and Renewals*
Phantom 'Rickshaw, The	1888	
Pig	1887	*Plain Tales from the Hills*
Pilgrim's Way, A	1918 (3 first stanzas 1914)	*The Years Between*
Pit that they Digged, The	1889	*The Phantom 'Rickshaw, Outward Bound ed. Under the Deodars 1895, and Sussex ed., vol. iii*
Plain Tales from the Hills	1888	
Playmate, The	1932	*Limits and Renewals*
Pleasure-Cruise, The	1933	*Sussex ed., vol. xxx*
Prairie, The	1908	*Letters to the Family*
Prayer of Miriam Cohen, The	1893	*Many Inventions*

LIST OF TALES AND POEMS

Press, The	1917	*A Diversity of Creatures*
'Priest in Spite of Himself, A'	1910	*Rewards and Fairies*
Proofs of Holy Writ	1934	*Sussex ed., vol. xxx*
Propagation of Knowledge, The	1926	*Debits and Credits*
Prophet and the Country, The	1924	*Debits and Credits*
Puck of Pook's Hill	1906	
Puzzler, The	1906	*Actions and Reactions*
Quiquern	1895	*The Second Jungle Book*
Rabbi's Song, The	1909	*Actions and Reactions*
Rahere	1926	*Debits and Credits*
Rebirth	1917	*A Diversity of Creatures*
Recantation, A	1919	*The Years Between*
Record of Badalia Herodsfoot, The	1890	*Many Inventions*
Red Dog	1895	*The Second Jungle Book*
Regulus	1917	*A Diversity of Creatures*
	(written 1908)	
Return of Imray, The	1891	*Life's Handicap*
Rewards and Fairies	1910	
'Rikki-tikki-tavi'	1893	*The Jungle Book*
Rout of the White Hussars, The	1888	*Plain Tales from the Hills*
Sahibs' War, A	1901	*Traffics and Discoveries*
Satisfaction of a Gentleman, The	1929	*The Complete Stalky & Co*
Schoolboy Lyrics	1881	*Sussex ed., vol. xxxv*
Sea Constables	1915	*Debits and Credits*
Sea Dog, A	1934	*Collected Dog Stories and "Thy Servant, a Dog"* (1938)
Sea Warfare	1916	
Second Jungle Book, The	1895	
Second-Rate Woman, A	1886	*Under the Deodars*
Sending of Dana Da, The	1888	*In Black and White*
Settler, The	1903	*The Five Nations*
Seven Seas, The	1896	
Ship that Found Herself, The	1895	*The Day's Work*

Simple Simon	1910	*Rewards and Fairies*
'Sleipner' late 'Thurinda'	1888	*Abaft the Funnel*
Soldiers Three	1888	
Some Aspects of Travel	1914	*A Book of Words*
Something of Myself	1937	
Son of his Father, The	1893–4	*Land and Sea Tales and The Day's Work,* Outward Bound ed.
Song of the English, A	1893	*The Seven Seas*
Souvenirs of France	1933	
Spring Running, The	1895	*The Second Jungle Book*
Stalky & Co	1899	
Steam Tactics	1902	*Traffics and Discoveries*
Storm-Cone, The	1932	*Verse,* Definitive ed.
Story of Muhammad Din, The	1886	*Plain Tales from the Hills*
Story of the Gadsbys, The	1888	
Story of Ung, The	1894	*The Seven Seas*
Strange Ride of Morrowbie Jukes, The	1885	*The Phantom 'Rickshaw*
Supports, The	1919	*Debits and Credits*
Surgeons and the Soul	1923	*A Book of Words*
'Swept and Garnished'	1915	*A Diversity of Creatures*
'Teem'—a Treasure-Hunter	1935	*Collected Dog Stories*
Tender Achilles, The	1929	*Limits and Renewals*
That Day	1895	*The Seven Seas*
'Their Lawful Occasions'	1903	*Traffics and Discoveries*
'They'	1904	*Traffics and Discoveries*
Threshold, The	1932	*Limits and Renewals*
Through the Fire	1891	*Life's Handicap*
Thrown Away	1888	*Plain Tales from the Hills*
'Thy Servant, a Dog'	1930	*Collected Dog Stories*
Tie, The	1932	*Limits and Renewals*
'Tiger—Tiger!'	1894	*The Jungle Book*
To be Filed for Reference	1888	*Plain Tales from the Hills*
To the Companions	1926	*Debits and Credits*
To the True Romance	1893	*Many Inventions*
Tomb of his Ancestors, The	1897	*The Day's Work*
Tomlinson	1892	*Barrack-Room Ballads*
Tour of Inspection, A	1904	*Sussex* ed., vol. ix

LIST OF TALES AND POEMS

Traffics and Discoveries	1904	
Treasure and the Law, The	1906	*Puck of Pook's Hill*
Tree of Justice, The	1910	*Rewards and Fairies*
Uncovenanted Mercies	1932	*Limits and Renewals*
Under the Deodars	1888	
Undertakers, The	1894	*The Second Jungle Book*
United Idolaters, The	1924	*Debits and Credits*
Unprofessional	1930	*Limits and Renewals*
Untimely	1926	*Debits and Credits*
Verse, Definitive ed.	1940	
Village that Voted the Earth was Flat, The	1917 (written 1913)	*A Diversity of Creatures*
Vortex, The	1914	*A Diversity of Creatures*
Walking Delegate, A	1894	*The Day's Work*
Watches of the Night	1887	*Plain Tales from the Hills*
Way through the Woods, The	1910	*Rewards and Fairies*
Wayside Comedy, A	1888	*Under the Deodars*
Wee Willie Winkie	1888	
Weland's Sword	1906	*Puck of Pook's Hill*
William the Conqueror	1895	*The Day's Work*
Winged Hats, The	1906	*Puck of Pook's Hill*
'Wireless'	1902	*Traffics and Discoveries*
Wish House, The	1924	*Debits and Credits*
With Number Three	1900	*Sussex ed., vol. xxx*
With the Main Guard	1888	*Soldiers Three*
With the Night Mail	1905	*Actions and Reactions*
Without Benefit of Clergy	1890	*Life's Handicap*
Woman in his Life, The	1928	*Limits and Renewals*
Wressley of the Foreign Office	1887	*Plain Tales from the Hills*
Wrong Thing, The	1909	*Rewards and Fairies*
Years Between, The	1919	
Young Men at the Manor	1906	*Puck of Pook's Hill*

Index

Main entries are indicated by figures in bold type. Passages where a tale, poem or author is alluded to (e.g. by the mention of a character or incident) are indexed under the name of that tale, poem or author whether it occurs in them or not. The sub-headings 'quoted' and 'also quoted' refer *only* to quotations which are given without any reference to their context.

Abaft the Funnel, 10, **100**
Actions and Reactions, 106, 128, 129–130, 158, 161, 164
Alcestis, 13, 208
'Alnashar and the Oxen', quoted, 106
'Among the Railway Folk', 62
Anstey, F. (Thomas Anstey Guthrie), **34–35**, 224
Arabian Nights, The, xiii, 58
'Arithmetic on the Frontier', quoted, 188
Arnold, Edwin Lester, **226–229**
'Arrest of Lieutenant Golightly, The', 47
'As Easy as A.B.C.', **95–96**, 131, 159, 236
'Astrologer's Song, An', 167, 170, 172
'At his Execution', 107
'At Howli Thana', 102
'At the End of the Passage', 50, 135, **199–202**, 205, 231, 244, 254; also quoted, 246
'At the Pit's Mouth', 187
'Aunt Ellen', 33, 36, 38, 42, 48, 49, 140, 141, 252, **255–256**
Austen, Jane, 86, 113, 190

'Baa Baa, Black Sheep', 8, **119–120**, 156, 158
Bacon, Francis, 104, 176
Bagehot, Walter, 11
Balestier, Wolcott, 1

'Ballad of East and West, The', 87–88
Bambridge, Mrs George, xiv
'Bank Fraud, A', 225
'Battle of Rupert Square, The', 47
'Beauty Spots', 35, 36, 101, 127, 132, **141–143**, 234, 236, 244
'Below the Mill Dam', 61, 98, 159
'Benefactors, The', 236
Beowulf, 99
Besant, Walter, **225–226**, 229
'Beyond the Pale', 233, **243**
'Bisara of Pooree, The', 233
'Bitters Neat', 223
Blake, William, 13, 92, 151, 219
Blücher von Wahlstatt, Gebhardt Lebrecht, 11
'Bonds of Discipline, The', 38, 103–104
Book of Words, A, 141, 231
Booth, General, 224
Brazilian Sketches, 62, 205
'"Bread upon the Waters"', xiv, 101, 119, **124–125**, 232
'Bridge Builders, The', 27–28, 63, 105, 119–120, 159, **190–193**, 197, 198, 215–216, 231, 238, 244, 255
'British-Roman Song, A', 78, 194
'Brookland Road', 204
'Brother Square-Toes', 3, 80, 226
Brown, C. Hilton, 26, 201
Browning, Robert, 8, 11, 13, 19, 102, 105, 207, **222–223**

INDEX

"'Brugglesmith'", 36, 37, **43–45**, 235
'Brushwood Boy, The', 3, 36, 98, 119, 159, 198, **205**, 220
'Bull that Thought, The', 106, 141, 154, **182–183**, 251
Bunyan, John, 213
'Burden, The', 106
'Burgher of the Free State, A' 84, 240
Burne-Jones, Sir Edward Coley, 58, 224–225
Burns, Robert 97, 247
Butler, Samuel, 61
'Butterfly that Stamped, The', 54, 59, 235
Byron, Lord, **210–213**, 259
'By Word of Mouth', 199, 202, 235

'*Captains Courageous*', xi, **2**, 3, 4, 63, 224, 234, 238; also quoted, 246
'Captive, The', 109, 159, 236, 257
'Carol, A', 83–84
Carrington, Charles E., xii, 9n, 19, 19n, 68, 182, 225, 228, 257
'Cat that Walked by Himself, The', 55–56, 164
'Centaurs, The', 60, 109
'Centurion of the Thirtieth, A', 74, 79, 80, 228
Charlemagne, xiii
'Charm, A', 160
Chaucer, Geoffrey, 7, 67
Chevrillon, André Louis, 65
'Children, The', 108, 189
'Children of the Zodiac, The', 50, 59, 88, 98, 159, **171–172**, 195
'Church that Was at Antioch, The', **145–146**, 235, 237, 251
"'Cities and Thrones and Powers'", 105; also quoted, 194
"'City of Dreadful Night, The'", 215, 254
'City of Dreadful Night and Other Places, The', 100
Civil and Military Gazette, The, 3, 101–102
'Cold Iron' (poem), 216
'Cold Iron' (tale), 57, 72, 76, 79, 114
Collins, Mortimer, 226–227

'Comforters, The', 107
'Conference of the Powers, A,' **105**, 193
Conrad, Joseph, 87, 155, 162
'Conversion of Aurelian McGoggin, The', 215, 235
'Conversion of Saint Wilfred, The', 57, 216–217
'Courting of Dinah Shadd, The', 188
'Crab that Played with the Sea, The', **55, 194–195**

Daily Telegraph, The, 39
'Daughter of the Regiment, The', quoted, 187
'Dayspring Mishandled', xiii, 4, 26–27, 89, 109–110, 111, 112–113 119, 127, 142, **146–155**, 159, 161 171, 224, 231, 237, 245, 251
Day's Work, The, 59, 159, **197–198**
'Deal in Cotton, A', 17
Debits and Credits, x, 3–4, 106, 159 250
'Death-Bed, A', 189
'Debt, The', 98, 170, 235
Definitive Edition of Rudyard Kipling's Verse, 104
Defoe, Daniel, 179
Delamere, Lord, 39
Departmental Ditties, 97, 205
De Quincey, Thomas, 19, 99, 204, 225, 230
'Devil and the Deep Sea, The', **125–126**
Dickens, Charles, 18, 19, 26, 62, 236, 245, 254, 256, 258
'Dinah in Heaven', 203
'Disturber of Traffic, The', **104–105**, 159, 193
Diversity of Creatures, A, 3–4, 106, **130–131**, 159, 162
Dobrée, Bonamy, x, xii, 138, 232
'Doctor of Medicine, A', 54, 75, 160, **167–170**
'Dog Hervey, The', 98, 107, 130, **162–167**, 185–186, 198, 237
Dowson, Ernest, 148n, 153
'Dray Wara Yow Dee', 101, 102, **121**

'Dream of Duncan Parrenness, The', 254
'Drums of the Fore and Aft, The', 240, **249–250**
Dryden, John, 213
'"Dymchurch Flit"', 75, 226

'Eddi's Service', 216–217
'Edge of the Evening, The', **108**, 109, 131, 236, 239
'Egypt of the Magicians', 14–15, 62–63, 216, 217; also quoted, 64
'Elephant's Child, The', 55, 59
Eliot, T. S., x, 13, 160
Emerson, Ralph Waldo, 105
'Enemies to Each Other, The', 50 59, 159, 181, 233
'Enlightenments of Pagett, M.P., The', 187
'Epitaphs of the War', **189–190**, 221
'Error in the Fourth Dimension, An', 198
Escarpit, Robert, x, 66n, 195
Eurich, Richard, 137
'Evarra and his Gods', 20, 215
Ewing, Mrs Juliana Horatia, 57, 179, 186, 230
'Expert, The', 142
'Eye of Allah, The', 12, 74, 107, 160–161, **167–170**, 251

'Fairy-Kist', 52, 94, 161, **177–179**, 234, 237, 244, 257
Fielding, Henry, 117
'"Finest Story in the World, The"', 93, 114, 218, **226–227**, 229, 251
'For One Night Only', 198, 202
'Four Angels, The', 193
'Friend of the Family, A', **127–128**, 205
'Friend's Friend, A', **34–35**, 105, 122
'Friendly Brook', 130, **132–134**, 236
Froissart, Jean, xiii
'From Lyden's "Irenius"', 90n, 109
From Sea to Sea, **11–12**, 29, 62, **100**, 224, 231; also quoted, 246
'From the Dusk to the Dawn', quoted, 201, 208

'From the Masjid-al-Aqsa of Sayyid Ahmed (Wahabi)', quoted, 109
'From the Unpublished Papers of McIntosh Jellaludin', 109
'From Tideway to Tideway', 84, 159–160

'Gardener, The', 94–95, 106–107, 110–111, 112, **115–118**, 159, 161, 172–173, **181–182**, **205–207**, 234, 245, 246–247, 255
'Garm—a Hostage', 257
Garrard, Florence, 9n
'Gate of the Hundred Sorrows, The', 187, 245
Gatty, Mrs Margaret, **59–60**
'Gemini', 225
'Gertrude's Prayer,' 110, 147, 154
'Gethsemane', 86, 204
Gilbert, W. S. and Sullivan, Sir Arthur, 35, 224
'Gloriana', 73
'Gods of the Copybook Headings, The', 197, 214, 215, 237
Goldsmith, Oliver, 64
'Gow's Watch', 109, 111
Gray, Thomas, 57–58
Grimble, Sir Arthur, 38–39
Grimm, J. and W., 226
Guthrie, Thomas Anstey, *see* Anstey, F.

'Habitation Enforced, An', 51, **159–160**, 162, 189, 247
Haggard, Lilias Rider, x, xiv, 196, 219
Haggard, Rider, x, xiv, 196, 219
'Hal o' the Draft', 72, 74, 80, 235
'Half-Ballade of Waterval', 157
Hardy, Thomas, **45–48**
Harte, Francis Bret, 61, 97, 223
'Haunted Subalterns', 198
'Head of the District, The', 188, 231, 237
'His Gift', 129
'His Private Honour', 232, 248, 255, **256**
'His Wedded Wife', 121
Home and Colonial Mail, The, 238

INDEX

'Honours of War, The', 34, 37, 38, 98, 108, 131, 232, 237
Hood, Thomas, 229
'Horse Marines, The', 34, 38, 40 131
Houseman, A. E., 204
'House Surgeon, The', 101, 106, 130, 143, **161–166**, 198, 202, 210, 232–233, 237, **238–240**, 257
'How Fear Came', 66
'How the Alphabet was Made', 41–42
'How the Whale got his Throat', 59; also quoted, 55
Huxley, Elspeth, 39
'Hymn of the Breaking Strain', 218
'Hymn to Physical Pain', 178

'If', 128
Illustrated London News, The, 226
In Black and White, 121, 147
'In Error', 223
'In Flood Time', 102
'"In the Interests of the Brethren"', 122, **175–176**, 177, 182, 233, 244
'In the Presence', 102–103, **121–122**, 131, 231, 235, 245
'In the Pride of his Youth', 50, 97, 156, 225
'In the Rukh', 26, **68–69**, 149n, 235
'In the Same Boat', 130, **162–167**
'Incarnation of Krishna Mulvaney, The', 225
'Independence', an address to the University of St Andrews, 223, 237
Ingelow, Jean, xiv

James, Henry, 93–94, 96, 155, 206
'Janeites, The', 103, 107, 140, 175–176, **190**
'Jews in Shushan', 225
'Jobson's Amen', 216–217
Johnson, Samuel, 86, 137, 254
Jonson, Benjamin, 26, 89
'Judgment of Dungara, The', 97, 121, 231

'Judson and the Empire', 27, 98, 240
Jungle Book, The, **56–58**, 64, **65–71**, 105–106, 128–129, 204, 222, 241
Just So Stories, **55–56**, **58–59**, 69, 76, 105, 194–195, 234

'Kaa's Hunting', 56, **67**, 70
'Kaspar's Song from "Varda"', 108–109
Keats, John, 17, **91–93**, 108–109
Kim, xi, 1, 2, 12, **21–32**, 86, 114, 143, 158, 170, 193, 206, 216, 234, 235, 238
'King's Ankus, The', 67, 70
Kipling, John Lockwood, 21, 76
'Knife and the Naked Chalk, The', 57, 76, 164, 231
'Knights of the Joyous Venture, The', 58

Lamb, Charles, 18, 230
'La Nuit Blanche', 205
'Lamentable Comedy of Willow Wood, The', 20
Land and Sea Tales for Scouts and Guides, 129
Lascelles, Mary, 113
'Last Ode, The', 107
'Last of the Stories, The', 236
'Last Relief, The', 201; quoted, 188
'"Late Came the God"', 110, 173
Léaud, F., xii
'Leaves from a Winter Note-Book', 84
'Legend of Mirth, The', 40, 59, 212, 235
'Legs of Sister Ursula, The', **52–53**
Leland, C. G., 225, 226, 229–230
Lescaut, Manon, 13, 224
'Letters of Marque', 1
'Letters on Leave', quoted, 188
'Letters to the Family', 62, 77, 101, 247
'Letting in the Jungle', 68, 70
Lewis, C. S., 89, 231
Life's Handicap, 121, 156

Light that Failed, The, 1, 2–3, **8–16**, **18–21**, 50, 101, 209, 219, 224, 225, 234, 254, 259
'Limitations of Pambé Serang, The', 121, 127
Limits and Renewals, x, 3–4, 33, 98, 106, 122, 158, 159, 250
Lippincott's Magazine, 19–20
'Little Foxes', 87
'Little Tobrah', 97, 156
Livingstone, Flora V., xii, 19n
Lockhart, Colonel W., 112
Longfellow, Henry W., 71
'Looking-Glass, The', 204
'Lost Legion, The', 166, **198–200**, 202, 208
'"Love-o'-Women"', 102, 120, **243–244**
Lynd, Robert, 41

Macaulay, Dame Rose, 26
'Madonna of the Trenches, A', 109, 171, **172–174**, **204–207**, 223, 235, 245
Malory, Sir Thomas, xiii
'Man who Was, The', **82**, 235
'Man who would be King, The', 110, **112**, 114, 234, 249, 256
Manchester Guardian, The, 7
Mandeville, Bernard, 60
'Manner of Men, The', xiii–xiv, 107, 114–115, 234, 237
Many Inventions, 159, 202, 209
'Mark of the Beast, The', 198, 202
'Marklake Witches', 86, 103, 160, **167–168**, 170, 235
'Marréd Drives of Windsor, The', 39
'Mary Postgate', 4, 112, 126, 128, 131, **134–137**, 140, 143, 159, 234, 243–244
'Matter of Fact, A', 250
Mead, Margaret, 39
Meredith, George, 20, 37, 179
Miller, Joaquin, 224
Milton, John, 60, 85
'Miracle of Purun Bhagat, The', 22–23, 27, 56, 65, 246
'Miracle of Saint Jubanus, The', 48, 52, 141, **176–177**, 178, 247, 256–257
'Moral Reformers, The', 124
'Mother Hive, The', 60, 129–130
Moran, Lord, 236
Morris, William, 194, 224–225
'Mother's Son, The', 161–162
'Mowgli's Brothers', 68, 69, 149n
'Mrs Bathurst', xi, **89–91**, 98, 109, 111, 163, 166, 182, 224, 232, 234, 236, 245
'Muse Among the Motors, The', 39
'Mutiny of the Mavericks, The', 16
'My First Book', 96–97
'My Lord the Elephant', 63
'My Own True Ghost Story', 199
'"My Son's Wife"', xiv, 2, 4, **50–52**, 67, 130, 131, 132, 160, **247–248**
'My Sunday at Home', 33, 37–38, **45–46**, 47, 48, 105, 198

'Naboth', **97–98**
'Namgay Doola', 156–157, 254
'Nativity, A', 216
Naulahka, The, 1–2
'Naval Mutiny, A', 238
'Necessitarian, The', 34, 36, 41–42, 48
Nesbit, E. E., 228
'New Knighthood, The', 17
Njål's Saga, 155, 224–225
Nodier, C., 151–152

'Of Those Called', 199–200
'Old Men at Pevensey', 57, 77, 81
Once a Week, 225–226
'On Greenhow Hill', 102, 114, **143**, 235, 239
'On the Gate', 161, 183, 193, 203, **209–214**
'On the Great Wall', 57, **71–73**; also quoted, 231
'On the Strength of a Likeness', 223
'Only a Subaltern', 156, 237
'.007', 60–61, 64, 65, 87
Orwell, George, 59
Osbourne, Lloyd and Stevenson, R. L., **42–43**, 223

INDEX

'Other Man, The', 187, 233
'Our Lady of the Sackcloth', 216
Outward Bound edition of the works of Rudyard Kipling, 88

'Palace, The', 224
Peacock, Thomas Love, 106, 127
'Penalty, The', 107
'"Phantom" Rickshaw, The', 120, **198–199**
'Pig', **126–127**, 132, 142
'Pilgrim's Way, A', 245
Pioneer, The, 10, 11–12, 100
'Pit that they Digged, The', 188
Plain Tales from the Hills, x, 33, 86, 97, 99, 101, 109, 132, 156, 214, 243
'Playmate, The', 49
'Pleasure-Cruise, The', 163
Potter, Beatrix, 56
'Prairie, The', 77
'Prayer of Miriam Cohen, The', 104, 159, 195
'Press, The', 107; also quoted, 131
'"Priest in Spite of Himself, A"', 3
'"Proofs of Holy Writ"', 89, 205
'Propagation of Knowledge, The', 76, **241–242**
'Prophet and the Country, The', **251–253**; also quoted, 246
Puck of Pook's Hill, 55, 57–58, 65, **71–82**, 88, 106, 128–129, 193, 204, 228–229, 234, 237, 241
'Puzzler, The', 36, 38, 39–40, 41

'Quiquern', 65

'Rabbi's Song, The', 106, 130, 143, 164, 212
'Rahere', 83, 173, 204
Reade, Charles, 3
'Rebirth', 108
'Recantation, A', 189–190
'Record of Badalia Herodsfoot, The', 105, 225
'Rector's Memory, A', quoted, 223
'Red Dog', 56, 65, **70–71**; also quoted, 129

'Regulus', 88, 123, 131, 232, 241–242
'Return of Imray, The', 166, 187, 200, 202, 254
Rewards and Fairies, 3, 54, 55, 57–58, 65, 69, **71–84**, 88, 106, 128–129, 158, 160, 204, 216–217, 228–229, 241
'"Rikki-tikki-tavi"', 67
'"Rimini"', 79
Ross, Martin and Somerville, E.Œ., 41
'Rout of the White Hussars, The', 33, 46–47

'Sahibs' War, A', **144–145**, 238
'Satisfaction of a Gentleman, The', **241–242**
'Schoolboy Lyrics', 198–199
Scott, Sir Walter, 74
'Sea Constables', 27, 112, 123, 128, **137–140**, 142
'Sea Dog, A', 42, 240–241, 251
Sea Warfare, 240
Second Jungle Book, The, 56–58, 64, **65–71**, 105–106, 128–129, 204, 222, 241
'Second-Rate Woman, A', 234
'Secret of the Machines, The', quoted, 215
'Sending of Dana Da, The', 121, 199
'Settler, The', 77
Shakespeare, William, 53, 61, 85, 99, 115, 116, 137, 143, 161, 182, 205, 213, 214, 228, 244, 247, 254, 255
Shaw, G. B., 193
'Ship that Found Herself, The', 61, 65, **196–197**
'Simple Simon', 57, **74**, 84, 225
'"Sleipner" late "Thurinda"', **198–201**
Smollett, Tobias, 19, 40
'Some Aspects of Travel', 237
Somerville, E. Œ. and Ross, Martin, 41
Something of Myself, ix, xiv, 1, 2, 3, 8–9, 17, 22, 33, 42, 45, 55, 60, 68, 74, 76–77, 79, 82, 87–88, 89, 119, 167, 186, 199, 202–203, 204, 215–

216, 221, **222–225**, **228–230**, 236, 241, 258; also quoted, 245, 252
'Son of his Father, The', 129, 186
'Song of the English, A', 188
'Song of Seven Cities, The', 106
Souvenirs of France, 154; also quoted, 259
'Spring Running, The', 68, 71
Stalky and Co., 58, 124, **241–242**
'Steam Tactics', 36, 48, 250
Sterne, Laurence, 53
Stevenson, R. L., **42–43**, 223, 253
'Storm-Cone, The', 220
'Story of Muhammad Din, The', 86–87, 156, 187, 234, 245–246
Story of the Gadsbys, The, 3, 87
'Story of Ung, The', 11, 59
'Strange Ride of Morrowbie Jukes, The', 199
Sullivan, Sir Arthur and Gilbert, W. S., 35, 224
'Supports, The', 193
'Surgeons and the Soul', 195–196
Surtees, Robert, 51
Sussex Edition of the complete Works in Prose and Verse of Rudyard Kipling, xiii
'"Swept and Garnished"', 131, **134–135**
Swift, Jonathan, 193
Swinburne, Algernon C., 111, 146, **223–224**

Taylor, John, 17
'"Teem"—a Treasure Hunter', 65, 113–114
'Tender Achilles, The', 98, 107, 112, 141, 177–178, **179–181**, 190, 212, 220, 231, 235, 237–238, 246–247
Tennyson, Lord Alfred, 230
Thackeray, W. M., 9, 18, 117
'That Day', 250
'"Their Lawful Occasions"', 3, 48, 63, **98–99**
'There runs a road by Merrow Down', 56
'"They"', 111, 164, **203–204**
'This Uninhabited Island', quoted, 55

'This ae Night', 210
Thomson, James, 100, **105**, 193
'Threshold, The', 107, **169–170**
'Through the Fire', 101, 233
'Thy Servant a Dog', 65
'Tie, The', ix, 34, 101, **122–123**, 137, 138, 224
'"Tiger—Tiger!"', 56, 67–68, 120; also quoted, 65–66
'To be Filed for Reference', 109, 214, 223–224, 243
Tolkien, H. R. R., 70
'Tomlinson', 210; quoted, 215
'Tom a' Bedlam's Song', 15, 114
'Tomb of his Ancestors, The', 27, 114
'Toomai of the Elephants', 56, 69
'To the Companions', 49
'To the True Romance', 209
'Tour of Inspection, A', 99
Traffics and Discoveries, 59, 90, 106, 159
'Treasure and the Law, The', 82, 128
'Tree of Justice, The', 57, **82–84**, 235; also quoted, 72
Trollope, Anthony, 26, 229, 230
Turner, W. J., 55
Twain, Mark, **29–32**

Uncle Remus, 59
'Uncovenanted Mercies', 159, 161, 183–184, **209–214**, 219, 220, 223, 224, 232, 234, 236–237
Under the Deodars, 100, 156
'Undertakers, The', 56, 70
'United Idolaters, The', 49, 59, 98, 109, **241–242**
'Unprofessional', 107, **167–171**, 182, 218, 234
'Untimely', 107, 169

'Village that Voted the Earth was Flat, The', 35, 107, **130–132**, 142, 148n, 224
'Vortex, The', 33, 36–37, 40, 41, 42, 48, 106

'Walking Delegate, A', 60, 61

INDEX

'Watches of the Night', 126
'Wayside Comedy, A', 156, 233-234, 238
'Way through the Woods, The', 86, 204
Webster, John, 19
'Weland's Sword, 69, 72, 76
Welch, Colin, 39
Wellington, 1st Duke of, 236
Wesley, Charles, 211–212
Westward Ho! (United Services' College), 59, 97, 242
'When Earth's last Picture is Painted' quoted, 183, 209
'White Seal, The', 56, 66
Williams, J. H., 69n
'William the Conqueror', 3, 4, 158, 232
Wilson, Edmund, 23, 171, 259
'Winged Hats, The', 27, 57, 72, **73**, 75
'"Wireless"', xiv, **90–94**, 108, 219, 236

'Wish House, The', ix, **4–8**, 83, 98, 109–110, 112, 154, 164, **171–173**, 198, **204–206**, **207–208**, 219–220, 231, 234, 236, 244–245
'With Number Three', 62, 240; also quoted, 138
'With the Main Guard', 187, 249
'With the Night Mail', 95, 193, 210, **217–218**, 236
'Without Benefit of Clergy', 101, 115–118, 234, 248; quoted, 187
'Woman in his Life, The', **177**, 178
Woodhouse, Richard, 17
Wordsworth, William, 67–68
'Wressley of the Foreign Office', 163 223, 233; quoted, 101
'Wrong Thing, The', 54, 57, 128, 146, 160

Yeats, W. B., 247
'Young Men at the Manor', 72, 77, 80–81